Virginia County Records

Volume VI

EDITED BY

William Armstrong Crozier

CLEARFIELD

Originally Published As
Virginia County Records
Volume VI
The Genealogical Association
Hasbrouck Heights, New Jersey, 1909

Reprinted
Genealogical Publishing Co., Inc.
Baltimore, Maryland
1971

Reprinted for
Clearfield Company, Inc. by
Genealogical Publishing Co., Inc.
Baltimore, Maryland
1993, 1994, 1998, 2001

Library of Congress Catalog Card Number 67-29835
International Standard Book Number 0-8063-0469-3

The publisher gratefully acknowledges
the loan of the original of this book
by the
George Peabody Branch
Enoch Pratt Free Library
Baltimore, Maryland

Vol. VI   MARCH, 1909   Part 1

Virginia
County Records

PUBLISHED QUARTERLY

EDITED BY

William Armstrong Crozier, F. R. S., F. G. S. A.

Published by
The Genealogical Association
211 West 101st Street
New York City

Five Dollars a Year   Single Copies, Two Dollars

𝔙𝔦𝔯𝔤𝔦𝔫𝔦𝔞 ℭ𝔬𝔲𝔫𝔱𝔶 ℜ𝔢𝔠𝔬𝔯𝔡𝔰

Published Quarterly

CONTENTS

Virginia County Records

QUARTERLY MAGAZINE

VOL. VI.	MARCH, 1909	No. 1

ELIZABETH CITY COUNTY WILLS

Wythe, Thomas. 12 March, 1693-4—18 Sept., 1694. Son Thomas; brother John Tomer; daughter Ann Wythe; to wife Ann after the decease of my mother; godson Francis Mallory, godson John Tomer, godson William Wilson; wife executrix; trustees Armiger Wade and John Tomer; witnesses Robert Creeke, Hugh Rose, John Allen.

Perrin, Sebastin. 5 March, 1691-2—19 Dec., 1692. Wife Esther; cousin William Wass to be brought up by Capt. William Wilson; witnesses Henry Turner, John Heyward.

Taylor, Thomas. 7 Jan. 1692-3—21 March 1692-3. To my son William in England; daughters Katherine, Elizabeth and Jane; sister Mary; Major William Wilson; Capt. Anthony Armistead; James Wallace; wife Frances Taylor, executrix; witnesses James Wallace, Roger Massenburg, Nathaniel Whitaker, Edward Powell.

Miller, John. 4 Feb., 1688-9—18 Nov., 1689. My two oldest sons, James and John; daughter Margaret to be executrix with William Wilson; witnesses William Cornish, George Digells, George Elyand.

Smythe, John. 11 Aug., 1690 ———. Estate to William Creeke; executors George Elyand and William Spicer; witnesses Thomas Bennet, William Bowless.

Barnes, John. 8 Dec., 1689—18 Feb., 1689. To brother Henry Barnes and his son John; witnesses Richard Jones, Thomas Wethersby.

VIRGINIA COUNTY RECORDS

Alson, John. 11 Dec., 1688—18 Feb., 1688-9. To Mary
Thurmore; James Cotsell; James Cotsell, Jr.; John
Barnes; Thomas, son of William Casey; John Barnes,
executor; witnesses Edward Loftis, Richard Jones.

Yeo, Leonard, Gent. 8 July, 1690—18 Nov., 1690. To wife
Mary all my estate and she to be executrix; witnesses
George Cooper, William Malory, Richard Parker.

Petter, Katherine. 20 Feb., 1688—18 July, 1690. To Catherine Shaw; to granddaughter Mary; John Tanner; Anthony King, executor; witnesses Mark Parrish, Bennet
Parrish.

Williams, John. 9 April, 1692—18 May, 1692. Son Robert;
daughters Ann and Mary; William Browne and John
Harron, executors; witnesses Robert Creeke, John Allen.

Copeland, Henry. 11 June, 1693; 18 Oct., 1693. William,
son of Christopher Copeland; Martha Daniell; brother
Samuel Daniell; my mother Ann Daniell; uncle Christopher Copeland, executor; witnesses Joseph Farnworth,
Darby Daniell, Henry Royall.

Dolby, Rebeccah, spinster. 22 April, 1693—19 Feb., 1693-4.
Friend George Eland, executor, and to have all my estate; witnesses John Dawson, Mary Dawson, John Hey-
wood.

Ruddell, Mary. 14 Jan., 1693-4—19 Feb., 1693-4. To daughter Hannah Rallison all my estate; witnesses Mary Price,
William Price, John Minson.

Jarvis, William. 14 Dec., 1693—19 Feb., 1693-4. Joseph
White, Jr.; William White; Christopher Goold; Jeremiah Smith; John Skally; Thomas Faulkner; John Rug-
gles; executors William Bowles and Joseph White; witnesses John Ellis, Barth. Witherby, William Smith.

Davis, Thomas. 26 July, 1694—18 March, 1694-5. Wife
Jane, executrix; my children; Edward Davis, overseer;
witnesses Augustine Moore, William Mallory.

Wythe, Thomas, Sr. 14 Dec., 1693—19 March, 1693-4. Grandson Thomas Wythe; son Thomas Wythe, Jr.; granddaughter Ann Wythe; my loving wife; Elizabeth Rus-

sell; Elizabeth Savory; Mr. Crooke; to G——— Rouse; to
son John Tomer; son Thomas and grandson Thomas
Wythe to be executors; overseers Mr. Armiger Wade
and John Tomer; witnesses John Bean, John Cheryton,
Francis Kneverton.

Browne, William. 4 Nov., 1694—11 Feb., 1694-5. Son William; Edward Jegetes; wife Susan; daughter Sarah;
Elizabeth Tully; executors wife and son William; overseer Thomas House; witnesses Thomas Francis, Thomas
Pool.

Miller, Robert, of Back River. 25 Jan., 1693—22 May, 1695.
Wife Ephica; goddaughter Margaret Lowry; friend Wil-
liam Lowry; godson Augustine Moore, Jr.; Mrs. Han-
nah Marshall; Frances Lowry; Ephica Prettyman;
Thomasine Prettyman; wife executrix; witnesses William
Marshall, John Phells.

Winterton, John. 5 July, 1694—26 July, 1694. Sons William
and John; daughters Rebecca and Elizabeth; wife executrix; witnesses Sedwell Minson, Charles Jones, John Minson.

Whitfield, Thomas. 26 July, 1694—18 Nov., 1694. Wife Ann
executrix; sons John and Thomas; daughters Mary and
Elizabeth; witnesses Thomas Taylor, Peter Manson,
Thomas Poole.

Naylor, John. 27 Sept., 1694—10 Oct., 1694. Son Thomas;
daughters Ann, Sara and Elizabeth Naylor; youngest
daughter Mary Naylor; wife Sarah; son James; to William and Thomas Sorrill; executors wife and son Thomas;
overseer Major William Wilson; witness Christopher
Copeland, Thomas House, Thomas Francis, Baldwin
Sheppard.

Harris, William. 14 Dec., 1695—18 May, 1696. Bert Servant; George Walker, Maddison Kelly; Maddison Servant; Francis Servant; Mary Servant; wife Judith; to
my daughter, name of whom is unknown to me, my wife
having been delivered since I left her; executor Bertram

Servant; witnesses George Walker, William Leader, John Smith, William Price.

Naylor, William. 15 Feb., 1695—18 March, 1696-7. Grandson Thomas Naylor; daughter Elizabeth Westwood; grandson James Naylor; granddaughter Sarah Naylor, granddaughter Ann House, granddaughter Mary Westwood; wife Mary and grandson Thomas Naylor executors; son Thomas House, trustee; witnesses Christopher Copeland, Edward Latymore, George Cooper.

Sheppard, Baldwin, Harris' Creek. 27 Feb., 1696-7—20 Feb., 1697-8. Daughter Elizabeth Cofield; my wife Elizabeth and my son John, executors; witnesses Henry Robinson, Thomas Francis, George Cooper.

Archer, John. 17 Feb., 1695-6—18 March, 1696-7. Son Thomas; daughters Hannah, Elizabeth and Sarah; wife Elizabeth executrix; witnesses Thomas Allen, William Williams, Thomas Williams.

Symons, Anthony. 18 June, 1698—18 July, 1698. Wife Mary; brother Richard Symons, executor; witnesses William Armistead, Daniel Preedy, Margaret Preedy.

Symons, John. 13 April, 1697—18 Oct., 1698. Brothers Richard and Anthony Symons; uncle Daniel Preedy; Matthew Watts, executor; witnesses William Armistead, Matthew Watts, Sr., Matthew Watts, Jr.

Creeke, William. 22 Sept., 1697—18 July, 1698. Wife Hannah executrix; sons William and George; daughters Elizabeth and Hannah; son Samuel; son-in-law Thomas Powell, son-in-law Mark Powell, son-in-law Matthew Powell; witnesses Thomas Powell, Matthew Powell, Charles Jennings.

Ferguson, Daniel. 28 July, 1697—20 Feb., 1697-8. Eldest daughter Ann Whitfield of Elizabeth City county; son John and my wife Katherine, executors; witnesses Christopher Copeland, Mary Robinson, Mary Copeland.

Sweney, Edmund, Gent. 19 Oct., 1696—18 May, 1697. Eldest son Edmund; wife Martha; Euphan Wallace, brother-in-law Augustine Moore; Alice Cole; Simon Hollier; goddaughter Martha Crook; estate in England and Virginia to be appraised; wife executrix; overseers Augustine Moore, James Wallace, Simon Hollier and Mr. Thomas Tabb; witnesses James Wallace, Augustine Moore, Robert Crooke.

Jenkins, Henry. 12 March, 1697—24 Sept., 1698. Brother Daniel; sister Mary Jenkins; son Henry; to Mr. Richard Trotter, Mr. James Scott, Mr. John Moore and Mr. John Howard, each a mourning ring; witnesses William Mallory, Thomas Hawkins, Francis Harlewit.

Field, Sarah. 1 April, 1698—18 May, 1698. Charles Jenings, executor and residuary legatee; my father Thomas Field, deceased; my brother Leonard Field, deceased; witnesses William Bowles, Thomas Hawkins, Sebastin Perrin, John White, Jane Gunnell, John Overton.

(Continued)

RAPPAHANNOCK COUNTY WILLS.

ORDER BOOK, 1656-1664.

Slaughter, Francis. No date. No date of probate. To mother-in-law Mrs. Margaret Upton; brother-in-law Col. Moore Fauntleroy; my wife Mrs. Elizabeth Slaughter; I appoint my good friend and loving brother ———; Humphrey Booth to be assistant to my wife.

Smith, Toby. 20 Dec., 1657. No date of probate. Land where I lived, called Rockingham, to my son ——— after the decease of his mother; to my son Henry; to my friend Henry Soane; to friend Col. Francis Morrison; to Thomas Lane; to my youngest children; my eldest son and my daughter ———; witnesses Neale Peterson, John Lacey, John Warner.

Thresh, Clement. 16 Feb., 1656. My daughter-in-law Ann Harris to go with Mrs. Peacock to school; to the children of Thomas Goodrich; godchild Ralph Warren; daughter Frances Thresh; godchild Benjamin Goodrich; Andrew

Gilson, Thomas Goodrich and John Gillet to be overseers
of my estate; witnesses Thomas Lidd, Thomas Powell.
Codicil, same date, mentions servant Robert Bennett; witness Thomas Powell.
Withey, Augustine. ——— 1659. My friend Moore Fauntleroy, gent., to be executor; debts I owe to Henry Nicholls to be paid; to Clement Herbert and to Thomas Griffin. (Witnesses' names not legible.)
Whitlock, Thomas. 9 Oct., 1659—20 Nov., 1659. Wife Mary
to be executrix; Thomas Writtle; son Thomas Whitlock;
mentions sons' godfather ——— Thatcher; my mate
Samuel Nicholls; witnesses Alexander Fleming, John
Richardson, James Yate.
Lawson, Richard. ——— 1658. To my dear wife; to Eliza-
beth Lawson, daughter of Epaphraditus Lawson; to James
Gaines; to John Taylor; to John Whitty; witnesses John
Catlett, John Pain.

ORDER BOOK, 1664-1673.

Berridge, John. 20 March, 1675—3 May, 1676. Friend Francis Suttle; friend Jane Barrett; friend Richard Mathews;
Francis Suttle to be executor; witnesses John Stone,
Walter Turner.
Bishop, Robert, Par. of Farnham. 21 April, 1676—20 Jan.,
1677. The land bought of Mr. Henry Newberry to be
given to John Gregory, Jr., and he to be executor; witnesses Thomas Wheeler, John Garner, John Burnett. Codicil with same witnesses, dated 24 May, 1676, mentions
John Jones, my brother-in-law.
Baxter, Nathaniel, Par. of Farnham, planter. 22 May, 1676—
2 May, 1677. Son Nathaniel; daughter Ann Baxter,
daughter Elithia Baxter; my wife and children to be
executors; my friends William Young, Sr., and Thomas
Roberts to be overseers; witnesses Thomas Jenkins, John
Jolly, Barbary Andrews.
Billington, Luke, Par. of Farnham. 13 Nov., 1671—23 May,
1672. Wife Barbara to be executrix; son Luke; daugh-

ter Eliza, daughter Elitia, daughter Jane, daughter Barbary, daughter Mary; grandchild William Daniell; friends William Travers, Mr. Gyles Cate and Dr. John Russell to be trustees; witnesses Henry Spears, John Russell.

Butler, Elizabeth, Sittingbourn Parish. ———— —16 June, 1673. Son Francis Slaughter; daughter Sarah; son John Catlett; daughter Elizabeth; son John, son William; my deceased husband John Catlett; cousin William Underwood, Sr.; cousin Humphrey Booth, cousin Katherine Booth; sister Peirce, money in Mr. Griffies' and Mr. Manford's hands in London; my husband Amory Butler to be executor; my cousin Capt. Thomas Hawkins, brother Edward Rowzee and Mr. Daniel Gaines to be overseers; brother Booth's children; witnesses Thomas Lucas, Sr., John Dawson.

Billington, Barbary. 7 Aug., 1674—21 Oct., 1674. Daughters Jane and Barbary; children Elishe Russell, Luke Billington and Elizabeth Billington; daughter Elishe and son Luke to be executors; Robert Bayley, Henry Clerk and Mr. Samuel Peachey overseers; witnesses John Stone, Henry Wilson, Nathaniel Richardson.

Blake, Elias. 11 June, 1674—6 Jan., 1674. My bodie to be buried at ye discretion of Henry Mouncaster and he to be executor; brother Walter Blake; witnesses John Goudy, Elizabeth Catlett.

Bollin, John. 27 Jan., 1674—5 May, 1675. Land to Matthew Harwood, and after the death of my mother to Martha Harod; Peter Harod; mother to be executrix; witnesses Richard King, Thomas Hines.

Cooper, Thomas. 29 July, 1675—16 Sept., 1675. Body to be buried by my wife in Piscateway churchyard; to John, eldest son of Richard Jones, deceased; to Richard, son of Richard Jones, deceased; Dorothy Petty, Denis Conniers; John Loper; Jane, daughter of Richard Jones, deceased; Avis Jone, widow, to be executrix; witnesses John Bagwell, Francis Webb.

Cox, Henry. 20 Feb., 1674-5—2 Nov., 1675. Mentions Edmund Craske, clerk of Rappahannock county; John Haselwood; Mr. James Miller; brother-in-law Richard Cawthorn; nephew Richard Cawthorn, Jr.; niece Aurelia Cawthorn; to Thomas Gordon and Jane, his wife; son William Cox; child my wife now goes with; father-in-law William Strachey of Gloucester county and my now wife Arabella Cox to be executors; witnesses Cornelius Melaghlein, William Harding, Thomas Hart.

De Young, John, Farnham Par. 5 March, 1671-2—6 Nov., 1672. Daughter Elizabeth De Young; my four children Elizabeth, Ann, Honora and John; brother-in-law George Knott and friend Thomas Freshwater, executors; witnesses Zachary Efford, William Davis.

Drewitt, John. 28 July, 1674—5 Aug., 1674. To Elizabeth Saxon; Annie, daughter of John Saxon; Richard Glover to be executor; witnesses John Jones, John Saxon.

Elder, Peter. 28 April, 1674—5 Aug., 1674. Son Peter and his godfather Mr. Richard Peacock, the latter to be executor; witnesses George Howell, Richard Applebee.

Ellwerd, Thomas. 23 Feb., 1675—2 May, 1677. Daughter Betty; my wife and son; witnesses Thomas Naylor, Susanna White.

Erwin, Thomas, Sittingbourne Parish. 19 Jan., 1675—30 May, 1676. My two eldest sons; two youngest sons; my daughters; wife Ann, executrix; William Sergeant and Henry Creighton, overseers; witnesses John Payne, Thomas Barker.

Gray, William. 25 July, 1673—3 Feb., 1673. Sons John, Warwick, William and Abner Gray; sons-in-law Toby and Thomas Ingram; daughter Mary Gray; grandchild Elizabeth Bowler; son-in-law James Bowler, and my wife Mandlin Gray, executors; witnesses Warwick Cammock, Francis Herne.

Hutson, Edward. 13 March, 1672—6 Nov., 1672. Son John Barton; Elizabeth Holt; wife Dorothy executrix; witnesses Arthur Hodges, Peter Hopgood.

Hardesty, John, planter. 8 Feb., 1672—6 April, 1673. Wife Mary, sole executrix; witnesses Robert Pley, Edward Rowzie.

Hodgkin, William. 22 March, 1671-2—7 May, 1673. Kinsman Samuel Peachey, Sr., and his eldest son Samuel, my godchild; to William Peachey, his youngest son; brother-in-law Henry Smith; Mr. Thomas Peenie; wife Phebe, executrix; witnesses Richard Bray, Ralph Graydon.

Hull, John. 26 June, 1675—2 May, 1677. Son-in-law John Carter and his wife; son Roger Hull; wife Elizabeth to be executrix; witnesses Thomas Collins, Thomas Smith.

James, Edward. 1 March, 1674—4 Nov., 1675. To children of Robert Welch, sailor, living in Back street in Bristol; Robert Peck, executor; witnesses John Phillips, Elias Yates.

Jackson, George. ———— —21 Jan., 1677. To Robert Eain, son-in-law to Edward Freeman; Edward, son of Edward Freeman, and latter to be executor; witnesses Thomas Harper, Symon Butler.

Lucas, Thomas, Sr., Sittingbourne Parish. 14 Oct., 1669. Son-in-law John Catlett; son-in-law Capt. Thomas Hawkins; granddaughter Mary Hawkins; son Thomas Lucas to be executor; witnesses Edmond Dobson, Richard West. Codicil, dated 24 March, 1673. Sister-in-law Mrs. Margaret Plaininer; son-in-law Thomas Hawkins and son Thomas Lucas to be executors; friend Daniel Gaines; witnesses Thomas Hawkins, Daniel Shipley.

Loes, Richard. 20 April, 1675—7 July, 1675. To son-in-law James Sacket, estate in Maryland; to son-in-law Henry Williamson, land in Rappahannock, formerly bought of Richard Bennett and Henry Corbin; executor Henry Williamson; witnesses Mary Hodges, Richard Grenstead, Edward Thomas.

Martin, Solomon. 23 Oct., 1671. Friend George Mott and his three children, Elizabeth, Margaret and Anne; said Mott to be executor.

Mansell, Capt. David. 24 July, 1672—20 Sept., 1672. God-- child Mansell Blagrane; friend William Wheeler to be executor; witnesses Jonas Page, Martha Lewis.

Mott, George, planter. 31 March, 1674—27 May, 1674. Brother John Mott; wife Elizabeth to be executrix; children Elizabeth, Margaret, Anne and Ellen; witnesses James Harrison, John Bowsier, Henry Hackney.

Maddison, Thomas. 19 Oct., 1674—4 Nov., 1674. Wife Catherine; friends Richard White and Thomas Bryant to be executors; godchild Rebecca Pettie, daughter of Robert Pettie; to wife the money which I have in England with my brother Leonard Maddison, which is the sum of seventy pounds sterling; witnesses Peter Calvin, John Biforest.

Mills, Peter. 2 Feb., 1676—2 May, 1677. Sister Elizabeth Mills; Mary, daughter of my brother John Barkett; Jane, wife of Samuel Ward; John Boyenton; Richard Middleton; to my father; to John Mills; to Joseph Shipp; witnesses Samuel Ward, John Mills.

Petus, Henry. 30 Jan., 1673-4—4 March, 1673-4. Two daughters Elizabeth Walker and Mary Petus; wife Jane; James Allen my wife's son; friends Mr. Lawrence Washington, John Meader, Francis Sterne and Warwick Cammock; wife executrix; witnesses Peter Dunnivan, John Gibson, Warwick Cammock. Codicil same date. Daniel Gaines and Warwick Cammock to be guardians of daughters Elizabeth Walker and Mary Petus.

Paxton, John. 18 April, 1673—27 May, 1674. My landlady Sarah Bowyer; to Samuel Flood; to Bridget Essex, daughter of John Essex; witnesses Joshua Lawson, Thomas Warring.

Payne, Robert, Gent. 24 March, 1671—4 Nov., 1675. Son Robert; William Clapham, Alexander Flemming and Mary Clapham; goddaughter Mary Meeder; Elizabeth Madehard; wife Elizabeth, executrix; witnesses Richard Barber, John Meader.

Page, Thomas. 10 March, 1676—20 May, 1676. Eldest
daughter Elizabeth West; Mary, eldest daughter of
Cornelius Noelle; grandson Samuel Allen; son Valentine
Allen; to William Hodges' children; daughter Mary Allen,
executrix; witnesses William Fogge, Robert Riderford.
Penn, John. 13 Jan., 1676-7—3 May, 1677. To Anne Sharp,
daughter of John Sharp money in England; to Judith
Sharp, daughter of John Sharp money in England; Eliza-
beth, daughter of Thomas Harward; Edward Dracas;
Thomas Cocker; Mary Peyton; Thomas, son of William
Talbutt; Thomas Harward, executor; witnesses Peter
Hopgood, Joseph Price.
Russell, John, Nuncupative will. 17 May, 1675—7 July, 1675.
Said Russell's son and daughter, William Sergeant and
his wife.
Sullivant, Cornelius, ———— Dec., 1672—19 Nov., 1673.
John Burridge; Patrick, son of Thomas Norton; John,
son of Matthew Kelly; John Douty; witnesses William
Major, John Orgill.
Stoakes, William, Nuncupative will. Probated 10 Nov., 1674.
Administration to Samuel Pary, Jr., upon the testimony
of John Stringer, nine months having expired since the
decease of said Stoakes.
Speede, John, Sittingbourne Parish. 18 April, 1675—5 May,
1675. To Sarah Allen; William Thorpe; John Evans;
witnesses Peter Cornwell, Francis Jenkins.
Sherman, Quintellian. 15 May, 1675—1 Sept., 1675. Son
Quintellian, son Martin; daughter Ann; wife Jane; witnesses Richard Dudley, Henry Tillery.
Sullivant, Dennis, Farnham Parish. 1 Dec., 1673—— Sept.,
1675. Sons Dennis and Daniel; wife Joane, executrix;
daughter Sarah, wife of Henry Lenton; grandson Anthony Lenton; friends Mr. Robert Baylie, James Samford, Henry Lenton and Thomas Freshwater overseers;
witnesses William Major, John Horsley.
Sherlock, John, Farnham Parish. 7 Jan., 1674—3 May, 1676.
Son Andrew, executor; son John and his children, Hanna

and John; son Bartholomew; Leabur's children, John and
Bartholomew; my wife; Thomas Freshwater and Hezekiah Turner; witnesses Edward Jones, William Bray.

Simms, Richard. 22 Jan., 1672-3—2 May, 1677. All personal
estate to my executor John Penn; witnesses Thomas Harward, Henry Williamson.

Wright, Thomas. 23 Oct., 1661—10 March, 1666. Wife Jane
and daughter Elizabeth Wright; Mr. John Washington to
be overseer; witnesses Roger Richardson, Robert Sisson.

Williams, Walter. 8 May, 1672—3 July, 1672. To Elizabeth Thatcher; John Cammock; Warwick Cammock to
be executor; Silvester Thatcher; Mathew Thatcher; witnesses Peter Duninan, Samuel Johnson.

Wright, Thomas of Moratico Creek, Planter. 8 May, 1672—
20 Sept., 1672. Wife Mary; to William Baldwyn's daughter living with Isaac Stannop; son-in-law Edward Poole;
Edward Kyles wife's daughter; cousin Edward Carter;
sons-in-law Thomas and Robert Bryant; Elizabeth, daughter of Edward Poole; Brian Stotts' children; witnesses
Brian Stott, Robert Briant.

Warriner, Ralph. 7 March, 1673-4—30 May, 1674. To
Frances Kayes; to William Dyer; Thomas Gouldman; my
sister; witnesses Robert Parker, William Dyer.

Washington, Laurence. 27 Sept., 1675—6 Jan., 1677. Daughter Mary Washington; son John; daughter Ann Washington; wife Jane; land in England to my son John and his
heirs; wife executrix; brother Col. John Washington and
my friend Thomas Hawkins, guardians of my children;
witnesses Cornelius Wood, John Barron, Henry Sandy,
Jr. Codicil same date and witnesses.

Nicholls, George, ——————6, June, 1677. Grandson
George Glascock; daughter Ann Glascock; son Zachariah;
granddaughter Anne Downing; son-in-law Thomas Glascock to be executor; witnesses Thomas Dewsin, Paul
Woodbridge.

Butler, John, Westmoreland Co., Planter. 26 Dec., 1676—6
Jan., 1676. Son Thomas; daughter Grace; wife to be

executrix with Henry Birsy of Rappahannock; witnesses James Taylor, John Thomas.

Kenny, William. 17 Jan., 1676—6 Jan., 1677. Son-in-law John Jackson; my wife; witnesses John Samson, Sarah Cannady, James Cheed, Jnr.

Williams, Roger. 26 Feb., 1675—6 Jan., 1677. Sons Roger and Shadrack; wife Jane; daughter Betty Williams; witnesses Gerard Greenwood, Robert Sisson.

Toone, James. 29 Aug., 1676—6 Jan., 1677. Sons James, William, John, Kaster and Mark; daughter Anne; sons-in law Andrew and Thomas Dew; wife Anne, executrix with friends William Barker, John Suggitt and Samuel Peckey; witnesses John Jacob, Robert Hughes, William Barber.

Toone, Anne, relict of James Toone. 29 May, 1677—6 Jan., 1677. Son Andrew Due; son Thomas Due; son-in-law James Toone; daughter Ann Toone; sons William, Kaster, Mark and John Toone; witnesses Samuel Griffen, Henry Willson, Edward Giffney, Robert Scott.

Rowze, Edward. 26 Dec., 1674—6 Jan., 1677. Wife Mary to be executrix; sons Edward, Lodowick and John; daughters Sarah and Elizabeth; witnesses Robert Pley, George Boyce.

Dempster, James. 15 Oct., 1676—6 Jan., 1677. John Fenner to be executor; godson John Braithatt; to John Fenners' three children; witnesses John Ryman, Alexander Marsh.

Killman, John. 19 Jan., 1676—6 Jan., 1677. Daughters Ann, Sarah and Mary; son George to be executor; John Dike, overseer; witnesses Thomas Coskin, Benjamin Randle.

Berry, Henry. 30 March, 1672— ————————Robert Peck, executor; William Kerton; John Rolt; my children; son Richard; witnesses John Rolt, Hannah Madding.

Prosser, John, Golden Valley, Rap. Co. 28 Aug., 1673—30 June, 1677. To be buried near my first wife Martha; my present wife Margaret to be executrix; eldest son John; second son Samuel; sons Roger and Anthony; sons-in-law

Robert Goffe and Thomas Goffe; witnesses John Waight, Hugh Palmer.

Ealles, William. 24 May, 1676— 4 July, 1676. All to friend John Mitchell; witnesses Peter Hopgood, John Fisher.

Newman, John. 2 April, 1676—4 July, 1677. Eldest son Alexander; sons John and Samuel; Capt. Leroy Griffin; Paul Woodbridge; Thomas Glascock; witnesses Richard Bowler, William Woodward, Thomas Banks.

Browne, William. 18 March, 1676—4 July, 1677. Three sons William, John and Maxfield; my wife Elizabeth and Evan Morgan executors; witnesses Mallachy Peale, Peter Butler.

Frith, Nathaniel. 3 Jan., 1676-7—4 July, 1677. Sons Nathaniel and William; wife Elizabeth, executrix; goddaughter Rebecca Williams; daughter Joan Williams; witnesses Rupert Berkerhead, Lewis Jones.

Bliss, Thomas. 7 Feb., 1676-7—4 July, 1677. John, son of Elias Wilson, and Susan, his wife; Phebe Wilson, daughter of same; Elizabeth Jones, daughter-in-law to George Taylor; Mrs. Mary Harper and her eldest daughter Elizabeth Boulware; Sarah Harper; Edward Freeman and William Sergeant, executors; witnesses John Savage, David Romer.

Evence, Anne, widow. 21 April, 1677—1 Aug., 1677. Daughter Sarah Cook; Anne Soaper; Dorothy Armstrong; Mary Armstrong; son William Young; witnesses John Soaper, John Patrick.

Pannell, Thomas. 11 May, 1676—1 Aug., 1677. Wife Katherine and my children William, Mary and Isabella, and the child my wife goes with; Anthony Prosser and his father John Prosser; friends Warwick Cammock and Daniel Gaines, overseers to my wife; witnesses John Powell, William Clapham.

Creighton, Henry. 20 Jan., 1676—6 Sept., 1677. Sons Henry, William and Thomas; wife Jane; Charles, John and Elizabeth Bridgar; executors friends Thomas Gouldman and

Robert Thomlin; witnesses Patrick Norton, John Hubbard.

Pells, Timothy. 8 Dec., 1676—5 Sept., 1677. Daughters Kezia, Susanna and Elizabeth; wife Alice executrix; witnesses Lawrence Rochefort, John Graves.

Godfrey, John, nuncupative will. 19 Dec., 1677. Estate to John Blaxson; Thomas Graham and Henry Woodnutt depose to above.

Scott, Samuel, of Headington, gent. 8 Sept., 1677—22 Nov., 1677. Servant William Glew; Nicholas Constable; Thomas Chelly (or Chitty) executor; witnesses Robert Scott, Edward Fryar.

YORK COUNTY WILLS

Abercrumway, John. 4 April, 1646. To Joseph Jolly and his wife; my countryman William Crumwell; Ralph Borer; witnesses Nich. Pescott, John Seeman, William Trumbull.

Bew, Robert. 29 Oct., 1645— — Dec., 1645. Brother Jeffry Bew, all my estate; witnesses George Westcombe, Charles Smith.

Baxted, John. 10 Dec., ——— —16 Jan., 1645. ——— to Elizabeth Clarke; John Pellam; Charles Smith; Mr. Lee; witnesses John Reade, Francis Browne.

Elkington, Richard. 26 May, 1646—6 June, ———. Mrs. Margaret and Mrs. Mary Pryor; Mrs. Mary Keton; Ann Claxton, servant to Mr. Pryor; John Flower; Mr. William Pryor, executor, for the use of Mrs. Mary Elkington; witnesses William Hockaday, Robert Lee.

Stookes, Christopher, of New Pawgusson, Co. of Charles River. 8 June, 1646—25 July, 1646. Wife Abeatoris; brother William Stookes; brother Francis Stookes; wife and brother William to be executors; witnesses Richard Watkins, John Madison, Edward Watts.

Death, Peter. 7 Oct., 1646—26 Oct., 1646. Henry Lee, executor and residuary legatee; witnesses John Conell, David Prichard.

Hines, William. 25 Oct., 1646—22 Dec., 1646. My three children; Samuel Elly, my wife's son; my two daughters Mary Hines and Jane Hines; wife Elizabeth, executrix; witnesses Rice Madox, Fr. Moxler, Law. Hulett.

Pryor, William. 21 Jan., 1646—30 Jan., 1646. Oldest daughter Margaret; daughter Mary; eldest son of my brother-in-law Joseph Clayton; wife of Richard Kemp, Esq.; Capt. Thomas Harrison of the ship "Hannor"; Capt. Thomas Harwood; to Mrs. Mary Kerton; two daughters to be executrixes; friends Joseph Clayton, Capt. Thomas Harrison and Capt. Thomas Harwood to be overseers; witnesses John Rose, William Hockaday.

Peaseley, Michell, of New Pawgusson. 22 May, 1647—4 Sept., 1647. Son Henry; daughter Elizabeth; wife Susanna, executrix; Augustus Warner and Armiger Wade, overseers; witnesses Henry Freeman, Robert Cade, Armiger Wade.

Weeke, Robert. 7 Nov., 1647—30 Nov., 1647. My wife executrix; witnesses Robert Lee, Robert Talafer.

Dale, Nicholas. 18 Feb., 1647—24 March, 1647. Eldest daughter Margaret; son Thomas; daughter Jeane; youngest daughter Sarah; wife's brother Richard Keye; wife Sarah; to son Thomas, 1,100 acres of land in Rappahannock; wife executrix; witnesses Richard Anderson, minister; John Clarkson, Law. Hulett.

Best, Thomas. 6 June, 1648—4 July, 1648. Cousin Thomas Jeffreys; godson Thomas Coxe, godson Thomas Heath; witnesses Francis Wheeler, Thomas Ramsey.

Simons, Richard, brother and heir, or Thomas Simons, deceased. 13 July, 1647— 10 Nov., 1648. Eldest son Richard Simons, in England, to be executor; my brother Francis Willis; Mr. Thomas Curtis of New Pawgusson; witnesses Francis Willis, David Lewis, John Barwus.

Waldron, Henry. 2 Jan., 1656—16 Nov., 1657. Capt. Robert Ellison, executor; my servant Jeremiah Rawlins; witnesses Robert Pyland, William Jones.

Broadnax, John. 23 July, 1657—16 Nov., 1657. Wife Dorothy; daughter Elizabeth; youngest sons William and Robert; eldest son Thomas, executor, who lives in ye "Golden Griffin" with Mr. Thomas Turges, in Fenchurch street; my son John Broadnax, living with Mr. Joseph King, in ye "Golden Sun," in Gratious street; friends Robert Baldrey and Edward Baptist of York; witnesses Henry Pictoe, Thomas Allen.

Fletcher, John. 12 Nov., 1657—21 Dec., 1657. Wife Katherine, executrix; daughter Elizabeth; Thomas Allen; witnesses John Wells, Thomas Atkinson.

Evans, William. 4 Nov., 1657—21 Oct., 1657. Wife Katherine; William Cox; William Douglas; James Tate; John Cotton; wife, executrix; witnesses John Cotton, Ann Cotton.

Baxter, Thomas (nuncupative will). Recorded 26 Jan., 1657. Estate to George Wale.

Gosling, John. 1 April, 1658—24 April, 1658. To my mother my three gold rings; Charles Dunne; Thomas Haynes, executor; witnesses George Castleton, Hugh Davis.

Clarke, John. 31 July, 1657—24 June, 1658. To my father, John Clarke, two houses in Bocking in ye county of Essex, one being in possession of my said father, and the other in possession of the widow How, which said houses were given me by my grandfather, John Clarke; sister Mary Pullum; my aunt Abigail, wife of Thomas Harper; witnesses Jerom Ham, Richard Webley, John Bogs.

Yates, Thomas. 16 Aug., 1657—24 Jan., 1658. To Susan and Katherine Fish in the county of Haddington, five acres, called by the name of Little Grounds, lying in Merryfields in ye parish of Wilney, which land was given me by my uncle, Mr. Thomas Yeates; Elizabeth, wife of Robert Vaulx; William Webb; Patrick Napier; Richard Webley; executrixes Susan and Katherine Fish; witnesses Richard Webley, Patrick Napier.

Barkeshyre, Richard, 16 Aug., 1658—10 Sept., 1658. Lewis Roberts, executor; witnesses John Claxon, John Morecroft, Thomas Hall.

Wentworth, Edward. 5 Oct., 1658—25 Oct., 1658. Son Robert in England; younger son William; wife executrix; witnesses Jeffrey Wilson, John Aduston.

Hulett, Lawrence. 3 Sept., 1658—17 Nov., 1658. Sons Augustine and Richard; to my unkind and unnatural wife Elizabeth, I desire that she have nothing to do with anything belonging to the children; friends Capt. Henry Gooch and Mr. Augustine Hodges, executors; witnesses William Crane, Lewis Atkins.

Spycer, William. 10 Feb., 1658—24 Feb., 1658. My servant Edward Kitchener; Daniel Tucker, executor; witnesses Robert Horsington, John Scarsbricke.

Davis, William. 20 Nov., 1658—24 Feb., 1658. William Saunders; goddaughter Anne Wolfe; godson William Chandler; Elizabeth Gyles; Thomas Hobson; wife, executrix; witnesses Thomas Hobson, Richard Evans.

Addams, Thomas. 27 Nov., 1655—10 Sept., 1659. To my mate Thomas Penkethman all my lands; witnesses Richard Fenne, George Turner, George Smith.

(Continued)

HANOVER COUNTY WILLS.

Hanover county was formed from New Kent county in 1720. Its records were seriously impaired during the Civil War. We give abstracts of the few wills remaining, previous to 1800.

Order Book for 1733.

Burridge, John. No date—3 May, 1734. To Lancelot Cookson a legacy, and he to be executor; to my godson John Keeling; witnesses William Ogletree, Johannah Knight.

Bouncher, William, St. Martin's Parish. 7 Jan., 1733-4—1 Feb., 1733-4. To Peter Garland; to Zebulon Skelton; to Mary Childs, daughter of John Childs, deceased; to William Mason, son of Peter Mason; executors Mary Childs and Peter Garland; witnesses Anne Gibson, Zebulon Skelton.

Searsey, Robert, St. Martin's Parish. 2 Aug., 1733—1 March, 1734. To wife Sarah; to daughter Susannah Singular; wife to be executrix; witnesses Edward Bullock, Jr., Thos. Hawks, Anne Bullock.

Harrelson, Peter, St. Paul's Parish. 21 Jan., 1733—1 March, 1733-4. To wife Mary; to son Paul, to son Burgess, to son John, to son Nathaniel; daughter Elizabeth, daughter Sarah; executors wife and children.

Harrelson, Paul, St. Paul's Parish, New Kent county. 18 Aug., 1718—5 April, 1734. To son Peter, to son Paul; granddaughter Rebecca Sims; daughter Anne Childs; daughter Judith Harrelson; my wife and my four children; executrix wife Rebecca; witnesses John Snead, John Meeks, John Snead, Jr.

Garland, John, St. Paul's Parish, Hanover county. 27 Feb., 1731—5 April, 1734. Wife Anne; son Peter, son Robert; twenty-five pounds to be laid out in land for John, James and Nathaniel Garland; executors Edward Nelson, Thomas Wingfield, James Garland; witnesses William Terrell, Cornelius Dabney, Peter Garland, Richard Find.

Horsley, Robert, St. Paul's Parish, Hanover county. 5 Feb., 1732—3 May, 1734. Son Rowland, son William, 200 acres of land in Goochland county; to nephew James Moore, land adjoining my son William; son Robert, son John; daughter Elizabeth Horsley, daughter Anne Horsley, daughter Mary Horsley; my wife Frances; daughter-in-law Frances Houl; executors wife Frances and son Rowland; witnesses Jane Crumpton, Ealse Wood, John Ryan.

Woody, Simon, St. Paul's Parish. 21 June, 1734—5 July, 1734. Son Moore Woody; wife Martha; daughter Rebecca, daughter Mary, daughter Martha, daughter Judith; executrix my wife; witnesses John Ryan, Mathew Turner, Hugh Moore, William Boskirk, Jr.

Brooks, Richard. 8 Oct., 1732—5 July, 1734. Son William; wife Mary; my four children Robert, Richard, Sarah and

Mascelina Brooks; executors Abraham Venable and Edward Hicks; witnesses Sarah Davis, Mary Banks, John Wright.

Snead, Alexander, St. Martin's Parish. 15 Oct., 1733—6 Sept., 1734. To son Mathew, to son Jacob; wife Mary; son Christopher; executors, sons Matthew and Christopher; witnesses Erasmus Harding, Elizabeth Lewis, Robert Thomson.

Woody, Moore. 27 Sept., 1734—7 Nov., 1734. To my four sisters Mary Woody, Martha Woody, Judith Woody and Susannah Woody; executrix mother Martha Woody; witnesses William Snead, John Cox, Jr.

Gibson, Thomas, Sr., St. Martin's Parish. 29 Oct., 1734—7 Nov., 1734. Son Thomas, son John; daughter Nice Nix, wife of Edward Nix; friends Humphrey and Mary Brock; executor Edward Nix; witnesses Isaac Johnson, James Phillips.

Rice, William, being in his perfect senses, gives and bequeaths all my land to my four sons David, William, Shadrach and Micajah Rice. 26 Feb., 1733. At a court, held for Hanover county, 6 Dec., 1734, the will of William Rice, deceased, was produced in court by Robert Clark, who lately married Elizabeth, the relict of said deceased.

Mullins, William, St. Martin's Parish. 2 Sept., 1734—2 Jan., 1734. Son Joshua, son William, son James; daughter Agnes Mullins, daughter Mary Mullins; son John; wife Katherine to be executrix; witnesses James Howard, John Heuson, A. Smith.

Pulliam, John. 4 Dec., 1734—6 Feb., 1734. My four sons William, John, James and Drewry Pulliam; my three daughters Agnes, Elizabeth and Sarah; my wife Agnes, executrix; witnesses John Bowles, Robert Allen, Charles Bailey, Robert Allen, Jr.

Glass, Thomas, Sr. 26 Feb., 1725-6—6 March, 1734. Son Robert, son Thomas; wife Elizabeth and son Thomas to be executors; witnesses Thomas Fitch, William Via, Mary Fitch.

Penix, Edward, St. Paul's Parish. 24 Dec., 1734—6 March, 1735. Sons George, John and Joseph; the child my wife now goes with; wife Esther and friend William Winston to be executors; witnesses V. Cobbs, Thomas Standley, James Wade.

Goodman, Benjamin, St. Paul's Parish. 29 March, 1729—1 May, 1735. Son Samuel, son Robert; wife Lucy; son Benjamin; wife Lucy and son-in-law John Turner to be executors.

Willis, Edward, St. Paul's Parish. 14 March, 1734—5 May, 1735. Wife Mary; grandson Daniel Harris; to Mary Bassett; to kinsman David Willis; wife Mary to be executrix; witnesses Hew Case, Elizabeth Acree, Edward Harris.

Deavenport, Martin, St. Martin's Parish. 4 May, 1735—2 Oct., 1735. Sons David and James; to sons Martin and William the land lying in King William county left by my father David Deavenport; wife Dorothy and son William to be executors; witnesses Garrett Connor, Henry Gambell.

EARLY SETTLERS IN VIRGINIA.

For the importation into the Colony of Virginia, the settlers were granted 50 acres of land for each person brought over. Upon making application for the grant, the name of the person imported had to be given. The following list of names has been taken from the records in the Land Office. The date in a large number of cases is probably not the year in which the immigrant arrived—he may have been in the Colony several years—but the date when the colonist made application for his importation grant. The abbreviation "tr." means transported.——(Editor).

Baldwin, William (servant), tr. by William Gany, Accomac county, 17 Sept., 1635.

Pursen, George, tr. by Jenkin Osborne, 9 July, 1635.

Bembridge, John, tr. by Maurice Thompson, Elizabeth City, 1624.

Harwood, Ralph, tr. by John Upton, 7 July, 1635.

Chandler, Thos., tr. by Capt. Adam Thorogood, in "Hopewell," in 1628.

Hasley, Elizabeth, tr. by Richard Bennett, 26 June, 1635.

Griffin, Reginald (servant), tr. by John Smith of Waricksqueake, in the "Bona Nova," in 1621.

Cowes, John, tr. by Capt. Adam Thorogood in "Bona Adventure"; grant 24 June, 1635.

Lacy, Richard, tr. by Samuel Weaver, 2 July, 1635.

Lane, Daniel, tr. by Thomas Harwood, 7 July, 1635.

Powell, Ann, tr. by William Prior, 11 July, 1635.

Baker, William (servant), tr. by John Vaster, Warwick county, 8 Nov., 1635.

Eastoote, John, tr. by Thomas Harwood, 7 July, 1635.

Eastwood, Edward (servant), tr. by George Sandys, of Archer's Hope, in 1621.

Bard, Robert, tr. by John Moone, 21 Oct., 1635.

Eagle, George, tr. by Capt. William Peirce, 22 June, 1635.

Dyer, John, tr. by Capt. Adam Thorogood in "Friendship," in 1629.

Abott, John, tr. by Sergt. Thos. Crompe, of James City county, 25 Sept., 1635.

Walton, George (servant), tr. by Alex. Stonar, 22 June, 1635.

Pattison, Thomas (servant), tr. by Capt. Francis Epes, 26 Aug., 1635.

Smalley, Margt., tr. by Capt. William Peirce, 22 June, 1635.

Powell, Hugh, tr. by Hugh Cox, 6 Dec., 1634.

Armetrading, Henry (servant), tr. by William Stone, Accomac, 4 June, 1635.

Greene, Dorothy (servant), tr. by Eliz. Clements, in the "George," 1611.

Armwood, Roger, tr. by Sergt. Thos. Crompe, James City county, 28 Sept., 1635.

Archer, George (servant), tr. by Capt. Francis Epes, 26 Aug., 1635.

Bussey, George, tr. by Richard Bennett, 26 June, 1635.

Parker, John, tr. by John Upton, 7 July, 1635.

Jones, Cath., tr. by Thacker Baldwin, Middlesex county, 7 Nov., 1700.

Churchill, Mary, tr. by Thacker Baldwin, Middlesex county, 7 Nov., 1700.

Hodgbins, John (servant), tr. by John Burnham, Elizabeth City, in 1624.

Whiting, James, tr. by George Keith, 29 July, 1635.

Baker, Daniel, tr. by William Wilkinson, minister, 20 Nov., 1635.

Swift, James, tr. by Henry Harte, 1 Aug., 1635.

Pattison, Henry, tr., by Hugh Cox, 6 Dec., 1634.

Bussey, Elizabeth, tr. by Richard Bennett, 26 June, 1635.

Gregory, Richard, tr. in "Temperance," 1621, by Lieut. Thos. Flint.

Greenfield, Robert, tr. by Thomas Phillips, 9 July, 1635.

Chelmedge, William, tr. in "Temperance," 1621, by Lieut. Thos. Flint.

Edwards, John, tr. by Thomas Harris, Henrico county, 11 Nov., 1635.

Jones, Thomas, tr. by Richard Bennett, 26 June, 1635.

Martledon, Math., tr. by Capt. William Peirce, 22 June, 1635.

Alice, Ellen (servant), tr. by William Spencer, 19 June, 1635.

Owles, Robert, tr. in "Southampton," 1622, by William Ferrar, Esq.

Hill, Henry, tr. in "John and Dorothy," 1634, by Capt. Adam Thorogood.

Grimes, John, tr. by George Menifee, 2 July, 1635.

Pullapin, John (servant), tr. by William Gany, Accomac county, 17 Sept., 1635.

Totman, Silvester, tr. by Thos. Harwood, 7 July, 1635.

Teffett, Robert, tr. by Thos. Harwood, 7 July, 1635.

Foster, Armstrong (servant), tr. by William Stone, Accomac county, 4 June, 1635.

Manning, Lazarus (servant), tr. by Charles Harmar, 4 July, 1635.

Bolton, Jane (servant), tr. by Lieut. John Cheesman, Charles River county, 21 Nov., 1635.

Chant, Andrew, tr. in "Hopewell," 1628, by Capt. Adam Thorogood.

Chawke, John, tr. by Rev. Willis Heyley of Mulberry Island, 8 Dec., 1635.

Thoroughgood, Thomas, tr. by Capt. Adam Thoroughgood, 24 June, 1635.

Fortescue, Nicholas, tr. by Capt. Thos. Willoughby, 19 Nov., 1635.

Smith, Thomas (servant), tr. by William Stone, Accomac county, 4 June, 1635.

Peale, Frances, tr. by Sergt. Thos. Crompe, of James City county, 25 Sept., 1635.

Fossett, Robert (servant), tr. by Capt. Francis Epes, 26 Aug., 1635.

Yates, Robert, tr. by William Barker, 26 Nov., 1635.

Warren, Susan, wife of Thos. Warren, Charles City county, and widow of Robert Greenleafe, 20 Nov., 1635.

Swan, John, tr. by William Swan, James City, 5 Nov., 1635.

Atkins, Silvester (servant), tr. by Capt. Francis Epes, 26 Aug., 1635.

Edwards, John (servant), tr. in the "Southampton," 1622, by John Sipsey of Elizabeth City.

Broade, Humphrey, tr. by William Eyres, 30 June, 1635.

Cowpeere, Ralph, tr. by Richard Bennett, 26 July, 1635.

Griffin, William, tr. by William Barker, 26 Nov., 1635.

Keth, Martha, wife of George Keth, clerk, tr. 29 July, 1635.

Gregory, George, tr. by William Barker, 26 Nov., 1635.

Burthen, Richard, tr. by Capt. William Peirce, 22 June, 1635.

Hickman, Henry, tr. by Christopher Stoakes, 28 July, 1635.

Withers, Francis (servant), tr. by William Beard, 19 June, 1635.

Prise, John, tr. by John Moone, 21 Oct., 1635.

Scot, John, tr. by Capt. Thomas Willoughby, 19 March, 1643.

Smith, Thomas (servant), tr. by William Spencer, 19 June, 1635.

Robinson, James, tr. in the "Charatie," in 1622 by Wm. Spencer, of James City.

Higginson, James, tr. by George Keth, 29 July, 1635.

Butler, Robert (servant), tr. by Edmund Scarbrough, Accomac county, 28 Nov., 1635.

Crouch, William, tr. by David Mansell, 22 July, 1635.

Petway, Richard, tr. by John Moone, 21 Oct., 1635.

Spencer, Nicholas (servant), tr. by William Spencer, 19 June, 1635.

Webstie, Robert (servant), tr. by Thos. Gray, James City, 27 Aug., 1635.

Lybing, Matt., tr. in "Neptune," in 1618 by Samuel Matthews, Esq.

Pharrin, Philip, tr. by Richard Bennett, 26 June, 1635.

Abbott, Christopher, tr. by Jeremiah Clement, 11 June, 1635.

Champin, Edward, tr. by William Swan, James City, 5 Nov., 1635.

Cripps, Katherine, tr. by William Swan, James City, 5 Nov., 1635.

Machin, Elizabeth, tr. by Edmund Scarburgh, Accomac county, 28 Nov., 1635.

Jenerie, Richard, tr. by Capt. Adam Thoroughgood, 24 June, 1635.

Feild, John, tr. by William Barker, 26 Nov., 1635.

Peeters, Edward, tr. by John Seaward, 1 July, 1635.

Trigg, Samuel, tr. by Thomas Harwood, 7 July, 1635.

Sweete, Robert, Elizabeth City, gent., tr. at own cost in "Neptune," 1618.

Fitchett, John, tr. by John Upton, 7 July, 1635.

Smith, Henry, tr. by Francis Fowler, James City county, 1635.

Panford, Thomas, tr. by William Ramshaw, 1 July, 1635.

Fitzgarret, Redman, tr. by John Brewer, 11 June, 1635.

Leading, James, tr. by Capt. Adam Thoroughgood, 24 June, 1635.

Parish, Edward, tr. by Capt. Adam Thoroughgood, 24 June, 1635.

Cugley, John, tr. by Jenkin Osbone, 9 July, 1635.

Abram, John, tr. by George Minifie, 2 July, 1635.

Bodin, John, tr. by John Parrott, 24 May, 1635.

Foster, Nicholas, tr. by William Swan, James City, 5 Nov., 1635.

Perry, Katherine, tr. by John Seaward, 1 July, 1635.

Savage, Francis, tr. by John Upton, 7 July, 1635.

Fowler, William, tr. by Richard Bennett, 26 June, 1635.

Austin, Richard (servant), tr. by Anthony Jones, 2 June, 1635.

Babbington, Michael, tr. by John Brewer, 11 June, 1635.

Warden, Thomas (servant), tr. by Capt. Francis Epes, 26 Aug., 1635.

Thomas, Richard, tr. by John Davis, James City, 14 July, 1635.

Bagley, Peter, tr. by Richard Bennett, 26 June, 1635.

Darby, Thomas, tr. by Samuel Weaver, 2 July, 1635.

Jackson, Richard, tr. by John Upton, 7 July, 1635.

Gun, William, tr. by Doctoris Christmas, Elizabeth City, 21 Nov., 1635.

Doe, John, tr. by George Minifie, 2 July, 1635.

Cocke, Lewis, tr. by Thomas Harwood, 7 July, 1635.

Browne, Antony, tr. by William Barker, 26 Nov., 1635.

Atwell, Nicholas (servant), tr. by William Spencer, 19 June, 1635.

Speed, William, tr. in "Hopewell," 1633, by Capt. Adam Thoroughgood.

Yates, John, tr. by William Barker, 26 Nov., 1635.

Brassey, Foulke, tr. by Thomas Harwood, 7 July, 1635.

Sparkes, Grace, tr. by John Sparkes, 3 June, 1635.

Power, Innocent, tr. in the "Southampton," in 1622, by John Cheeseman, Elizabeth City.

Cole, Robert, tr. by Thomas Shippey, 14 Nov., 1635.

Carter, Henry, tr. in the "James" in 1624, by Capt. William Epes, Accomac county.

(Continued)

———

SURRY COUNTY RECORDS.

Surry county was formed from Isle of Wight in 1652. The earliest entry in the first book of records is dated 1650.

The first three clerks were: Robert Stanton, from 1652 to 1653; George Watkins, from 17 Nov., to 20 Nov., 1652, and William Edwards, from 1652 to 1697.

Book I.

3 Feb., 1650. Convy. from Mary Crafton, relict of Thomas Crafton, to John Cooper.

3 Nov., 1652. Dep. of Capt. George Jordan.

7 May, 1652. Dep. of Francis Norton.

14 ——, 1651. Convy. from John Blackburne, Par. of Southwarke, taylor, to Jno. Dibdall, of same place. Wit.: Morris Rose, Richard Dibdall.

4 Feb., 1652. Agreement bet. Thos. Felton, carpenter, and Jno. Holmewood. Wit.: Geo. Stephens, Sack. Brewster.

15 Dec., 1652. Dep. of Jno. Flood, aged 30.

15 Dec., 1652. Dep. of John Blackborne, aged 33.

15 Nov., 1652. Jury impaneled to give verdict upon the body of Robert Woodford, a Northamptonshire man, servant to Mr. Emline. Jurors: Mr. John Bishopp, Mr. Jas. Macom, Mr. Thos. Binns, Mr. Jno. Phibbs, Mr. Jno. Courtman, Mr. Jno. Leake, Mr. Jno. Hitchcock, Mr. Robert Major, Mr. Thos. Hadlye, Mr. Edmund Howell, Mr. Robert Palmer.

16 Feb., 1651. Ind. bet. Richard Banin, par. of Southwarke, planter, and Jno. Flood, same par., planter. Wit.: Daniel Hutton, Jno. Dibdall, Jno. Dobbs, Richard Dibdall.

26 Oct., 1652. Ind. bet. John Gittings and Frances Howgood, of 1st pt., and Wm. Murrell, of 2nd pt. Wit.: Grigonge Rawlins, Jno. Howard.

5 Jan., 1652. Ind. bet. Robt. Shepard, of Lawnes Creek, gent., and Lieut. Wm. Canfield. Wit.: Jas. Taylor, Wm. Batt.

21 Feb., 1652. Ind. bet. Jno. Brutin and Jno. Holmwood, gent. Wit.: Robt. Stanton.

1 March, 1652. Convy. bet. Timothy Jessall and Jno. Holmwood. Wit.: Robt. Stanton.

28 Feb., 1652. P. of atty. from Jno. Jennings to Jno. Orchard.

4 Feb., 1652. P. of atty. from Jno. Jennings to Wm. Rose.

28 Feb., 1647. Convy. from Wm. Batt to Jno. Bishopp of a cow formerly belonging to Wm. Ewen. Wit.: Jno. Jennings, Wm. Lea.

2 Aug., 1653. Certificate to Jonathan Newell and Edmond Patin to depart out of this country in ship "Two Brothers," Capt. Richard Waters, commander.

5 Feb., 1652. Ind. bet. Thos. Warringe, gent.; James Masom, planter; Jno. Watkins, cooper, unto Jno. Spilltimber, planter.

1 March, 1652. Sale by Capt. Benj. Sidway of piece of land in Co. Surry, belonging to Peter Harrison, orphan of Benj. Harrison, gent., decd., to Mr. Wm. Thomas. Wit.: Wm. Batt, Robt. Stanton.

17 March, 1652. Confession of judgment by Daniel Barwick to Karbye Kiggan, atty. for Capt. Whittye of London, mariner. Wit.: Martin Hammond, Wm. Marriott.

21 March, 1652. Deed from Robt. Bateman, of Smithport, to Thos. Warringe, of same place.

25 Feb., 1652. Deed from Jas. Mason to Thos. Felton, carpenter. Wit.: Robt. Stanton, Sack. Brewster.

5 April, 1653. Dep. of John George, aged 50.

6 April, 1653. Deed from Hy. Meddowes to Robt. Spencer and Robt. Atkins. Wit.: Jno. Holmwood, Robt. Morslay.

5 April, 1653. Convy. from Col. Henry Browne, Esq., 1st pt., and Col. Geo. Ludlowe, Esq., Capt. Geo. Jordan and Wm. Brown, gent., 2nd pt., for love and affection, etc., to his wife, Ann Browne. Wit.: Law. Baker, Robt. Stanton, Sack. Brewster.

9 April, 1653. Convy. from Wm. Edwards, atty. for Mr. Wm. Cooke, 2 men servants, Louis de Cortell and Francis Ware, to Mr. Walter Childs. Wit.: Jas. Jaty, Sarah Edwards.

7 Sept., 1653. Petition of Thos. Swann, sheriff of co., agst. Karbye Kiggan.

3 June, 1653. Petition of Wm. Lea, executor of Gregory Rawlins, to pay debt due to Robt. Fox, of Wapping co.,

Middlesex, mariner. Wit.: Steven Yates, Jno. Heiward, Sack. Brewster.

3 June, 1653. Bill of sale from Wm. Lea to Wm. Thomas.

5 May, 1653. Bill of sale from Anthony Trivett to Wm. Murrell.

4 Sept., 1653. Convy. from John Blackburn to Wm. Jennings.

5 July, 1653. Convy. from John Johnson, James City co., planter, to Robert Roberts. Wit.: Hy. Randolph, Samuel Taylor.

5 Jan., 1653. Convy. from Robert Roberts to Mr. Geo. Stephens, Wit.: Geo. Jordan, Thos. Warringe.

6 Sept., 1653. Convy. from Henry Bannister of 275 acres of land, possessed by will of Wm. Shepard, decd., and petitioned by him in 1640, and now assigned to Wm. Batt, of Surry county. Wit.: Jno. Board, Jno. Price, Sack. Brewster.

2 Oct., 1653. Jury to inquire into death of Jno. Briant, a boy, and late servant to Jno. Spilltimber and Jno. Bradye. Jury: Wm. Agborowe, Wm. Gassinge, Nich. Perry, Jno. King, Thos. Woodhouse, Jno. Hux, Jno. Saines, Jno. Bishoppe, Thos. Binns, Peter Greene, Robt. Warren, Rich. Shortland, Wm. Marriott, Henry Bannister, Jno. Board, Jno. Price, Thos. Dinnetys, Richard Blunt, Austin Honnicott.

2 Oct. 1653. Petition of Karbye Kiggan, atty. for Capt. Jno. Whittye, of London, mariner, against Lieut.-Col. Thos. Swann, sheriff of Surry co.

2 Oct., 1653. Convy. from Anthony Trivett, planter, to Richardina Field, now wife of John Gittings, planter. Wit.: Jno. Corker, Sack. Brewster.

3 Oct., 1653. Convy. from Edward Hurlston to Mr. Jno. Price. Wit.: Wm. Edwards.

4 Jan., 1653. Quit claim from John Cogan to Anthony Trivett.

15 June, 1653. Convy. from Eliz. Simpson to Thos. Welch,

of Portsmouth, chirergeon; also to Hy. Jones and Jno.
Saynes.

28 Nov., 1653. Convy. from Matthew Battell, cooper, to
Wm. Hemlock, planter. Wit.: Robert Bloyse.

5 Dec., 1653. Convy. from Christopher Vaughan of right of
land leased from Daniel Massingall, the title of same belonging to Christopher Lawson, unto Francis Farrington,
planter. Wit.: Thos. Pittman, Jno. Rawlings, Daniel Massingall.

19 March, 1653. Receipt of Robt. Digby, of Bristol, mariner,
to Wm. Batt, of 320 lbs. of tobacco. Wit.: Wm. Edwards, Thos. Culmer.

4 Jan., 1653. Convy. from Christopher Boaz, planter, to
Nicholas Perry, merchant, of land, etc., in James City co.
Wit.: Nich. Reynolds, Sack. Brewster.

17 May, 1653. Convy. from Hy. Randolph to Richard Atkins, of Chard, in county of Somerset, merchant. Wit.:
Ab. Wood, Sack. Brewster.

3 Oct., 1653. Bond of Geo. Raymond to Mr. Peter Mack-
rell, merchant. Wit.: John Kent, Robt. Stanton.

9 July, 1654. Certificate that Geo. Browne is lawfully in-
trusted with the estate of Capt. Wm. Cox, decd.

23 March, 1653. Attestation of Mr. Edwd. Sanderson, that
he came to Va. and met his brother, Montague Sanderson,
and that he was familiar and associated with Mr. Daniel
Coates and his wife, and that his brother told him, Mr.
Coates' wife was in Va., and that she was married to
to Mr. Richard Hill, notwithstanding her husband was
living in London, and that he did, accordingly, wonder at
it, knowing the woman by sight, and knowing her said
husband, Coates, to be alive, all of which the witness is
ready to depose.

23 March, 1653. Convy. of John Holmwood, atty. for Mr.
Theodorick Bland, merchant, to John Barker. Wit.: Benj.
Sidway, Robt. Stanton.

5 May, 1654. Petition of Randall Holt.

5 May, 1654. Convy. of Thos. Woodhouse to John Zanes.

21 March, 1653. Convy. from Wm. Rose to Matthew Battell and Richard Tias.

26 March, 1654. Petition of Edward Skynner, in behalf of the Commonwealth of England, that James Taylor, of county of Surry, chyrugeon, hath lived in the loathesome sin of adultery with his late servant, Ursula Kettle, and that she was delivered of a bastard child, the 18 Oct. last past.

26 March, 1654. Deposition of Ursula Kettle, aged 20 years.

26 March, 1654. Petition and complaint of Mrs. Elizabeth Taylor, wife of James Taylor, for a separation.

22 March, 1653. Release from Richard Shortland to Mrs. Cicilye Dunstan.

7 March, 1653. Deposition of Thos. Gray, Sr., aged 60 years, or thereabouts, that Daniel Hutton, in the time of his sickness, did bequeath his whole estate unto Rebeccah, his wife, verbally.

7 March, 1653. Dep. of William Rose, aged 38 years, or thereabouts.

27 March, 1654. Dep. of Randall Holt and William Marriott.

2 May, 1654. Dep. of Wm. Coates, Sr., aged 54, or thereabouts, that when Mary Powell died, she was near upon 15 years of age, and that Richard Powell, her father, gave her four head of cattle a little before the death of him, the said Richard Powell.

2 May, 1654. Dep. of Alice Carter, aged 55, or thereabouts, in re. the above.

16 April, 1654. Bond of Jno. Gittings to Wm. Jennings. Wit.: Wm. Flood, Wm. Browne.

7 July, 1654. Bond of Jno. Dibdall and Capt. Jno. Frame to Richard Dibdall.

2 May, 1654. Bond of Andrew Robinson and Dorothy Kew to Alex. Matrick.

2 May, 1654. Bond of Robt. Morsley to Jno. Felton. Wit.: John Harris, Sack. Brewster.

7 Oct., 1650. Ind. bet. Martin Hammond and Jane, his wife, and Wm. Hammond, for latter's apprenticeship.

Wit.; John Hammond, Thomas ap Thomas, Law. Little-
boy.

1 July, 1651. Ind. bet. Nich. Reynolds and Edwd. Hurlstone, carpenter. Wit.: Eustace Grimes, John Gossall.

23 Feb., 1651. Conv. from Edwd. Hurlstone to Thos. Cov-
ington. Wit.: Eustace Grimes, Elizabeth Hardinge.

6 May, 1654. Convy. from Jas. Masonn, of Mathews
Mount, co. of Surry, planter, to Richard Marydall. Wit.:
Sack. Brewster, Edward Petway.

17 July, 1652. Letter from Wm. Edwards to John Medmore.
Teste: Mrs. Sarah Edwards.

4 July, 1654. Deed from William Gassinge to John King.
Wit.: Nich. Perry, Peter Adams.

9 Jan., 1653. Agreement bet. John Sames and John Berrye.

1 Aug., 1654. Convy. from Wm. Rickett to Wm. Marriott.

(Continued)

VIRGINIA REVOLUTIONARY SOLDIERS.

There is deposited at the Land Office, Richmond, a record
of the name and services of over 12,000 officers and men, who
served on land or sea from the State of Virginia, during the
Revolutionary War. By permission of Col. Richardson, their
custodian, we are now placing in print these valuable records.
—(Editor).

In the House of Delegates, 30 Dec., 1784.

Resolved, that any person who has served in the armies
of the United States from the first day of May, 1779, until
the close of the late war between America and Great Britain,
and who is possessed of a land warrant in his own right, or
by assignment before the first day of May, 1779, issued agreeable to the Proclamation made by the King of Great Britain
in the year 1763, may exchange the same with the Register of
the land office for a warrant agreeable to this resolution, which
warrant he shall be permitted to locate on any vacant lands
reserved by an act of this Assembly on the eastern side of the

River Ohio, for the officers and soldiers of this Commonwealth on continental establishment.

(*Test*) JOHN BECKLEY, C. H. D.

1785, Jan. 1st.

Agreed to by the Senate,

WILL DREW, C. S.

ENTITLED TO LAND WARRANTS.

Shelton, Clough, Capt., 1st Lieut., Va. Contl. Line, 13 Nov., 1776; Capt., 1 March, 1777; in service until 18 Jan., 1783.

Hoffler, William, Capt., State Line from 9 Jan., 1777, to June, 1780.

Pendleton, James, Capt., Va. Artillery, Jan., 1776, to 24 Jan., 1783.

Moore, Thomas, Private, State Line 3 years ending 17 Jan., 1783.

Moseley, William, Major, Contl. Line, 5 Feb., 1776, to 12 April, ——.

Webb, John, Col., 7th Va. Regt., 5 Feb., 1776, to ——.

Wiley, George, Jr., Sgt.-Major, 9th Va. Regt., 10 Aug., 1776, to 10 Sept., 1779.

Savage, Nathaniel, Lieut., State Cavalry, 28 July, 1779.

Graves, William, Cornet of Cavalry, Aug., 1779, to this day, ——, 1783.

Wyatt, Capt.-Lieut., State Artillery, 6 Dec., 1778, to this day, ——.

Davis, John, Sgt., Va. Line, 3 years ending 28 July, 1781.

Allison, John, Col., ——.

Maury, Abraham, Lieut.,——, 14 Nov., 1776,——.

Rice, Nathaniel, Lieut., Artillery, 7 Dec., 17—.

Weedon, George, Jr., Brig.-Genl., Contl. Line, 1776 to present day.

Roane, Christopher, Capt., State Artillery, 1777; is now a captain in legion commanded by Col. Dabney.

Boswell, Machen, Capt., State Line; service ended 6 Feb., 1781.

Dillon, Jesse, Corpl., Contl. Line, 3 years, and died in service; Warrant issued to Benjamin Dillon, his heir-at-law.

Spiller, William, Capt., State Artillery, 3 years.

Hill, Baylor, Capt., Light Dragoons, Contl. Line, Dec., 1776, to 15 Jan., 1783.

Vawter, William, Lieut., Contl. Line, Feb., 1777, to Feb., ——.

Rucker, Angus, Capt., State Infantry, ——.

Hill, Thomas, Major, Contl. Line more than 3 years.

Dandridge, John, Capt., Artillery, from Nov., 1776, to present time.

Armistead, Thomas, Capt., State Line, Aug., 1776, to 21 May, ——.

Mallory, Philip, Capt., Contl. Line, 22 Nov., 1776, to present time.

Lipscomb, Bernard, Capt.-Lieut., Artillery, Dec., 1778, to March, 1782.

Lipscomb, Yancey, Capt.-Lieut., State Line, May, 1778, to March, 1782.

Davies, Joseph, Surgeon to the 1st Va. Contl. Regt., April, 1778, to present time.

Quarles, James, Capt., State Line, April, 1776, to Nov., 1780.

Gary, John, Sgt., Artillery, 3 years, ending 27, Nov., 1780.

Swope, John, Dr., Surgeon in Navy from 24 May, 1776, to Nov., 1781.

Towers, John, Private, State Line, 3 years, ending 1 March, 1780.

Bayler, George, Col., Light Dragoons, Contl. Line, Jan., 1777, to present day.

Wallace, Gustavus B., Lieut.-Col., Va. Line, 7 years' service.

Callender, Eleazer, Capt., State Navy, 3 years' service.

Roberts, John, Dr., Surgeon in Va. State Line from —— to March, 1780.

Brodie, Lodowick, Dr., Surgeon in Va. State Line from 15 Aug., 1776, to Aug., 1782.

Green, John, Col., Va. Line, 4 Sept., 1775, and is now in service.

Green, John, Lieut., entered the service July, 1776, and died in service, 3 April, 1778; warrant issued to William Green, his heir-at-law.

Hall, William, 3 years in service in 2nd State Regt.

Askew, James, Private, in Va. Contl. Infantry prior to 1 Dec., 1780.

Wilson, Willis, Lieut., Va. Contl. Regt., 3 years from 2 July, 1779.

Hendricks, Elijah, Sgt., Contl. Line, 3 years' service.

Puckett, Woman, Private, 3 years in Va. Contl. Line, to his discharge, 25 July, 1781.

Downs, John, 3 years' service in Va. Contl. Line.

Ewing, Alexander, Lieut., Va. Contl. Line, 3 years' service prior to his resignation, 1 Jan., 1781.

Marks, John, Capt., Contl. Line, 3 years' service.

Holmes, Benjamin, Capt., 3 years' service prior to Sept., 1778.

Cabell, Samuel J., Col., Va. Infantry, from 11 March, 1776.

Campbell, William, Capt., State Line, 3 years' service.

Brush, James, Sgt., Contl. Line, 3 years prior to 3 Dec., 1779.

Hoomes, Thomas Claiborne, Lieut., 3 years' service ending July, 1779.

Pugh, Willis, Ensign, late of 15th Va. Regt., deceased in service; warrant to William Pugh, his heir-at-law.

Oldham, Conway, Capt. killed at Battle of Eutaw, Sept., 1781; Contl. Line from April, 1777, to time of his death; warrant to Samuel Oldham, his heir-at-law.

Phillips, Samuel, Ensign, Va. Line; killed in service at Charleston, 3 May, 1780; warrant to Sally Phillips, devisee of Samuel Phillips, deceased.

Ray, William, Private, 2nd Va. Regt., 3 years' service.

Campbell, Samuel, Lieut., Contl. Line, from Sept., 1777, until his death, Aug., 1778; warrant to William Campbell, his heir-at-law.

Nevill, Presley, Col., Aug., 1775, to 7 Nov., 1782.

Morgan, Daniel, Brig.-Genl., Contl. Line, from June, 1775.

Voglusan, Armand, Capt., 3 years' service in State Cavalry.

Meriwether, Thomas, Major, State Line, March, 1776, to 6 Feb., 1781.

Drew, Thomas Haines, Capt., Feb., 1777, to Feb., 1781.

Carrington, Mayo, Capt., Contl. Line, Feb., 1776, to present time.

Croghan, William, Major, Contl. Line, Feb., 1776, to present time.

Stith, John, Capt., State Line, from March, 1777, to present time.

Dudley, Henry, Capt., State Line, 3 years' service.

Dabney, Charles, Lieut.-Col., State Line, from Dec., 1776, to this day.

Morgan, John, disabled soldier, enlisted in Contl. Line for the war.

Marshall, John, Capt., 3 years' service.

Coombes, Francis, soldier in Contl. Line for the war.

Consolver, John, soldier in Contl. Line for the war.

Reddy, Dennis, Sgt., Contl. Line, 3 years ending 25 July, 1781.

Hunter, John, Capt., State Line for 3 years.

Anderson, Richard C., Col., Contl. Line, 6 March, 1776, in service and taken prisoner in Charleston, 12 May, 1780.

Thomson, William, State Legion of Artillery as Cadet, Aug., 1777; officer, 18 June, 1778; Captain, 23 April, 1780.

Moody, Edward, Capt., decd., State Artillery in year 17—; died in Halifax, March, 1781; warrant to Eliz. Moody, his devisee.

Hall, John, 3 years in State Artillery.

Stewart, William, 3 years in State Artillery.

Edmunds, Thomas, Capt., in service since 10 March, 1777, and still continues in same.

Wright, Patrick, Midshipman, from May or June, 1776, and continued in service until 2 Aug., 1777, when he was appointed Lieut. of State Artillery; Capt. of same, 1778 until his resignation in 1780.

Muter, George, appointed to command "New Galley," 14 March, 1776 with rank equal to Major in land forces; resigned commission in Navy, July, 1777; appointed to receive recruits of State Artillery, 27 Aug., 1777; Lieut.-Col. of same 15 Nov., 1777, until 8 Nov., 1779; then in command of State Garrison Regt., which command he still retains.

Blair, John, Capt.-Lieut., Contl. Artillery; killed at Sumter's defeat, 18 Aug., 1780; warrant to Archibald Blair, his heir-at-law.

Overton, Thomas, Lieut., Contl. Line, 10 June, 1776, resigned 8 July, 1779.

Slayden, Daniel, soldier in 4th Va. Regt., 1776, 2 years; 4th Regt. Light Dragoons, 3 years.

Read, Isaac, Col., died in the service; warrant to Clement Read, eldest son and heir-at-law, 14 Dec., 1782.

Drew, Thomas H., Lieut., Contl. Line, 1776; Capt. in State Garrison Regt., 3 July, 1779.

Bentley, William, Capt., 5th Va. Regt., Jan., 1776, and is still in service.

Archer, Joseph, Lieut., Contl. Line, 1776, until his death; warrant to John Archer, his heir-at-law.

Archer, Peter Field, Lieut., Va. Line, June, 1779, and still continues.

Scott, Joseph, Sr., Capt., 1st Va. Regt., Sept., 1775, and still in service.

Clay, Matthew, Lieut., Va. Line, Jan., 1776, and still in service.

Reade, Edmund, Capt., officer in 4th Va. Regt., 1775; Capt. in Nelson's Corps State Cavalry, 26 June, 1779.

Conner, John, Sgt., 1st Va. Regt., 3 years prior to 20 Dec., 1779.

Payne, Thomas, Capt., 9th Va. Contl. Line, 14 June, 1776.

Peyton, John, Capt., Contl. Line, 2 Jan., 1776, to Oct., 1778.

Porterfield, Robert, Capt., 24 Dec., 1776, to this day.

Porterfield, Charles, Lieut.-Col., died in service from wounds; warrant to Robert Porterfield, his heir-at-law.

Tunstall, Edward, Sgt., 3 years in State Artillery.

Jones, Samuel, Capt., Va. Line, 1776 to 1781.

Marshall, Thomas, Jr., Cadet in State Artillery, 1777; Officer, 1778; Capt., 23 April, 1780.

Marshall, Humphrey, Cadet, State Artillery, 1777; Capt., 18 Dec., 1779.

Sansum, Philip, Capt., Va. Contl. Regt., March, 1777, and is still in service.

Bowne, Thomas, Capt., 1st Va. Regt., May, 1777, and is still in service.

Linton, Michael, Private, 3rd Va. Regt., wounded at defeat of Col. Buford, and served 4 years.

Kennedy, James, Officer, from Jan., 1776; State Garrison Regt., July, 1779, when he was commissioned a Lieut., and is now supernumary.

Giles, John, Ensign, Contl. Line, 1780, until his death; warrant to William Giles, his heir-at-law.

Read, Clement, Lieut., in Major John Nelson's Va. Cavalry, until his death, in Aug., 1781; warrant to John Read, eldest brother to Clement Read.

Slaughter, Philip, Capt. in Contl. Line, July, 1776; resigned in Feb., 1781.

Smith, Francis, Lieut. from 1 Feb., 1777, until this day.

Booker, Samuel, Capt. Contl. Line, Nov., 1776, and in service ever since.

Lewis, William, officer in Contl. Line, from Sept., 1775 until present time.

Hogg, Samuel, Capt., 1st Va. Contl. Regt., 11 June, 1777, and still in service.

Morton, James, Lieut. 4th Va. Regt., 1 Jan., 1776, and is still in service.

Moseby, Benjamin, Lieut. Va. Line, 10 Sept., 1778, and still in service.

Hardyman, Lieut. State Line, 3 Sept., 1777, to Feb., 1782.

Smith, Gregory, Col. State Line, 3 years.

Fenn, Thomas, Capt.-Lieut. State Artillery from 13 Jan., 1777, to this day.

Prior, John, Capt.-Lieut. Contl. Artillery, 13 Jan., 1777, and is now in service at Winchester, this day, 30 Dec., 1782.

Smith, Jonathan, Lieut. Va. Line, March, 177—, to 12 March, 1783.

Rudder, Epaphroditus, Lieut. Va. Cavalry, April, 1778 to this day.

Gordon, Allen, Sgt., Contl. Cavalry, 3 years, ending 10 Feb., 1781.

Digges, Dudley, Lieut., Contl. Cavalry, June, 1779, to present day.

Whiting, Francis, Lieut., Contl. Cavalry, 3 years' service.
Taylor, William, Major, Va. Line, 29 Jan., 1776, to 10 Feb., 1781.
Taylor, Richard, Capt., Navy, from 6 Feb., 1776, to Nov., 1781.
Whitton, Francis, Private, State Line, 3 years.
Washington, George, Lieut., Va. Line, 16 Feb., 1780, to this day, 20 Feb., 1783.
Rucker, Elliott, Lieut., State Line, 3 years' service.
Stark, Richard, Lieut., Va. Line, 28 Dec., 1776, to 15 Feb., 1783.
Leigh, John, Sgt., Va. Line, Feb., 1776, to Feb., 1781.
Vanduvall, Markes, Lieut., Va. Line, 11 June, 1777, to 13 Dec., 1782.
Cash, Warren, Private, Va. Line, 3 years' service.
Moore, Alexander, Midshipman, 3 years' service in the navy.
Driver, Thomas, Sgt., State Line, 3 years' service, ending 23 June, 1782.
Collingsworth, Edmund, Private, State Line, 3 years' service.
Collingsworth, John, Private, State Line, from Dec., 1776, to Dec., 1779.
Fowler, William, Capt., Va. Line, 3 years' service.
Smith, William S., Lieut., 6th Va. Regt., Feb., 1777, to 29 Nov., 1782.
Gist, Nathaniel, Col., Contl. Line, 10 Jan., 1777, to 24 Feb., 1783.
Rogers, John, Capt., State Line, 1778, to 14 Feb., 1782.
Quarles, James, Major, State Line, for proportion of land, together with a former allowance as Capt. in State Line.
Miller, William, Lieut., Artillery, 13 Jan., 1777, to 27 Feb., 1783.
Dix, Thomas, Capt.-Lieut., Artillery, 13 Jan., 1777, to 27 Feb., 1783.
Overton, John, Capt., 14th Va. Regt., Dec., 1776, to 25 Dec., 1782.
Roy, Beverley, Capt., Va. Line, Aug., 1777 to March 31, 1783.
Williams, John, Capt., Artillery, Aug., 1777, to 8 Feb., 1781.
Coleman, Samuel, Lieut., Artillery, 13 Jan., 1777, to 15 Feb., 1783.

Dugar, Robert, Sgt., Contl. Line, 3 years' service.

Cowne, Robert, Capt.-Lieut., State Artillery, 3 years' service.

Cowne, Augustus, Lieut., State Line, 3 years' service.

Vowles, Charles, Lieut., State Line, 3 years' service.

Vowles, Henry, Capt.-Lieut., Artillery, 3 years' service.

Vowles, Walter, Capt., State Line, died in service; warrant to Henry Vowles, his heir-at-law.

Young, William, Corpl., Contl. Line, 3 years' service.

Rankins, Robert, Lieut., Contl. Line, 4 July, 1779, to 28 Dec., 1782.

Edmonds, Elias, Lieut.-Col., State Line, from 1777 to ——— (record torn).

Ransdall, Thomas, Capt., Va. Line, July, 1776, to 4 March, 1783.

Crockett, Joseph, Lieut.-Col., State Line, Sept., 1775, to 6 Feb., 1781.

King, John, Private, Contl. Line, 3 years' service.

Kelly, Thaddy, Capt., State Line, 3 years' service.

Harrison, John Peyton, Capt., Contl. Line, 3 years' service.

Clark, Jonathan, Lieut.-Col., State Line, 4 March, 1776, to ——— (torn).

Cowherd, Francis, Capt., Contl. Line, from 6 July, 1776, to 11 March, 1783.

White, William, Capt., Contl. Line, from 8 May, 1776, to 11 March, 1783.

Saunders, Celey, Capt., State Navy, 3 years' service.

Muhlenberg, Peter, Brig.-Genl., Contl. Line, from Jan., 1776, to 10 March, 1783.

Huffamn, Philip, Lieut., Contl. Line, 3 years' service.

Anderson, Isaac, Private, State Line, Jan., 1777, to 12 March, 1783.

Valentine, Jacob, Capt., State Line, 3 years' service.

Woodson, Robert, Capt., Contl. Line, from 29 Jan., 1776, to 10 March, 1783.

Brooks, Nathaniel, Private, Contl. Line, 3 years' service.

Worsham, Richard, Lieut., Contl. Line, from 20 Nov., 1776, to 3 March, 1783.

Smith, Aaron, Private, Contl. Line, 3 years' service.

Humphreys, Reuben, soldier in State Cavalry, 3 years' service.

Craddock, Robert, Lieut., Contl. Line, from 1 Jan., 1777, to 19 March, 1783.

Crule, John, Lieut., Contl. Line, 3 years' service.

Craddock, Henry, Sgt., Contl. Line, 3 years' service.

Kirby, John, Drummer in Contl. Line, from 10 Dec., 1779, to 17 March, 1783.

Kemp, Peter, Capt., State Artillery, 3 years' service.

Jameson, John, Lieut.-Col., Contl. Cavalry, from 13 June, 1776, to 19 March, 1783.

Chavoiz, John, soldier for 3 years.

Galt, Patrick, Dr., Surgeon in 9th Va. Regt., 1776 until his death at Morristown, N. J., 13 Feb., 1777; warrant to James Galt, heir-at-law.

Brown, Windsor, Capt., State Line from March, 1776, to 25 March, 1783.

Mabin, James, Capt., Va. Line, 3 years' ending April, 1780.

Pointer, William, Lieut., Contl. Line, 3 years' service.

Beale, Robert, Capt., Contl. Line, from 10 Feb., 1776, to 26 March, 1783.

Butler, Lawrence, Capt., Va. Line, from 2 Dec., 1776, to 26 March, 1783.

Smith, Ballard, Lieut., Va. Line, from 11 June, 1777, to 12 March, 1783.

Yancey, Robert, Capt., Light Dragoons, Va. Line, from March, 1779, to 15 Jan., 1783.

Terry, Stephen, Corporal, 3 years ending 24 Feb., 1781.

Hays, John, Major, Va. Line, from 6 March, 1776, to 14 Feb., 1781.

Thweatt, Thomas, Capt., Va. Line, from 24 Feb., 1777, to 4 May, 1782.

Padens, Samuel, Capt., Artillery, Contl. Line, from 7 March, 1776, to 28 Dec., 1782.

Dickerson, Edmund, Major, Va. Line, 3 years' service.

Baughan, Avis, Private, State Line, 3 years' service.

Bland, Theodorick, Col., Va. Cavalry, from June, 1776, to Jan., 1780.

Moulden, Thomas, Corporal, State Line, from Jan., 1777, to 12 March, 1783.

Barns, Robert, Private, Contl. Line, 3 years' service.

Slaughter, William, Lieut., State Line, 3 years' service.

Tupman, John, Master in State Navy for 3 years.

Holmes, David, Surgeon in Contl. Line, 3 years ending 7 May., 1782.

Knight, John, Surgeons-Mate, Contl. Line, 3 years ending 1 Jan., 1780.

Gibson, John, Col., Contl. Line, 3 years, ending Nov., 1779.

Springer, Uriah, Capt., Contl. Line, 3 years, ending Dec., 1779.

Biggs, Benjamin, Capt., Contl. Line, 3 years, ending 27 Dec., 1779.

Coleman, Jacob, Lieut., Contl. Line, 3 years, ending 21 Dec., 1779.

Springer, Jacob, Lieut., Contl. Line, 3 years, ending 16 Dec., 1779.

Mills, John, Lieut., Contl. Line, 3 years, ending 21 Dec., 1779.

Dawson, Henry, Lieut., Contl. Line, 3 years, ending 16 Dec., 1779.

Tannehill, Josiah, Lieut., Contl. Line, 3 years, ending 6 Aug., 1782.

Harrison, John, Lieut., Contl. Line, 3 years, ending, 16 Dec., 1779.

Winlock, Joseph, Lieut., Contl. Line, 3 years, ending 1 Feb., 1780.

Posey, Thomas, Lieut.-Col., Va. Line, 7 years' service.

Barbee, Thomas, Capt., Va. Line, 3 years, ending 22 March, 1780.

Gray, George, Capt., Contl. Dragoons, 3 years, prior to June, 1779.

Gray, William, Lieut., Va. Line, 3 years, prior to Jan., 1782.

Field, Reuben, Capt., Va. Line, 3 years, ending 10 March, 1780.

Triplett, George, Lieut., Va. Line, 3 years' service.

Slaughter, Lawrence, Lieut., decd., 3 years' service; warrant to Thomas Slaughter, his heir-at-law, 1 April, 1783.

Evans, William, Lieut., Va. Line, 3 years, ending 10 Dec., 1779.

Russell, Charles, Lieut., State Line, 3 years' service.
Orr, Samuel, soldier in 2nd Va. Regt., serving 3 years.
Woodward, Charles, Private, State Line, 3 years' service.
Stewart, Solomon, Private, State Line, 3 years' service.
English, Charles, Private, State Line, 3 years' service.
Townshend, George, Private, State Line, 3 years' service.
Redden, Robert, Private, State Line, 3 years' service.
Mansfield, Thomas, Private, State Line, 3 years' service.
Carrick, Patrick, Private, State Line, 3 years' service.
Burris, Frederick, Private, State Line, 3 years' service.
Williams, Zebulon, Private, State Line, 3 years' service.
Williams, Thomas, Private, State Line, 3 years' service.
Creekman, William, Private, State Line, 3 years' service.
Williams, William, Private, State Line, 3 years' service.
McDaw, Daniel, Private, State Line, 3 years' service.
McClanachan, Elijah, Armorer in State Navy, 3 years' service.
Colden, James, Private, State Line, 3 years' service.
Thompson, Littlebury, Private, State Line, 3 years' service.
Hampten, William, Private, State Line, 3 years' service.
King, Francis, Private, State Line, 3 years' service.
Wade, David, Private, State Line, 3 years' service.
Bigley, Lewis, Private, State Line, 3 years' service.
Heaken, William, Private, State Line, 3 years' service.
McHene, John, Private, State Line, 3 years' service.
Dunn, Richard, Private, State Line, 3 years' service.
Ricketts, William, Private, State Line, 3 years' service.
Young, Frederick, Sgt., Va. Line, 3 years.
McDugal, John, Drummer, State Line, 3 years' service.
Austin, John W., Sgt.-Major, State Line, 3 years' service.
Russell, John, Lieut., State Line, 3 years' service.
Pelham, Charles, Major, Contl. Line, 7 years' service, ending
    5 Feb., 1783.
Kelley, John, Private, State Line, 3 years' service.
Bland, James, Private, State Line, 3 years' service.
Walden, Zachariah, Private, State Line, 3 years' service.
Phillips, Larkin, Private, State Line, 3 years' service.
Fortune, Gardner, Private, State Line, 3 years' service.

Bohannon, Ambrose, Capt.-Lieut., Cont. Line, from Feb., 1776, to 25 March, 1783.

Balmain, Alexander, Revd., Brigade-Chaplain, from 20 Feb., 1777, to 9 Jan., 1783.

Guthrie, John, Fifer, Va. Line, 3 years' service.

Lovely, William S., Capt., 4th Va., Contl. Line, from March, 1776, to 29 Nov., 1783.

Baldwin, Cornelius, Dr., Surgeon, Contl. Line, 3 years, ending 1780.

Shepherd, Abraham, Capt., Contl. Line, 3 years' service.

Bedinger, Henry, Capt., Contl. Line, 3 years, ending 9 July, 1779.

Bendinger, Daniel, Private, Contl. Line, 3 years' service.

Palmer, William, Corporal, Contl. Line, 3 years' service.

Eastin, Richard, Lieut., Contl. Line, 3 years' service.

Eskridge, William, Lieut., Contl. Line, from 3 Sept., 1775, to 28 Dec., 1782.

Wood, James, Col., Contl. Line, from Nov., 1776, to 7 April, 1783.

Hite, Abraham, Capt., Contl. Line, 3 years, ending 8 Jan., 1780.

Eastin, Philip, Lieut., Contl. Line, from March, 1776, to 6 Jan., 1783.

White, Robert, Capt., Contl. Line, 3 years, ending Dec., 1779.

Reardon, George, Sgt., State Line, 3 years' service.

Bell, Thomas, Capt., Contl. Line, 3 years, ending 8 March, 1780.

Carter, John C., Capt., Contl. Artillery, 7 years, ending March, 1783.

Clark, John, Capt., Contl. Line, 3 years.

Crawford, John, Lieut., Contl. Line, 3 years, ending 4 May, 1780.

Christie, James, Private, State Line, 3 years, ending 1 Sept., 1782.

Miller, David, Lieut., Contl. Line, 7 years, ending Jan., 1783.

Westcott, Wright, Capt., State Navy, 3 years' service.

Tyree, William, Private, Va. Cavalry, 3 years' service.

Tabb, Augustine, Capt., State Line, 3 years' service.

Mann, David, Private in Artillery, Aug., 1776; Ensign in State Garrison, 24 June, 1778; Lieut., 1 June, 1779, and is now 1st Lieut. in Legion of Colonel Dabney.

Nowell, Lipscomb, Lieut., Contl. Line, 3 years, ending 9 Sept., 1781.

Harper, James, Lieut., State Line, 3 years' service.

Miller, James, Private, State Cavalry, 3 years' service.

Boston, Adam, Private, State Cavalry, 3 years' service.

Cole, William, Private, State Cavalry, 3 years' service.

Lock, William, Private, State Cavalry, 3 years' service.

Bartlett, John, Private, State Cavalry, 3 years' service.

Bronn Le, John, Corporal, State Cavalry, 3 years' service.

Green, Robert, Lieut., Contl. Line, 3 years, ending 23 Dec., 1782.

Leplong, Joseph, Corporal, State Cavalry, 3 years' service.

Calmes, Marquis, Capt. Contl. Line, 3 years' service.

Wood, Edward, Private, State Line, 3 years, ending Jan., 1783.

Barnes, William, Private, State Line, 3 years' service.

Clarke, Edward, Private, Va. Artillery, 3 years' service.

Blackwell, Joseph, Capt., Contl. Line, from Feb., 1776, to 6 Jan., 1783.

Davis, John, Private, State Cavalry, 3 years, ending May, 1782.

Rings, Burtus, Private, State Cavalry, 3 years' service.

Punter, Henry, Sgt., Va. Artillery, 3 years' service.

Taylor, Bartholomew, Private, State Cavalry, 3 years' service.

Taylor, Samuel, Private, Contl. Line, 3 years' service.

Franklin, James, Private, Va. Line, 3 years' service.

Taylor, Major, Private, State Cavalry; discharged by order of the Gov. in Council.

Nickins, William, Drummer, State Line, 3 years' service.

Hebron, John, Private, State Line, 3 years' service.

Emry, Thomas, Private, State Line, 3 years' service.

Upshaw, Thomas, Capt., State Line, 3 years' service.

Swearingen, Joseph, Capt., Contl. Line, 3 years, ending 9 Dec., 1779.

Russell, Albert, Lieut., Contl. Line, 3 years, ending 9 Dec., 1779.

Williams, John, Private, State Line, 3 years' service.

Massey, Theodorick, Private, State Line, 3 years' services.

Lind, Arthur, Capt., Contl. Line, from Feb., 1776, to Feb., 1781.

Duel, Henry, Private, State Cavalry, 3 years' service.

Stephenson, David, Major, Contl. Line; warrant for Surveyor's service.

Curry, James, Capt., Contl. Line, 3 years, ending June, 1780.

Graham, Arthur, Sgt., State Line, 3 years' service.

Bradford, Samuel K. Capt.-Lieut., Va. Artillery, 3 years' service.

Simms, Charles, Lieut.-Col., Va. Line, 3 years' service.

Griffith, David, Rev., Brigade Chaplain, Contl. Line, 3 years' service.

Carrol, Edward, Sgt., State Line, 3 years' service.

Rose, George, Private, State Line, 3 years' service.

Howell, Phillison, Corporal, State Line, 3 years' service.

Highland, William, Private, State Line, 3 years' service.

Dean, John, Private, State Line, 3 years' service.

Hobbs, Thomas, Private, State Line, 3 years' service.

Brimer, Isaac, Private, State Line, 3 years' service.

Woodcock, John, Private, Contl. Line, from Sept., 1775, to Sept., 1780.

Hendren, Ephraim, Private, State Line, 3 years' service.

Hill, Amos, Private, State Line; died in service; warrant to his widow, Nancy Hill.

Alexander, Ellis, Private, State Line, 3 years' service.

Tyser, Cornelius, Private, State Line, 3 years' service.

Morris, John, Private, State Line, 3 years' service.

Williams, Philemon, Private, State Line, 3 years' service.

Lewis, George, Capt., Va. Cavalry, 3 years' service.

Nixon, Andrew, Capt., Va. Cavalry, 3 years' service.

Tutt, Charles, Lieut., Contl. Line, 3 years' service.

Goodman, Daniel, Private, State Line, 3 years' service.

Raynor, John, Private, State Line, 3 years' service.

Loden, Jesse, Private, State Line, 3 years' service.

Flecher, Thomas, Private, State Line, 3 years' service.

Porter, Daniel, Sgt., State Line, 3 years' service.

Nepier, James, Sgt., State Line, 3 years' service.
Reynolds, Bernard, Private, State Line, 3 years' service.
Griffith, David, Regimental Surgeon, State Line, for 3 years.
Quarles, Nathaniel, Sgt., State Line, 3 years' service.
Kelly, Benjamin, Private, State Line, 3 years' service.
McCarty, Charles, Private, State Line, 3 years' service.
Atkinson, John, Private, State Line, 3 years' service.
Connor, Philip, Sgt., State Line, 3 years' service.
Fling, James, Private, Contl. Line, 3 years' service.
Porter, Calvert, Sgt., Contl. Line, 3 years' service.
Walker, William, Private, State Line, 3 years' service.
Pritchett, John, Sgt., State Line, 3 years' service.
Lapsley, Samuel, Capt., Va. Line, 3 years' service.
Lapsley, John, Lieut., Va. Line, 3 years' service.
Nickelson, William, Private, Va. Line, 3 years' service.
Jones, William, Private, Va. Line, 3 years' service.
Dunton, Stephen, Private, State Cavalry, 3 years' service.
Weaver, John, Private, State Line, 3 years' service.
Wills, John, Private, State Line, 3 years' service.
Hughes, Nathaniel, Private, Va. Line, 3 years' service.
Locke, Joseph, Private, Va. Artillery, 3 years' service.
Lewis, Addison, Capt., Contl. Cavalry, 3 years' service.
Ragsdale, Drury, Capt., Artillery, from 13 Jan., 1777, to 20
    Jan., 1783.
Pemberton, Thomas, Capt., Light Dragoons, Contl. Line, from
    17 Dec., 1776, to 15 Jan., 1783.
Webb, Richard, Private, State Line, 3 years' service.
Gaskey, Richard, Private, State Line, 3 years' service.
Newman, Thomas, Sgt., State Line, 3 years' service.
Highland, Robert, Drummer, State Line, 3 years' service.
Simms, Edward, Sgt., State Line, 3 years' service.
Tompkins, Robert, Lieut., decd., Contl. Line, 3 years' service;
    warrant to William Tompkins, heir-at-law.
Brown, John, Private, State Line, 3 years' service.
Tompkins, Henry, Ensign, decd., Contl. Line, 3 years' service;
    warrant to William Tompkins, heir-at-law.
Hadly, Isaac, Private, State Line, 3 years' service.
Lyon, Thomas, Sgt., State Line, 3 years' service.

Martin, Alexander, Drummer, State Line, 3 years' service.
Camban, John, Private, State Line, 3 years' service.
Maxwell, William, Private, State Line, 3 years' service.
Evans, Thomas, Private, State Line, 3 years' service.
Smith, William, Private, Va. Line, 3 years' service.
Robertson, William, Lieut., Contl. Line, 3 years' service.
Mosses, John, Private, State Line, 3 years' service.
Jeffries, Thomas, Sgt., State Line, 3 years' service.
Davis, Lewis C., Private, State Line, 3 years' service.
Manning, Samuel, Private, State Line, 3 years' service.
Staves, William, Private, State Line, 3 years' service.
Love, John, Sgt., State Line, served to end of the war.
Kemdy, Moses, Private, State Line, served to end of the war.
Summers, James, Private, State Line, served to end of the war.
Palmer, David, Corporal, State Line, 3 years' service.
Phipps, George, Private, State Line, 3 years' service.
Winston, Benjamin, Ensign, Contl. Line, 3 years' service.
Davis, Joseph, State Line, 3 years' service.
Moore, Lewis, Private, State Line, enlisted for the war.
Granger, William, Private, State Line, 3 years' service.
Miles, James, Private, State Line, 3 years' service.
Perry, Hildey, Sgt., State Line, enlisted for the war.
Wood, Robert, Private, State Line, 3 years' service.
Austin, John Wilson, Sgt.-Major, State Line, 3 years' service.
New, Jesse, Private, Contl. Line, 3 years' service.
Carroll, John, Private, State Line, enlisted for the war.
Rowe, John, Private, State Line, enlisted for the war.
Vickers, John, Private, State Line, 3 years' service.
Mansfield, Thomas, Private, State Line, enlisted for the war.
Tate, Adam, Fifer, State Line, 3 years' service.
Lee, Edward, Private, State Line, 3 years' service.
Whetter, John, Private, State Line, 3 years' service.
Whale, John, Private, State Line, 3 years' service.
Powell, John, Private, State Line, 3 years' service.
Welch, Nathaniel, Capt., State Line, 3 years, ending 4 Feb.,
    1780.
Davis, William, Private, State Line, enlisted for the war.
Williams, Christopher, Private, State Line, enlisted for the war.

Randolph, Adam, Private, State Line, enlisted for the war.
Waller, William, Private, State Line, enlisted for the war.
Porter, William, Private, died in the service; warrant to David
    Porter, his heir-at-law.
Watson, William, Corporal, State Line, enlisted for the war.
Colden, James, Private, State Line, enlisted for the war.
Hays, Joseph, Private, State Line, enlisted for the war.
Murray, Francis, State Line, 3 years' service.
Cromlier, Charles, Private, State Line, enlisted for the war.
Lambert, John, Sgt., State Line, enlisted for the war.
Phillips, Benjamin, Private, State Line, enlisted for the war.
Fleming, William, Capt.-Lieut., Va. Artillery, from Jan., 1777,
    to Jan., 1783.
Boulware, Obadiah, Private, State Line, 3 years' service.
Roberts, Anthony, Private, State Line, 3 years' service.
Martin, James, Corporal, State Line, 3 years' service.
Rhoads, Hohn, soldier, died in the service; warrant to John
    Rhoads, his representative.
Atkinson, Thomas, Corporal, State Line, enlisted for the war.
Welday, George, Corporal, State Line, enlisted for the war.
Jouitt, Mathew, Capt., decd., Va. Line, for 3 years; warrant
    to John Jouitt, his heir-at-law.
Butler, John, Sgt.-Major, Va. Artillery, 3 years' service.
Finch, James, Private, State Line, enlisted for the war.
Russell, Thomas, Private, State Cavalry, enlisted for the war.
Triplett, Daniel, Sgt., State Line, 3 years' service.
Feagan, John, Private, State Line, 3 years' service.
Fleet, John, Lieut., State Line, 3 years' service.
Woodson, Frederick, Capt., State Line, 3 years' service.
Belvin, William, Sgt., State Line, 3 years' service.
Drewry, Benjamin, Private, State Line, 3 years' service.
Williamson, Lawrence Lot, Private, State Line, 3 years' service.
Lee, John, Major, State Line, 3 years' service.
Garrett, Mark, Sgt., State Line, 3 years' service.
Baker, James, Drummer, State Line, 3 years' service.
Lynch, Timothy, Private, State Line, 3 years' service.
Coggin, Herbert, Private, State Line, enlisted for the war.
Penny, John, Private, State Line, 3 years' service.

Breadlove, William B., Private, State Line, enlisted for the war.

Pickett, Francis, Drummer, State Line, 3 years' service.

Courtney, Thomas, Private, State Line, 3 years' service.

Cutts, William, Private, State Line, 3 years' service.

Cutts, Shadrack, Private, State Line, 3 years' service.

Falvey, Patrick, Private, State Line, enlisted for the war.

Bozwell, Robert, Private, State Line, 3 years' service.

Hail, Leonard, Private, State Line, 3 years' service.

Messaw, Joseph, Private, State Line, 3 years' service.

Reardon, George, Sgt., State Line, enlisted for the war.

Hodgins, Joseph, Private, State Line, 3 years' service.

Pickett, George, Drummer, State Line, 3 years' service.

Wood, Philip, Private, State Line, 3 years' service.

Frogett, William, Private, State Line, enlisted for the war.

Bailey, Michael, Private, 3 years' service.

Mitchell, James, Corpl., State Line, 3 years' service.

Whitakes, James, Private, State Line, 3 years' service.

Pollard, Braxton, Corpl., State Line, 3 years' service.

Carter, James, Private, State Line, 3 years service.

Johnson, Joseph, Private, State Line, 3 years' service.

Sanderford, Samuel, Private, State Line, 3 years' service.

Gardner, George, Corpl., State Line, 3 years' service.

Oliver, John, Private, State Line, 3 years' service.

Getten, Casper, Private, 3 years' service.

Brooks, John, Private, State Line, 3 years' service.

Crump, Abner, Capt., State Line, 3 years' service.

Masten, John, Lieut., State Line, 3 years' service.

Dunn, John, Private, State Line, 3 years' service.

Huddleston, John, Private, State Line, 3 years' service.

Shelton, Thomas, Private, State Line, 3 years' service.

Farrow, Robert, Private, State Line, 3 years' service.

Scott, James, Private, State Line, 3 years' service.

Whitmore, William, Corpl., State Line, 3 years' service.

Lucas, Samuel, Fife-Major, State Line, 3 years' service.

Liggett, Owen, Private, State Line, enlisted for the war.

Carver, Lawrence, Private, State Line, 3 years' service.

Crump, Benjamin, Sgt., State Line, 3 years' service.
Watkins, William, Private, State Line, 3 years' service.
Edwards, Benjamin, Private, State Line, enlisted for the war.
McValley, James, Private, State Line, enlisted for the war.
Fears, Thomas, State Cavalry, 3 years' service.
Lorde, John, Sgt., State Line, 3 years' service.
Sheffield, Peter, Private, State Line, enlisted for the war.
Heyward, John Hall, Private, State Line, 3 years' service.
Sanford, John, Private, State Line, 3 years' service.
Jourden, Michael, Private, State Line, 3 years' service.
Thomas, William, Corpl., State Line, 3 years' service.
Corder, James, Corpl., State Line, 3 years' service.
Kendall, George, Private, State Line, 3 years, service.
Angel, John, Private, State Line, 3 years' service.
Moore, William, Sgt., State Line, enlisted for the war.
Parks, Henry, Private, State Line, 3 years' service.
Cole, Thomas, Private, State Line, 3 years' service.
Elliott, Jeremiah, Private, State Line, 3 years' service.
Spratley, Richard, Corpl., Contl. Line, 3 years' service.
Booth, James, Private, State Line, 3 years' service.
Forrest, George, Private, Contl. Line, 3 years' service.
Cavander, James, Private, State Line, 3 years' service.
Hill, James, Sgt., State Line, 3 years' service.
Thomas, Amos, Private, State Line, 3 years' service.
Thomas, William, Private, State Line, 3 years' service.
Croker, William, Drum-Major, State Line, 3 years' service.
Smith, Underwood, Private, State Line, 3 years' service.
Burnett, William, Private, State Line, 3 years' service.
Gunnett, Joseph, Private, State Line, 3 years' service.
Fair, James, Sgt., Contl. Line, 3 years' service.
Pursley, William, Sgt., State Line, 3 years' service.
Henry, Christopher, Private, State Line, 3 years' service.
Carnes, Daniel, Private, 3 years' service.
Flax, John, Private, State Line, 3 years' service.
Lucas, Thomas, Private, State Line, 3 years' service.
Hardy, Rhodius, Private, State Line, 3 years' service.
Broadus, Robert, Private, Contl. Line, 3 years' service.
Elmore, Daniel, Private, State Line, 3 years' service.

Anderson, Charles, Sgt., Contl. Line, 3 years, ending Jan., 1780.

Kays, Robert, Lieut., Contl. Line, 3 years, ending 4 July, 1782.

Conner, John, Sgt., State Line, 3 years' service.

Anderson, Isaac, Private, State Line, for the war.

Taliaferro, Benjamin, Capt., Contl. Line, 7 years' service.

Garland, Peter, Capt., Contl. Line, 3 years' service.

Gentry, James, Corpl., Contl. Line, 3 years' service.

Cawthon, Christopher, Sgt., Contl. Line, 3 years' service.

Blakey, John, Private, Contl. Line, 3 years' service.

Cary, James, Private, Contl. Line, 3 years' service.

Graves, William, Private, State Line, 3 years' service.

Owen, Charles, Private, State Line, 3 years' service.

Scott, William, Sgt., State Line, 3 years' service.

Carrington, Mayo, Capt., Contl. Line, 7 years' service.

Simmons, George, Private, State Line, 3 years' service.

Elmore, William, Sgt., State Line, 3 years' service.

Blankenship, Womack, Capt., Contl. Line, from Sept., 1775, to 1779.

Singleton, Joshua, Lieut., State Navy, 3 years' services.

Smaw, John, Sgt., Contl. Line, 3 years' service.

Palmer, Thomas, Private, Contl. Line, 3 years' service.

Elzey, Edward, Private, State Line, 3 years' service.

Bacon, Burwell, Corpl., Va. Artillery, 3 years' service.

Welch, Lang, Private, State Line, 3 years' service.

Kelly, Benjamin, Private, Contl. Line, 3 years' service.

Anderson, Matt., Private, Contl. Line, 3 years' service.

Hardyman, John, Sgt., State Line, 3 years' service.

Hart, James, Private, Contl. Line., 3 years' service.

Ewell, Charles, Capt., State Line, 3 years' service.

Norvell, Aquilla, Sgt., Contl. Line, 3 years' service.

Blakey, John, Corpl., State Line, 3 years' service.

Duff, Edward, Dr., Regimental Surgeon, Contl. Line, 3 years' service.

Blackwell, John, Capt., Contl. Line, 7 years' service.

Gillison, John, Capt., Contl. Line, 3 years, ending 18 Nov., 1779.

Cofer, George, Corpl., Contl. Line, 3 years' service.

Underwood, Gideon, Sgt., Contl. Line, 3 years' service.
Duffey, James, Private, Contl. Line, 3 years' service.
Treekle, John, Private, Contl. Line, 3 years' service.
Hudgins, Moses, Private, Contl. Line, 3 years' service.
Manning, Jesse, Private, Contl. Line, enlisted for the war.
Harwood, Littlebury, Sgt., State Line, 3 years' service.
Hackley, John, Lieut., Contl. Line, 3 years' service.
Spotswood, John, Capt., Contl. Line, 3 years, ending 19 Nov.,
   1779.
Williams, James, Capt., Contl. Line, 7 years, ending April,
   1783.
Fox, Thomas, Capt., Contl. Line, 3 years, ending 4 Dec., 1779.
Hord, Thomas, Capt., Contl. Line, 7 years' service.
Reid, Nathan, Capt., Contl. Line, 3 years' service.
Steel, John, Lieut., Contl. Line, 3 years, ending 4 April, 1780.
Peace, Samuel, Sgt., State Line, 3 years' service.
McDorman, James, Private, Va. Artillery, 3 years' service.
Saunders, William, Capt., State Navy, 3 years' service.
Bowser, James, Private, Contl. Line, 4 years' service.
Wyat, Benjamin, Private, Contl. Line, 3 years' service.
Pavi, George, Private, Contl. Line, 3 years' service.
Link, John, Private, Contl. Line, 3 years' service.
Winston, John, Capt., 4th Va. Line, from 6 Dec., 1776, to 13
   Feb., 1781.
Burnes, Jeremiah, Private, Contl. Line, 3 years' service.
Young, Henry, Capt., Contl. Line, 3 years' service.
Gates, John, Private, State Line, 3 years' service.
Moss, Henry, Capt., Contl. Line, 3 years, ending 19 Nov.,
   1779.
Tinker, William, Private, State Line, 3 years' service.
Stubbs, Francis, Private, State Line, 3 years' service.
Laurence, Thomas, Private, Contl. Line, 3 years' service.
Brakenridge, Alex., Capt., Va. Line, 3 years' service.
Dihouse, Edward, Private, State Line, 3 years' service.
Smith, Larkin, Capt., Contl. Line, 3 years' service.
Warman, Thomas, Capt., Contl. Line, 3 years' service, ending
   July, 1779.
Shearman, Robert, Fife-Major, Contl. Line, 3 years' service.

Foster, Robert, Lieut., Contl. Line, 3 years' service.

Ross, John, Private, Contl. Line, discharged on account of wound in the service.

Brewer, Henry, Drummer, Contl. Line, 3 years' service.

Murry, Duncan, Private, Contl. Line., 3 years' service.

Baylor, Walker, Capt., Cavalry, Contl. Line, 3 years' service.

Brown, Jacob, Lieut., Contl. Line, 7 years' service.

Baskerville, Samuel, Lieut., Contl. Line, 7 years' service.

Holt, Thomas, Capt., Contl. Line, 3 years' service, ending Nov., 1779.

Langford, Euclid, Private, Contl. Line., 3 years' service.

Denholm, Archibald, Capt., Contl. Line., 3 years' service.

Robertson, George, Private, Contl. Line, 3 years' service.

Mills, Nichols, Private, State Line, 3 years' service.

Marrow, Robert, Capt., Va. Cavalry, 3 years' service.

Wheeley, John, Private, State Line, 3 years' service.

Hardaway, Joseph, Private, Va. Cavalry, for the war.

Cox, Radford, Corpl., Contl. Line, 3 years' service.

Winter, George, Private, Contl. Line, 3 years' service.

Martingly, John, Private, State Line, 3 years' service.

Slaughter, John, Private, Contl. Line, 3 years' service.

Crump, Jesse, Sgt., State Line, 3 years' service.

Maderson, John, Private, Contl. Line, 3 years' service.

Legg, John, Private, Contl. Line, 3 years' service.

Edwards, Thomas, Private, State Line, 3 years' service.

Alexander, William, Private, Va. Artillery, 3 years' service.

Brooks, George, Private, Contl. Line, 3 years' service.

White, John, Lieut., Va. Cavalry, died in service; warrant to John White, his heir.

Hire, William, Private, State Line, 3 years' service.

Cross, Samuel, Sgt., Contl. Line, 3 years' service.

Goff, Samuel, Private, Contl. Line; warrant to Abram Goff, his heir.

Fisher, John, Private, State Line, 3 years' service.

Landrum, Thomas, Private, State Line, 3 years' service.

Maxwell, James, Private, Contl. Line, 3 years' service.

Johnson, Edward, Private, State Line, for the war.

Bowyer, Thomas, Capt., Contl. Line, 3 years, ending Dec., 1779.

Morton, Hezekiah, Capt., Va. Infantry, Contl. Line, 30 Aug., 1777, to 28 Dec., 1782.

McIlhany, John, Capt., State Line, April, 1777, to May, 1780

Thompson, Daniel, Private, State Line, 3 years' service.

Clod, Robert, Corpl., State Line, 3 years' service.

Patterson, John, Sgt.-Major, State Line, 3 years' service.

Angel, Robert, Private, Va. Cavalry, 3 years' service.

Anderson, Robert, Private, Va. Contl. Artillery, 3 years' service.

Martin, John, Private, State Line, for the war.

Towers, John, Private, State Line, for the war.

Trent, Laurence, Capt., Va. Cavalry, 3 years' service.

Burton, James, Private, State Line, 3 years' service.

Quarles, Henry, Capt., State Line, 3 years' service.

Meriwether, David, Officer, 14th Va. Contl. Regt., Nov., 1776, and is still in service, Dec., 1782.

McDonald, Terence, Private, Va. Artillery, 3 years' service.

Treacle, John, Private, State Line, 3 years' service.

Treacle, Dawson, Private, State Line, 3 years' service.

Taylor, Humphrey, Private, State Line, 3 years' service.

Johnston, Gideon, Capt., Va. Artillery, 3 years' service.

Porter, William, Lieut., Contl. Line, 3 years' service.

Branham, Eben, Sgt., Contl. Line, 3 years' service.

Brown, Henry, Sgt., State Line, 3 years' service.

Buford, Abraham, Col., Contl. Line, 3 years' service.

Epps, William, Capt.-Lieut., Contl. Line, 3 years' service.

Pool, Robert, Private, Va. Cavalry, 3 years' service.

Treacle, William, Private, State Line, 3 years' service.

Roberts, Gerrard, Sgt., State Line, 3 years' service.

Asselin, Thomas, Sgt., Contl. Line, 3 years' service.

Powell, Thomas, Lieut., State Artillery, and died in service; warrant to Seymour Powell, his heir-at-law.

Jett, John, Seaman, State Navy, 3 years' service.

Brownlee, William, Capt.-Lieut., Contl. Line, 3 years' service.

Davies, Richard, Sgt., Va. Cavalry, 3 years' service.

Lipscomb, John, Corpl., Va. Cavalry, 3 years' service.

Wyatt, John, Private, Contl. Line, 3 years' service.

Smith, Obadiah, Lieut., Contl. Line, 3 years' service.

Fox, Lewis, Private, Contl. Line, 3 years' service.

Hamilton, James, Lieut., Contl. Line, 3 years, ending Jan.,. 1780.

Hopkins, Samuel, Lieut.-Col., Contl. Line., 7 years' service.

Atkinson, Reuben, Private, Contl. Artillery, 3 years' service.

Graham, Walter, Capt.-Lieut., State Artillery, 3 years' service.

Carter, John, Private, State Artillery, 3 years' service.

Clark, James, Private, State Line, 3 years' service.

Oliver, William, Capt.-Lieut., State Artillery, 3 years' service.

Brown, William, Private, Contl. Line, 3 years' service.

Richeson, James, Sgt., State Line, 3 years' service.

Flourney, Jacob, Private, State Artillery, 3 years' service.

Cole, Hamlin, Sgt., Contl. Line, 3 years' service.

Brent, William, Col., State Line, 3 years' service.

Payne, Tarlton, Capt., Contl. Line, 3 years' service.

Green, Jesse, Private, Va. Cavalry, 3 years' service.

Cannon, Luke, Lieut., Contl. Line, 3 years, ending 21 July, 1780.

Wallace, William B., Lieut., Contl. Line, 3 years, ending March, 1780.

Elzey, Edward, Private, State Line, for the war.

Sykes, George, Private, State Line, 3 years' service.

Guthrie, John, Private, State Line, 3 years' service.

Guthrie, James, Sgt., State Line, 3 years' service.

Fox, Nathaniel, Capt., Contl. Line, 3 years' service.

Gammells, Nathan, Sgt., Contl. Line, 3 years' service.

Robinson, Cole, Sgt., Contl. Line, 3 years' service.

Robinson, William, Private, Contl. Line, 3 years, and killed in service; Cole Robinson is his legal representative.

Barron, James, Commodore, State Navy, 25 Dec., 1775, to 7 April, 1783.

Brown, William, Dr., Regt. Surgeon, Va. Line, 3 years' service.

Dagnell, Stephen, Private, State Cavalry, for the war.

McMeekin, Joseph, Drum-Major, Va. State Artillery, 3 years' service.

Perry, William, Drummer, Contl. Line, 3 years' service.

Harper, John, Corpl., State Line, 3 years' service.

Emmins, William, Sgt., Va. Artillery, 3 years' service.

McCall, Samuel, Sgt., Contl. Line, 3 years' service.

Harden, James, Private, Contl. Line, 3 years' service.

Edwards, Richard, Private, Contl. Line., 3 years' service.

Barron, Richard, Capt., State Navy, 3 years' service.

Colbert, John, Private, State Line, for the war.

Gibson, John, Sailing Master, Va. Navy, 3 years' service.

White, James, Private, State Cavalry, for the war.

White, James, Private, Contl. Line, 3 years' service.

Dandridge, Robert, Lieut., Va. Artillery, 3 years' service.

Lewis, Andrew, Lieut., Contl. Line, 3 years' service.

Casey, Archibald, Private, State Line, for the war.

Depriest, John, Sgt., State Artillery, 3 years' service.

Long, William, Capt., State Line, 16 April, 1777, to 6 Feb., 1781.

Parker, Thomas, Capt., Contl. Line, 3 years, ending Jan., 1780.

Ranger, Joseph, Sailor, State Navy, 3 years' service.

Morris, John, Private, State Line, for the war.

Parker, Richard, Col., decd., Contl. Line, 3 years' service; warrant to Alex. Parker, heir-at-law.

Skinner, Alex., Dr., Regt. Surgeon, Contl. Line, 3 years' service.

Triplett, William, Sgt., State Line, 3 years' service.

Clements, Mace, Dr., Regt. Surgeon, Contl. Line, 7 years' service.

Vawter, Benjamin, Private, State Line, 3 years' service.

Beaver, Samuel, Corpl., State Line, 3 years' service.

Bowen, John, Lieut., Va. Line, 1 May, 1777, to 24 Jan., 1783.

Mars, Barnabas, Private, State Line, 3 years' service.

Williams, Edward, Ensign, Contl. Line, 3 years' service.

Vanmeter, Joseph, Ensign, Contl. Line, 3 years' service.

Casey, Benjamin, Capt., Va. Line, 3 years' service.

Lord, Roberson, Private, State Line, for the war.

Evans, Charles, Private, State Line, 3 years' service.

Atkinson, Major, Private, Va. Artillery, 3 years' service.
Mills, John, Private, Contl. Line, 3 years' service.
Cratton, William, Private, Contl. Line, for the war.
Chamberlane, George, Lieut., State Navy, 3 years' service.
Smart, Richard, Master's Mate, State Navy, 3 years' service.
Willis, John, Major, Contl. Line, 7 years' service.
Munden, Edward, Private, Contl. Line, 7 years' service.
Wyatt, William, Private, Contl. Line, 3 years' service.
Newby, Thomas, Private, State Artillery, 3 years' service.
Worth, William, Sailor, State Navy, 3 years' service.
Higden, John, Sailor, State Navy, 3 years' service.
Hughes, Pratt, Lieut., State Line, 7 years' service.
Lawson, Benjamin, Lieut., Contl. Line, March, 1777, to 1
    Jan., 1782.
Russell, William, Private, State Artillery, 3 years' service.
Yarrington, Oliver, Private, Va. Artillery, 3 years' service.
Brown, Berryman, Sailor, State Navy, 3 years' service.
Gaskins, Thomas, Lieut.-Col., Contl. Line, 3 years, ending 1
    Feb., 1779.
Jones, Alex., Private, State Line, 3 years' service.
Smith, Michael, Sgt., Contl. Line, 3 years' service.
Pate, Matt., Private, State Line, 3 years' service.
Minnis, Francis, Capt., Contl. Line, 7 years' service.
Wallace, John, Private, State Line, 3 years' service.
Higgins, Peter, Lieut., Contl. Line, 3 years' service.
Gresham, John, Private, Contl. Line, 3 years' service.
Beasley, Richard, Private, State Line, 3 years' service.
Bowen, Francis, Drummer, State Line, 3 years' service.
Carter, Charles, Private, State Line, 3 years' service.
Wright, Robert, Private, Contl. Line, 3 years service.
Moss, Henry, Private, Contl. Line, 3 years' service.
Gibson, Robert, Corpl., State Line, 3 years' service.
Powell, Aaron, Sgt., State Artillery, 3 years' service.
Parker, Robert, Corpl., State Line, 3 years' service.
Elliott, Wyatt, Sgt., State Line, 3 years' service; warrant to
    William Elliott, June 10, 1783.
Ravenscraft, Thomas, Private, Contl. Line, 3 years' service.
Cunningham, William, Major, Contl. Line, 3 years' service.

Bentley, William, Capt., Contl. Line, 7 years' service..
Bernard, William, Lieut., decd., Contl. Line, 3 years' service;
  warrant to John Bernard, 10 June, 1783.
Lynch, Patrick, Private, Contl. Line, 3 years' service.
Dickie, William, Private, Va. Artillery, 3 years' service.
Morris, Robert, Private, State Line, 3 years' service.
Chapman, John, Capt., decd., State Line, 3 years' service;
  warrant to Joseph Chapman, heir-at-law, 12 June, 1783.
Varden, John, Corpl., State Line, 3 years' service.
Gilchrist, George, Major, Contl. Line, 3 years' service.
Poulson, John, Major, Contl. Line, Jan., 1776, to 3 Jan., 1783.
Stokely, Charles, Lieut., Contl. Line, 22 June, 1776, to 28
  Dec., 1782.
Clayton, Philip, Lieut., Contl. Line, 3 years' service.
Wade, Moses, Private, Contl. Line, 3 years' service.
Norvall, Henry Holdcraft, Sgt., Contl. Line, 3 years' service.
Crutchfield, Stapleton, Private, Contl. Line., 3 years' service.
Weedon, George, Brig.-Genl., Contl. Line, 7 years' service.
Quarles, Thomas, Lieut., State Line, 3 years' service.
Parker, Wyatt, Private, State Line, 3 years' service.
Abbett, Robert, Sgt., State Line, 3 years' service.
Gates, Horatio, Major-Genl., Va. Line, May, 1776, to 13
  June, 1783.
Randolph, Robert, Capt., Va. Cavalry, 3 years' service.
Darke, William, Lieut.-Col., Contl. Line, Feb., 1776, to Dec.,
  1782.
Blake, Charles, Private, State Artillery, 3 years' service.
Walker, Jacob, Capt., State Artillery, 3 years' service.
Scott, Charles, Brig.-Genl., 20 Sept., 1775, to 14 June, 1783.
Collins, Mason, Private, Va. Artillery, 3 years' service.
Hines, James, Corpl., Va. Artillery, 3 years' service.
Ludeman, William, Lieut., Contl. Line, 3 years' service.
Rydman, John, Gunner, State Navy, 3 years' service.
Cooley, James, Private, Contl. Line, 3 years' service.
Hawes, Samuel, Lieut.-Col., 7 years, ending 2 Feb., 1783.
Martain, John, Private, Contl. Line, 3 years' service.
Richards, Thomas, Sgt., Contl. Line, 3 years' service.
Rycroft, Thomas, Private, Conl. Line, 3 years' service.

Joliff, John, Lieut., decd., Contl. Line, 3 years; warrant to
  Job Joliff, heir-at-law, 14 Jan., 1783.
Steed, John, Capt., Contl. Line, 3 years' service.
Halcomb, John, Capt., Contl. Line, 3 years' service.
McDowell, John, Lieut., Contl. Line, 3 years' service.
Warneck, Frederick, Lieut.-Col., State Line, 3 years' service.
Hunt, James, Private, Contl. Line, 3 years' service.
Colquehon, James, Private, Contl. Line, 3 years' service.
Estes, Elisha, Sgt., Contl. Line, 3 years' service.
Carney, Martin, Lieut., Contl. Line, 3 years' service.
Warick, William, Sgt., State Artillery, 3 years' service.
Perryman, Philip, Private, State Line, 3 years' service.
Collins, John, Private, Contl. Line, 3 years' service.
Puryear, Thomas, Private, Contl. Line, 3 years' service.
Davis, William, Private, Contl. Line, 3 years, ending 4 Feb.,
  1782.
Halloly, Thomas, Sgt., Contl. Line, 7 years, ending 8 March,
  1783.
Crowley, David, Private, Contl. Line, 3 years' service.
Thornton, Presby, Capt., Va. Cavalry, 3 years' service.
Royal, Grief, Private, State Artillery, 3 years' service.
Allen, Joseph, Private, State Line, 3 years' service.
Mitchell, William, Corpl., Contl. Line, 3 years' service.
Vance, Robert, Capt., Contl. Line, 3 years' service.
Crawford, William, Col., Contl. Line, 3 years' service.
Beck, John, Lieut., Contl. Line, 3 years' service.
Bealle, Robert, Capt., Contl. Line, 3 years' service.
Taliaferro, Nicholas, Lieut., Contl. Line, Nov., 1776, to Jan.,
  1783.
Towles, Oliver, Lieut.-Col., Contl. Line, Feb., 1776, to 1 Jan.,
  1783.
Rice, George, Capt., Contl. Line, 3 years' service.
Dowell, William, Private, Contl. Line, 3 years' service.
Parker, Nicholas, decd., Contl. Line, 3 years' service; war-
  rant to Josiah Parker, heir-at-law, 18 June, 1783.
Rogers, William, Capt., Contl. Line, 3 years' service.
Williams, David, Lieut., Contl. Line, 3 years' service.
Meanly, Robert, Private, decd., State Line, 3 years' service;

warrant to Deveaux Gonott Meanly, heir-at-law, 18 June, 1783.

McDowell, Matt, Private, Contl. Line, 3 years' service.

Becam, Robert, Private, Contl. Line, 3 years' service.

Norwood, Joseph, Private, Va. Cavalry, 3 years' service.

Shurls, Benjamin, Private, Va. Artillery, 3 years' service.

Danelly, John, Private, decd., Contl. Line, 3 years' service; warrant to John Danelly, heir-at-law, 19 June, 1783.

Floyd, Thomas, Private, State Artillery, 3 years' service.

Chambers, Alex., Private, Contl. Line, 3 years' service.

Ironmunger, Robert, Fife-Major, Contl. Line, 3 years, ending Jan., 1780.

Heally, William, Private, Contl. Line, 3 years, ending 25 March, 1783.

Archer, Isaac, Private, Contl. Line, 3 years, ending 19 March, 1781.

Barnes, John, Private, State Line, 3 years' service.

(Continued)

INDEX TO LAND GRANTS
ISLE OF WIGHT COUNTY
BOOK No. 1.

495	Hugh Wynn	1637	200
497	Epaphroditus Lawson	1637	50
498	Nathaniel Floyd	1637	850
500	John Taylor	1637	50
502	Thomas Davis	1637	100
502	Henry Snaile	1637	50
506	Joseph Cobb	1637	400
509	John Moone	1637	550
517	Charles Bancroft	1637	350
529	Arthur Smith	1637	1450
529	Ambrose Bennett	1638	300
540	Robert Pitts, merchant	1638	550
544	John Seaward	1638	400
560	Sarah Cloyden	1638	200
588	Gresham Coffield and Thomas Stamp	1638	200
605	Lieut. John Upton	1638	1500
626	Richard Bennett	1638	300
628	Peter Knight	1638	200
633	Nicholas George and John Grymsditch	1638	300
634	John Seaward	1638	400
669	John Lewin	1639	200
670	John Lewin	1639	50
671	Robert Eley	1639	600
679	Samuel Jackson	1639	200
681	Justinian Cooper	1639	850
681	Edmund Porter	1639	100
686	Wm. Crannage	1639	300
694	Wm. Yarrett	1641	150
714	Wm. Denham	1639	200
728	Gresham Coffield	1640	200
735	Wm. Crannage	1640	700
745	John Roe	blank	350
747	Thomas Morrey	1641	300
747	Same	1641	300
746	Ambrose Bennett	1641	1150
748	James Hawley	1641	300
750	Thomas Grinwood	1641	150

751	Robert Burnett	1641	200
755	John Seaward	1641	1300
772	Richard Jackson	1641	450
793	Robert Lawrence	1642	100
793	Same	1642	200
798	Wm. Barnard	1642	1200
820	Wm. Lawson	1642	491
820	John Stocker	1642	200
840	Timothy Fenn	1642	300
848	John Vallentine	1642	119
849	Same	1642	50
855	John Styles	1642	200
857	Francis England	1642	746
860	Henry Hird	blank	350
860	John Moone	1642	2250
904	Robert Lawrence	1643	150
871	Wm. Pudivatt	1642	200
871	Same	1642	200
874	Justinian Cooper	1642	2400
876	Capt. John Upton	1643	3289
895	Robert Pitt	1643	209
901	Joseph Cobb	1643	400
907	Richard Jackson	1643	110
911	John Sweete	1643	1540
912	Henry Watts	1643	157
913	James Hawley	1643	300
914	Robert Burnett	1643	200
928	Tristam Nosworth	1643	150
937	Silvester Thacker and Anthony Fulliamb	1643	100

BOOK No. 2.

2	Wm. Mills	1643	450
12	Robert Lawrence	1644	200
32	Justinian Cooper	1645	2450
38	Wm. Smith	1645	700
60	Thomas Davies, or Davis	1648	600
62	Thomas Hinson	1646	209
71	Thomas Davis	1646	200

76	Lawrence Ware and John King	1645	100
84	Elizabeth Barcroft	1647	1200
85	Thomas Parker	1647	300
86	Peter Knight	1643	255
87	John King and Lawrence Ward	1648	500
93	James Hawley	1648	300
98	Robert Byrd	1646	150
107	Richard Wilkinson	1646	236
116	John Seward	1648	1200
117	Same	1648	400
118	Robert Pitt	1648	300
126	James Mason	1647	450
142	George Hardy, Thomas Wombwell and Peter Hall	blank	1100
240	Robert Blake and Samuel Eldridge	1650	560
289	Thomas Parker	1650	380

Book No. 3.

5	Gregory Perrot	1653	150
11	Robert Flake	1653	600
32	John Joliffe	1653	150
78	James Watson	1653	345
109	Christopher Lewis	1652	750
110	Francis England	1652	120
110	Same	1652	946
177	Thomas Greenwood	1652	300
180	John Oliver	1652	100
189	Nathaniel Bacon	1652	1075
205	Thomas Harris	1652	40
206	Thomas Taberer and Francis Higgins	1652	250
213	James Tooke	1653	178
271	Lieut. Col. Robert Pitt	1654	1200
315	John Gutteridge	1654	350
315	Elizabeth Gwin	1654	700
323	Daniel Boucher	1654	200
354	John Marshall	1654	1655
385	Job Bearly	1656	600

Book No. 4.

3	Daniel Bouther	1655	200
39	Nichols Smith	1655	200
140	Wm. Yarret	1657	500
243	Christopher Reynolds	1657	350
250	Giles Driver	1657	200
252	Same	1657	100
265	Wm. Smith	1657	300
357	Thomas Harris	1657	1000
377	Thomas Woodward	1659	100
389	Wm. Body	1661	550
487	Henry Watts	1661	457
522	Wm. Smith	1661	300
551	Thomas Woodward	1662	100
558	John Marshall	1662	200
576	Thomas Poole	1662	100
613	Col. Robert Pitt and Wm. Burgh	1664	1200
613	Same	1664	1800
614	Col. Robert Pitt, Capt. Joseph Bridger and Wm. Burgh	1664	3000

(Continued)

ELIZABETH CITY COUNTY

Book No. 1.

Page	Name	Date	No. acres
26	John Taylor	1624	50
27	John Powell	1624	150
29	Capt. Wm. Tucker	1624	150
31	John Bush	1624	300
32	Wm. Julian	1624	150
33	Lieut. Albiano Lupo	1624	350
34	Elizabeth Lupo	1624	50
35	Thomas Spilman	1624	50
37	Alexander Mountney	1624	100
38	Elizabeth Dunthorne	1624	100

39	Wm. Gainye	1624	200
40	Wm. Lansden	1624	100
41	Wm. Clayborne, of James City	1624	150
42	Mary Bouldin	1624	100
44	Peter Arundell, of Buckroe	1624	200
45	Bartholomew Hoskins	1624	100
61	Ensign Thomas Willoughby	1624	50
73	Mary Flint	1628	100
77	Thomas Flint (lease)	1626	50
77	Edward Johnson (lease)	1627	50
78	Doctoris Christmas	1627	50
79	Jonas Stockden	1627	50
80	David Poole (lease)	1627	60
81	John Arundell (lease)	1627	12
82	James Bonall (lease)	1627	50
83	John Henry (lease)	1627	150
84	Wm. Hampton (lease)	1627	50
84	Richard Ball (lease)	1627	6
88	Lieut. Thomas Purfory	1628	100
89	Wm. Cox (lease)	1628	100
90	Christopher Windmill (lease)	1628	60
91	Walter Heyley (lease)	1628	50
93	Edward Waters (lease)	1628	100
93	Christopher Windmill (lease)	1628	50
96	Nicholas Roe (lease)	1628	40
99	Elias La Guard	1628	100
101	Nicholas Browne (lease)	1630	50
109	John Arundell	1632	100
116	Same	1632	100
117	Bartholomew Hoskins	1632	100
119	John Robins (the younger)	1632	300
122	Capt. Wm. Tucker	1632	100
133	James Knott (lease)	1632	50
136	Wm. Hampton (lease)	1632	50
135	John Neale (lease)	1632	50
139	James Bonall (lease)	1633	50
141	Elias La Guard	1633	12

142	Lancelott Barnes (lease)	1633	100
145	Joseph Hatfield, of Elizabeth City	1633	50
147	Henry Coleman	1634	60
149	Thomas Watts (lease)	1634	50
152	Wm. Conner (lease)	1634	60
153	Wm. Hampton (lease)	1634	100
193	Wm. Ranshaw	1635	200
226	Thomas Vicount	1635	100
227	Capt. Christopher Calthorpe	1631	500
264	Thomas Ranshaw	1635	250
265	Christopher Stoakes	1635	300
290	Robert Glascocke	1635	200
309	Wm. Woolritch	1635	400
310	Wm. Clarke	1635	100
312	Capt. Thomas Willoughby	1635	300
313	Thomas Keeling	1635	100
317	Doctoris Christmas	1635	300
323	Thomas Purifye	1635	100
334	Thomas Normanton	blank	50
334	James Knott	1635	1200
340	John Yates	1636	150
340	Same	1636	200
341	Christopher Burroughs	1636	200
342	Robert West	1636	100
342	Thomas Watts	1636	50
356	John Place	1636	150
357	Joseph Moore	1636	200
360	Wm. Coleman	1635	100
368	John Chandler	1636	1000
370	Wm. Armestead	1636	450
381	Thomas Allen	1636	550
382	Thomas Beast	1636	200
382	Wm. Rainshaw	1636	150
383	Same	1636	100
383	John Roberts	1636	100
385	Thomas Burbage	1636	300
387	Samuel Stephens	1636	2000

388	Wm. Julian	1636	600
389	John Gater	1636	300
389	Same	1636	300
389	Same	1636	200
394	Cornelius Loyd	1635	800
395	Thomas Bernsted	1636	50
396	James Vanerit	1636	1000
401	George Sapheir	1636	300
403	Thomas Andrews (lease)	1636	50
426	William Morgan alias Brookes	1637	100
443	John Graves	1637	600
444	Leonard Yeo	1637	850
445	Capt. Francis Hooke	1637	100
446	Same	1637	50
473	Same, parcel of land	1637	
476	John Gundry	1626	150
477	John Gundry	1626	150
479	Wm. Lansden	1624	100
481	Capt. Adam Thorogood	1637	200
481	Same	1637	200
501	George Slaughter	1637	200
503	Robert Partin (lease)	1637	40
505	Humphrey Tabb	1637	50
506	Nicholas Hill	1637	100
516	Capt. Adam Thorogood	1637	200
518	Same	1634	200
542	Thomas Eaton	1638	650
542	Same	1638	400
556	John Graves	1638	200
557	Peter Stafferton	1638	200
564	John Powell	1638	50
567	Humphrey Tabb	1638	100
564	Wm. Armestead	1638	300
594	Joseph Moore	1638	200
601	John Gibbs	1638	300
601	Thomas Boulding	1638	200
620	John Laydon	1638	500

629	Aron Corsetam and Derrick Corsestam ..1639	860
638	John Robins 1639	200
654	George Hull 1639	50
655	John Graves 1639	150
663	Christopher Dawcey 1639	50
675	Wm. Parry 1639	350
679	John Smith and Christopher Bea 1639	100
680	Marke Johnson 1639	50
680	Thomas Baulding 1639	400
688	Doctoris Christmas 1639	300
716	Thomas Oldis (lease) 1639	50
737	Wm. Armestead 1641	20
752	Wm. Hampton 1640	550
760	Thomas Oldis 1641	50
776	Richard Greyson 1642	400
795	Wm. Morgan, als Booth 1642	50
824	Humphrey Tabb 1642	100
825	Same 1642	150
834	Henry Poole 1642	116
836	Henry Coleman 1642	104
890	Adam Thorogood 1637	200

(Continued)

NORTHUMBERLAND COUNTY

Book No. 2.

Page	Name	Date	No. acres
156	Richard Thompson 1649		560
186	Wm. Presly 1649		1150
187	Wm. Pierce and Francis Symons 1649		220
187	Ralph Horsly 1649		130
189	Francis Broune 1649		500
202	Wm. Nesum, Thos. Sax, Miles Battersby and Jno. Pyne 1649		800
203	Wm. Nesum, Thos. Sax, Miles Battersby and Jno. Pyne 1649		550

206	John Robins	1649	400
206	Thomas Spake	1649	400
207	Same	1649	600
218	Thos. Kirby and John Johnson	1650	227
225	Andrew Munrow	1650	200
225	John Hallows	1650	328
225	Henry Brooke	1650	658
226	Capt. Henry Fleet	1650	1750
246	James Metgrigar and Hugh Foutch	1650	300
246	Wm. Presley	1650	100
247	John Mottrum·	1650	963
248	Edward Walker	1650	900
249	Thomas Gerrard	1650	1000
250	Lewis Burwell	1650	1600
258	George Ludlow	1650	1000
260	George Read	1650	500
273	James Cloughton	1650	250
273	Mr. Joane Powell	1650	288
274	Wm. Minson, Sr.	1650	150
274	John Rosier	1650	550
275	Hugh Lee	1650	100
275	John Trussell	1650	200
275	Gervace Dodson	1650	1600
277	John Hull	1650	200
277	Samuel Smith	1650	529
278	Richard Hawkins	1650	100
278	John Armsbee	1650	250
279	John Bayles	1650	300
279	Jefferie Gooch	1650	500
279	Richard Budd	1650	350
280	John Cooke	1650	450
280	Thomas Blagg	1650	500
281	John Essix	1650	500
281	John Hany	1650	950
281	John Hallowes	1560	600
282	John Hallowes	1650	1600
283	Same	1651	200
283	Nathaniel Jones	1650	600

VIRGINIA COUNTY RECORDS   71

283	Thomas Vaus	1650	500
285	Mrs. Francis Townshend	1650	2200
300	Thomas Orley	1651	100
300	Robert Newman	1651	814
300	Robert Newman	1651	550
301	Richard Wooton	1651	300
301	Christopher Boyce	1651	1250
301	Palmer Hinton	1651	300
302	Wm. Hoccaday	1651	1000
303	Wm. Vincent	1651	640
303	George Colelough	1651	500
305	David Phillips	1651	400
305	Hugh Fench and James Magregory	1651	800
305	Henry Hust	1651	350
306	Mrs. Anna Bernard	1651	1000
307	James Baldridge and Capt. Thomas Baldridge	1651	840
311	Thomas Thornbrough	1651	700
311	Thomas Watts, Jr.	1651	200
312	Richard Walker	1651	200
312	Wm. Rennolds	1651	650
314	Capt. Stephen Gill	1651	900
317	John Ingram and Richard Flint	1651	406
317	John Hull	1651	500
322	Wm. Newman and John Meekes	1651	1000
322	Antho. Steevens	1651	500
333	Richard Burney	1651	2109
333	John Rookwood	1651	708
333	Lieut.-Col. Giles Brent	1651	768
335	Wm. Betts	1651	100
337	Thomas Speake	1651	1000
337	Same	1651	900
338	Thomas Yowell	1651	300
339	Thomas Hales and Thomas Sheppard	1651	300
341	Robert Bradshaw	1651	400
349	Wm. Parry	1651	550
354	Humphrey Tabb	1651	1000

354	Capt. Thomas Davis	1651	600
359	Lieut.-Col. Giles Brent	1651	1040

Book No. 3.

1	Roger Walter	1653	600
3	John Bennett, of Nomany, carpenter	1653	150
3	Anthony Lawton	1653	1025
3	John Wood	1653	600
3	Nathaniel Hickman	1653	450
3	Richard Wells	1653	500
4	William Walker	1653	639
4	Thomas Wilsford	1653	26
5	Wm. Whitbye	1653	1800
9	Thomas Saffall	1654	850
12	Edward Cole	1653	300
12	Wm. Bacon	1653	300
13	John Haney	1652	500
14	Thomas Shepherd	1653	66
14	John Shakly	1653	350
14	Thomas Kidley	1653	300
15	Wm. Reynolds	1653	92
15	Francis Symons	1653	91
15	Thomas Salisbury	1653	300
15	Richard Holden	1653	600
15	Thomas Philpot	1653	100
15	Francis Symons	1653	224
17	Carbet Piddel	1653	1000
17	Matthew Tomlin	1653	200
17	David Phillips	1653	200
18	Thomas Mallerd	1653	300
18	Samuel Bonam	1653	300
19	Major George Read	1653	500
20	Thomas Youl	1653	500
25	James Allen	1653	300
28	Maj. Wm. Lewis	1654	800
28	Hugh Lee	1654	288
35	John Wood	1653	1200
37	John Rosyer	1653	700

```
38  Col. George Ludlow ..................1653   1000
38  John Earle .........................1653   1000
45  John Medstard and John Edward .......1653    300
47  Peter Knight .......................1653    500
50  Francis Clay .......................1653    200
51  Thomas Youl ........................1653    150
52  Wm. Freeke .........................1653    300
53  Roger Walter .......................1653    600
61  Thomas Keene .......................1653    527
62  John Faucett Freeman Connaway and John
       Howard ..........................1653   1000
```

(Continued)

WESTMORELAND COUNTY.

Book No. 3.

Page	Name	Date	No. acres
14	Gervase Dodson	1653	1300
272	Vallentine Patton	1654	1000
273	John Walton and John Bagnall	1654	3900
275	Richard Hawkins	1654	500
275	Mrs. Margaret Brent	1654	700
276	Richard Browne	1654	200
278	Thomas Frizzar	1654	300
279	Nathaniel Pope	1654	1000
280	Robert Yoe	1654	650
284	Richard Codsford	1654	400
284	William Robinson and Cornelius Johnson	1654	400
285	Major Miles Cary	1654	3000
297	David Mansell	1654	600
299	William Beach	1654	700
301	Thomas Fowke	1654	3350
302	Humphrey Higgenson and Abraham Moone	1654	2000
303	Lieut.-Col. Giles Brent	1654	1518
306	Col. John Matrom	1654	3609
308	Capt. Giles Brent	1654	300

312	Nicholas Marteaw	1654	2000
313	Robert Hubard	1654	1600
319	Mrs. Francis Harrison	1654	1000
325	Richard Browne	1654	650
328	Christopher Boor	1654	300
328	Edward Parker	1654	300
329	Ann Bernard	1654	1500
356	George Wall	1655	1200
357	William Gooch and Robert Vauly	1655	6000
363	Nicholas Marteaw	1655	2000
363	Thomas Wilsford	1655	50
364	Richard Codsford	1655	400
363	John Withers	1655	150
373	John Withers	1654	1000
373	Mr. Giles Brent	1654	1000
374	Francis Smith, Ingeenr., and John Smith, of Stanly Hundred	1654	3000
376	Nicholas Merywether	1654	3000
376	Same	1654	1350
391	David Philips	1656	400
391	John Harrison	1655	1000

Book No. 4.

7	Robert Vauly	1655	6000
18	William Botham	1655	500
23	Richard Coale and David Anderson	1655	150
51	Nathaniel Pope	1656	1550
59	John Lear	1655	100
63	Lieut.-Col. Nathaniel Pope	1656	1050
75	John Rosier, clarke	1656	1050
84	Herbert Smith	1656	500
98	Margaret Miles	1656	1200
99	Robert Hubbard and William Lewis	1656	2000
103	Robert Hubbard	1654	500
103	Robert Hubbard	1654	500
125	Thomas Graves	1656	300
133	Mrs. Mary Brent	1657	1250
134	Henry Footman	blank	300

134	Giles Brent	1657	1340
173	John Wood	1657	500
175	William Thomas	1657	1000
183	Lieut.-Col. Miles Cary	1657	3000
191	George Seaton	1657	300
210	Capt. Ed. Streater	1657	3000
220	Richard Hubord	1657	250
230	John Bennett	1658	150
234	William Martin	1657	1000
241	Anthony Stephens	1657	850
255	Henry Payton	1657	400
257	Robert Vauly	1657	2000
262	Henry Roach	1657	140
262	John Bennett	1658	210
263	Richard Searle and William Spence	1658	60
265	John Lewis and Robert Joanes	1658	2000
270	John Williams and Stephen Norman	1657	1200
279	Maj. James Goodwin	1657	1000
281	John Drayton	1657	2000
283	William Strowder	1658	500
284	David Phillips	1657	350
286	Richard Searle	1657	550
293	Lieut.-Col. Nathaniel Pope	1657	1500
294	Gervase Dodson	1657	5200
305	Richard Wright	1658	2200
306	Christopher Harris	1658	2000
309	Charles Ashton	1658	400
312	Capt. Peter Ashton	1658	2000
316	William and John Heabord	1658	300
318	Richard Wells	1658	100
324	Henry Roach	1658	1700
337	Gervase Dodson	1658	600
338	Mr. John Ellis	1658	1400
338	John Evans	1658	1650
341	Maj. James Goodwin	1658	400
342	John Withers	1658	320
342	William Withers	1658	400
353	John Curtis	1657	1300

369	John Maddison	1658	300
371	Col. Thomas Pettus	1658	1000
371	Col. George Read	1657	2000
383	John Dodman	1662	350
417	Giles Brent, Jr.	1662	1800
421	Arthur Shore and Henry Cossum	1662	350
426	Valentine Payton	1662	1600
430	Richard Browne	1662	300
434	Isaac Allerton	1662	500
441	Giles Brent	1662	1000
446	William Drummond	1661	4750
447	Col. Richard Lee	166–	4000
450	Richard Bushrod	1660	2000
456	Peter Ashton	1661	2550
492	William Overed	1661	400
550	Walter Broadhurst	1662	300
553	Gerrard Broadhurst	1662	500
555	Katherine Brent	1662	1050
555	William Hallows	1662	3900
571	Henry Vincent	1662	550
611	George Wading	1664	600
612	Thomas Butler	1664	391
623	William Struder	1664	500

BOOK No. 5.

14	Richard Bushrod	1662	2000
36	Anthony Arnold	1665	500
36	John Alexander	1664	550
37	John Beard	1664	245
37	John and Thomas Palmer	1664	365
38	Maj. John Washington	1664	320

(Continued)

YORK COUNTY

Book No. 1.

Page	Name	Date	No. acres
803	Thomas Mooreland	1642	100
812	Wm. Ireland and Robt. Wallis	1642	700
813	John Hartwell	1642	50
829	Ellis Richardson	1642	150
856	Stephen Hamblyn	1642	400
857	Luce Webster	1642	250
873	Stephen Gill	1642	2500
874	Wm. Smoote	1642	400
884	Rowland Burnham	1643	450
886	James Besouth	1643	100

Book No. 2.

Page	Name	Date	No. acres
18	Richard Lee	1644	91
23	John Shepard	1644	179
37	David Mansell	1644	72
51	George Ludlow	1644	1927
53	Lucis Webster	1644	200
56	George Lake	1645	250
55	Nicholas Wattkins	1642	100
59	George Lake and George Wyatt	1642	400
74	George Ludlow	1646	1452
86	Robert Vause	1647	400
90	Nicholas Brooke, Jnr	1647	500
90	Nicholas Brooke	1645	blank
93	Wm. Hockaday	1646	500
94	John Broach	1646	300
106	James Stone and Nicholas Jernew	1647	564
107	John Flynn	1646	50
108	Wm. Blackey	1647	300
121	Francis Fludd	1647	300
133	John Davis	1647	150
135	Thomas Gibson	1647	600
135	Hugh Allen	1647	420

156	Thomas Bourne	1648	200
160	Lieut. Stephen Gill	1649	25
163	Stephen Gill	1649	1150
163	John Bide	1648	50
192	Nicholas Brooke, Sr	1649	500
195	Manwarring Hamon	1649	3760
201	Joseph Croshaw	1649	1350
202	Richard Croshaw	1649	750
202	Henry Lee	1649	247
207	Nicholas Jernew	1649	1000
208	Nicholas Jernew	1649	200
208	John Holding	1649	850
209	Timothy Lodell	1649	575
226	William Hodgson	1650	500
270	Capt. Charles Leech	1650	1250
276	Capt. Ralph Wormeley	1649	1645
285	George Gill	1650	700
301	John Perines	1651	400
302	Thomas Bell	1651	200
304	Thomas Gibson	1651	900
304	Joseph Hayes	1651	300
309	Robert Abrall	1651	300
309	Same	1651	200
310	Same	1651	900
310	Wm. Ginsey	1651	300
313	John West	1651	1550
316	Edward Diggs	1651	1200
317	Arthur Prise	1651	1700
323	Robert Vaus	1651	150
324	Ashwell Battin	1651	1000
334	Henry Lee	1651	126
352	Joseph Croshaw	1651	750
352	Same	1651	1000
360	Nicholas Brooke, Jnr	1649	500

Book No. 3.

1	Joseph Croshaw	1653	700
4	Robt. Priddy	1653	377

5	Thomas Dunkleton	1653	50
9	Thomas Whitehead	1653	162
16	John Hope	1653	537
20	Henry Lee	1653	350
23	Col. Geo. Ludlow	1652	1500
28	Thomas Holmes	1654	434
30	Same	1654	300
30	Capt. Robt Abrahal	1653	160
33	Thomas Willis	1653	170
39	James Besouch	1652	98
51	Joseph Croshaw	1652	1750
54	Joseph Croshaw	1653	700
59	Major Wm. Lewis	1653	50
68	Robt. Wild and Philip Chesley	1653	100
72	John Holding	1653	389
76	Charles Kiggin	1653	100
89	Wm. Cox	1653	312
93	Capt. John West	1653	850
96	Robert Bauldry	1653	100
118	Wm. Bauldwin	1653	600
125	John Flett	1653	130
188	John Thomas	1649	350
192	John King	1649	500
139	Nicholas Sebrell	1653	200
146	Edward Overman	1653	1000
93	Edward Wright	1653	50
155	Thomas Holme	1652	200
161	Hannah Clarke	1652	800
161	Same	1652	1300
194	Robert Bouth	1653	880
201	Same	1652	400
202	Same	1652	400
238	Robert Vaus	1654	550
263	Robt. Wild	1654	800
274	Philip Chesley and Dan Wilde	1654	750
301	George Leddall	1654	1750
305	Francis Hamon	1654	2000
323	William Hoccaday	1654	200

358	Mathew Huberd	1655	590
268	Thomas Pencherman	1654	80
370	Obed Williams	1654	440
387	Lieut.-Col. Wm. Barber	1656	538

Book No. 4.

14	Robert Bourne and Daniel Parke	1655	580
19	Wm. Graves	1655	80
45	Thomas Bromfield	1656	315
126	Robert Vaux	1657	330
194	Edward Moalson	1657	50
275	Wm. Hay	1658	250
315	Mathew Sandever and Richard Addams	1658	200
334	Robert Bourne and Daniel Parke	1658	580
343	John Hansford	1658	850
422	Capt. Daniel Parke	1662	580
435	John Underhill	1662	250
437	Ralph Elkins	1661	30
452	Peter Efford	1660	900
561	John Sandavor and Richard Addams	1662	200
562	John Baisby	1662	350
564	Thomas Pinkeman	1662	125

(Continued)

HENRICO COUNTY.

Book No. 1.

Page	Name	Date	No. acres
118	Seth Ward	1634	60
155	Christopher Branch	1634	100
304	Thomas Harris	1635	750
326	Christopher Branch	1635	250
330	Elizabeth Parker, widow	1635	200
351	Alice Edloe, widow	1635	350
351	Hannah Boyse	1635	300
352	John Baker	1636	50
353	Wm. Hatcher	1636	200

VIRGINIA COUNTY RECORDS 81

355	Mary Box, widow	1636	300
356	Nathan Martin	1636	500
358	Robert Hollom	1636	1000
358	Edward Osborne	1636	400
571	Thomas Markham	1636	300
373	Elizabeth Parker	1636	500
581	Christopher Branch	1636	100
592	Wm. Clarke	1636	450
593	Same	1636	1100
597	Edward Tonstall	1636	450
403	Alice Edloe, widow	1636	50
403	Wm. Cox	1636	150
405	James Place	1636	550
413	Elizabeth Ballhash	1636	450
433	Alice Edloe, widow	1637	350
433	Wm. Hatcher	1637	850
434	John Baker	1637	200
436	Thomas Shippey	1637	300
436	Thomas Markham	1637	300
437	Richard Greete and Margin Thomas	1637	300
437	Wm. Farrar	1637	2000
438	Mary Box	1637	300
440	Richard Ward	1637	100
438	Capt. Thos. Harris	1637	700
441	Alice Edloe	1637	100
451	Robert Craddock and John Davis	1637	300
452	Joseph Royall	1637	300
454	Elizabeth Parker	1637	950
455	Edward Tunstall	1637	400
491	Robert Hollom	1637	1000
492	Wm. Cox	1637	150
512	Thomas Osborne, Jnr.	1637	500
512	Arthur Bayly	1637	200
512	Arthur Bayly and Thomas Crosby	1637	800
513	Arthur Bayly	1637	300
519	Capt. Thomas Osborne	1637	1000
537	Robert Craddock	1638	300

547	Wm. Clarke	1638	1100
547	Ann Hallom	1638	1000
551	Elizabeth Balhash	1638	300
552	Bryan Smith	1638	140
555	John Cookeney	1638	20
553	Christopher Branch	1638	250
555	John Cookeney	1638	150
558	Mathew Price	1638	150
559	John Baugh	1638	250
559	Wm. Hatcher	1638	150
567	Thomas Ellis	1638	50
599	Alice Edloe, widow	1638	150
608	Christopher Branch	1638	250
608	Howard Horsey	1638	1400
615	Capt. Thomas Harris	1638	820
634	Christopher Branch	1638	450
646	Thomas Mathews, Surgeon	1639	1100
653	Abraham Wood	1639	200
658	Ambrose Cobbs	1639	350
658	Mathew Gough	1639	350
659	Edward Tunstall	1639	150
661	John Howell	1639	150
662	Richard Johnson	1639	350
665	Thomas Sheppey	1639	250
668	Richard Johnson	1638	30
689	Dorothy Clarke	1639	800
707	Richard Cocke	1639	2000
711	Samuel Almond	1639	600
712	Same	1638	400
715	Richard Nance	1639	300
783	Bryant Smith	1641	100
815	Edward Tunstall	1642	100
836	Thomas Osborne	1642	400
839	Abraham Wood	1642	700
842	John Davis	1642	200
842	Cornelius De Hull	1642	502
862	John Pratt	1642	298
946	Seth Ward	1643	350

Book No. 2.

26	Michael Masters	1645	413
27	John Baugh	1645	100
75	Jeremy Blackman, Marinor	1646	1400
219	John Baugh	1650	100
262	Nicholas Perkins	1650	170
344	Major Wm. Bellew	1651	406

Book No. 3.

11	Wm. Johnson	1653	550
23	Wm. Worsnam and George Worsnam	1652	400
32	Richard Thomas	1652	185
41	Henry Lowne	1652	300
114	Robert Elam	1652	503
133	Richard Cocke	1652	2482
143	John Greenhough	1652	400
172	Christopher Robinson and John Sturdevant	1652	600
318	Maj. Abraham Wood	1654	406

Book No. 4.

9	Gilbert Deacon	1655	324
65	Isaac Hutchings	1656	378
67	Peter Lee	1656	126
149	Henry Randolph	1655	150
178	Wm. Waltham	1657	1600
583	Capt. Thomas Stegg	1662	800
599	Thomas Ludwell	1663	961
607	John Beauchamp	1664	56

Book No. 5.

4	Thomas Gazecomb	1664	150 A. 6 P.
43	Richard Ward	1665	1337 A. 1 P.
44	John Cox	1665	550
61	Wm. Stinton and Robt. Nurse	1665	204
62	John Knowles	1665	220
62	John Knowles	1665	100
69	George Archer	1665	550

90	Thomas Jones	1663	420
119	John Grenhough	1665	400
133	George Bullington	1664	503
155	Thomas Taylour	1662	281
278	Maj. Wm. Harris	1663	450
344	John Field	1662	400
399	John Beachamp and Richard Cocke	1664	2993
416	Capt. Wm. Farrer	1664	375
417	Thomas Liggon and Capt. Wm. Farrer	1664	335
517	James Adkin	1665	250
517	Thomas Webster	1665	251
527	George Archer	1663	250
528	Capt. Thomas Stegg	1663	1850
528	John Knowles	1663	100
534	John Brown and Edward Hatcher	1663	500
538	Amey Butler	1663	400
584	Thomas Wells	1665	260
585	John Burton	1665	700
589	John Pockett	1665	500
590	Christopher Branch	1665	1380
616	John Wilson	1666	100
618	Thomas Webster	1666	251

(Continued)

LANCASTER COUNTY.

Book No. 2.

Page	Name	Date	No. acres
341	Abraham Moone and Thomas Griffin	1651	1400
344	Capt. George Read	1651	600

Book No. 3.

2	John Edwards	1653	350
5	John Nichols	1653	50
6	Dennis Conniers	1653	1000
6	Richard Lake	1653	950
6	Wm. Tidner	1653	650

13	Randall Chamly	1654	100
15	Col. Richard Lee	1653	300
18	John Phillips	1652	100
18	Margaret Upton	1653	700
20	Robert Chowning	1653	250
20	Wm. Thomas	1653	100
20	John Phillips	1653	400
21	Patrick Miller	1653	150
21	Wm. Harper and Henry Rye	1653	550
21	John Bebey	1653	700
22	David Fox	1653	300
24	Toby Smith	1652	681
30	Thomas Kidd	1653	200
34	Capt. Wm. Brocas	1653	190
35	Dennis Conniers	1653	700
35	Elinor Brocas	1653	250
35	Abraham Moone	1653	400
35	Henry Deadman	1653	400
36	George Taylor	1653	542
40	Dennis Coniers	1653	223
40	Same	1653	194
45	John Edwards	1653	700
45	Robert Parfitt and Wm. Thatcher	1653	300
46	Thomas Bourn	1653	220
46	John Merryman and Morgan Heynes	1653	700
47	Col. Hugh Gwynn	1653	200
50	James Bonner	1653	650
56	Francis Gower	1653	280
57	John Cable	1653	250
58	John Sherlock	1653	200
69	Abraham Moon	1653	1700
69	Same	1653	300
71	George Wadding	1653	600
73	Charles Grymes	1653	960
73	Same	1653	1000
74	Same	1653	1000
74	John Bell	1653	150
75	John Phillips	1653	250

75	Same	1653	100
79	Thomas Griffin	1653	1064
80	Wm. Johnson	1653	350
81	Samuel Parry	1652	1250
83	Edmond Kemp, Geo. Cortlough and John Meradith	1653	800
86	Evan Davis and Henry Nicholls	1653	542
87	Nicholas Meriwether	1653	300
88	Maj. John Carter	1653	1600
90	Wm. Leech	1653	300
90	John Robinson	blank	300
97	Capt. Henry Fleete	1652	750
97	Teague Floyne	1652	300
99	Elias Edmonds	1652	600
99	John Sharpe	1652	300
100	Capt. Henry Fleet	1652	200
113	Thomas Lucas	1652	600
118	Tobias Horton	1652	500
119	David Fox	1652	800
119	John Taylor	1652	400
120	Thomas Steevens	1652	1400
124	John Bayles	1652	250
128	Isaac Richeson	1652	300
129	Richard Hutton and Lambett Lambettson	1652	600
130	Mrs. Elinor Brocas	1652	800
151	John Philips	1652	200
153	Thomas Paine	1652	600
154	Thomas Stevens	1652	600
156	John Fleet	1652	200
167	Thomas Brice	1652	1650
165	Francis Brown	1652	300
172	David Fox	1652	600
173	Mrs. Elinor Brocas	1652	700
174	Toby Smith	1652	900
187	Thos. Hoane	1652	130
195	Thomas Glasscock	1652	600
195	David Fox	1652	300

196	David Fox	1652	80
196	Daniel Welch	1652	537
197	Same	1652	600
200	Henry Nicholls	1652	200
206	Capt. Thomas Hackett	1652	800
207	John Phillips	1652	200
208	Rice Jones	1652	88
208	Enoch Hawkins and Anthony Doney	1652	1000
209	Evan Griffith	1652	100
220	Oliver Seager	1653	200
221	Oliver Segar	1653	250
224	Capt. Wm. Brocas	1653	950
228	Charles Grimes	1653	600
229	John Gillett	1653	400
234	Richard Hacker	1653	1653
235	Abraham Moone	1653	800
235	Humphrey Haggett	1654	450
239	John Robinson	1652	250
266	Dame Eliza. Lunsford	1654	500
266	Toby Horton	1653	350
266	Eppy Bonison	1653	400
269	Peter Rigby	1653	186
274	Sir Henry Chickly, Kt.	1653	950
275	John Phillips and John Batts	1653	500
276	Edwin Connaway	1654	1250
280	Abraham Moone	1654	2500
281	John Sharpe	1654	500
282	Clement Thrush	1654	150
292	Maj. John Carter	1654	1600
297	Charles Grymes	1654	600
297	Same	1654	600
300	Anthony Stephens	1654	500
298	Thomas Salsbury	1654	300
309	Robt., Thomas and Wm. Moss, brothers	1654	800
309	Alex. Portus and Thos. Williams	1654	271
310	Richard White, cooper	1654	500
318	Wm. Savadge	1654	100

324	Robert Younge	1654	400
325	John Cox	1654	600
327	Walter Dickenson	1654	800
328	Toby Smith	1654	1600
331	Wm. Thatcher	1654	300
331	Col. Fra. Morrison (lease)	1654	120
336	John Wyere	1655	300
343	Jer. Dodson	1655	600
343	John Bell	1655	200
344	Cyprian Bishopp	1655	200
345	Thomas Roots	1655	50
350	Wm. Johnson	1655	176
350	John Sharp, Jr.	1655	400
351	Wm. Johnson	1655	176
351	John Sharpe, Jr.	1655	400
352	Frauncis Gower	1655	530
353	Thomas Read	1655	300
356	John Watson	1655	300
356	Wm. Thatcher	1655	200
360	John Catlett and Ralph Rouzee	1655	1542
362	John Sharpe	1655	500
365	Mrs. Margaret Brent	1655	1000
365	Thomas Wills	1655	450
365	Walter Dickenson	1655	500
366	George Kible	1655	350
367	Edward Grimes	1655	390
372	Wm. Mells	1654	400
374	Thomas Hobkins	1654	1400
378	Capt. Henry Fleet	1654	1000
380	Alexander Porteus	1656	600
384	Peter Rigby and George Kibble	1656	600
386	David Fox	1656	800
390	Sarah Phillips	1656	250
392	Thomas Harris	1656	650

(Continued)

FAUQUIER COUNTY.

BOOK No. I.

Page	Name	Date	No. acres
69	Thos. Bryan Martin	1761	343
70	Benj. Snelling	1761	38
71	John Morgan	1761	36
79	Robt. Embry	1761	482
81	John Garner	1762	150
91	John Hitt	1762	53
92	Wm. Thornton	1763	212
104	Danl. Newland	1764	190
106	John Bell	1764	187
116	Wm. Obannon	1764	258
128	Richard Taylor	1765	127
136	Michael Luttral	1765	109
143	Herman Fishback	1765	179
144	George Lamkin	1765	17
149	Isaac Adams	1766	170
151	Betty and Peggy Mauzy	1766	14
153	George Neavill	1766	270
169	James Siers	1769	122
172	Jas. Foley, Sr.	1770	117
182	Jas. Stewart	1770	49
183	Geo. Williams	1770	231
185	Thos. Williams	1770	196
191	Benj. Crump	1771	132
194	Joseph Taylor	1771	270
201	Jeremiah Darnall	1771	35 2/3
203	Wm. Asbury	1772	301
209	Carr Bailey	1772	57
213	Robert Donaldson	1772	62
220	Wm. Blackwell	1772	60
228	Jas. Bashaw	1772	60
241	Andrew Cocran & Co., merchants in Glasgow	1773	370
260	Minor Winn, Jr.	1774	25

264	Reuben Wright	1775	420
266	Cuthbert Harrison	1775	1350
268	Henry Lee	1775	100
269	Richard Parker	1775	111
275	Thomas Barbey	1776	83
284	Augustine Jennings	1776	20
284	Augustine Jennings	1776	20
288	Lynaugh Helm	1777	233
289	Henry Mauzy	1777	312
294	Margaret Reynolds	1777	25
295	Wm. Barkley	1777	92
296	John Peter Kemper	1777	70
300	Edwd. Dixon and, after his death, to son, Turner Dixon	1777	4406
302	Wharton Ransdell	1777	500
306	Thos. Bryan Martin	1777	255
307	Wm. Lynn	1777	282
312	Capt. James Scott	1778	18
320	John Monroe	1778	416
321	John Monroe	1778	86
332	Wm. Pickett	1778	340
333	Brereton Jones	1778	185
341	Abner Smith, heir of Joseph Smith, Jr., decd.	1779	25
344	Wm. Eliott	1779	15
350	John Moffett	1779	513
350	John Moffett	1779	513
352	Yelverton Peyton	1779	270
355	Augustine Jennings	1779	18½
356	Capt. Peter Grant	1779	52
358	Wm. Grant	1779	298
359	Thos. Stone, Jr.	1779	320
362	Pearson Chapman	1779	372
363	Reuben Wright	1779	470
364	Thomas James	1779	76
369	Wm. Hamilton	1779	315
372	Robert Hinson	1779	47
375	Martin Pickett	1780	243

376 Wm. Pickett 1780 420
377 Jonathan Gibson 1780 56
379 William Conway 1780 70
374 Thomas Barbey 1776 12

BOOK N.

329 John Lee, Henry Lee and Thos. Lawson,
    exrs. of Allen Macrae, decd. 1766 432
330 John Lee, Henry Lee and Thos. Lawson,
    exrs. of Allen Macrae, decd. 1766 1277

BOOK O.

76 Thos. Bryan Martin 1767 119,927
80 Thos. Bryan Martin 1767 26,535

BOOK S.

194 Martin Pickett 1786 798
223 Simon Morgan 1787 332
225 Simon Morgan 1787 200
264 John Withers 1787 30
315 Wm. Smith 1787 32
319 Benj. Thomas 1787 98
382 John Ashbey, Jr. 1788 285
491 Martin Pickett 1788 150
532 Thomas Saunders 1788 78½
545 James Dowdall 1788 586

BOOK T.

28 John Wilkinson 1788 100
64 Gustavus Scott 1788 383
79 Thos. Bryan Martin 1788 912
145 Thos. Fitzhugh 1788 931
176 Wm. Skinker 1788 308
199 John Ringo 1788 142
539 Charles Martin 1789 282
584 Martin Pickett 1789 183
400 Roger West 1789 295

BOOK U.

341 Wm. Carr 1789 248

371	Charles Duncan	1789	14
431	Wm. Conway	1789	24
591	Martin Pickett, Thos. Keith and Chas. Chilton	1790	93
601	John Woodsydes	1790	382
603	Benj. Crump	1790	60
604	Benj. Crump	1790	131
605	Benj. Crump	1790	37
613	Thos. Nugent	1790	95
630	Capt. Peter Grant	1790	64

Book V.

300	George Williams, Sr.	1791	7
313	William Carr	1791	97½
404	Lot Hackley	1792	334
554	John Nelson, Jr.	1792	98
558	Thomazen Ellsey	1792	158

Book W.

87	Wm. Conway	1792	48
91	John Crump	1792	113½
103	Peter Wagener	1792	90
104	Peter Wagener	1792	73
143	James Wright	1792	166
144	Elijah Edwards	1792	50
158	Martin Pickett	1792	139
159	Hy. Mauzy, Jr.	1792	10
202	Thos. and Robert Embry	1793	144
245	Joshua King, Sr.	1794	385
272	Thos. Keith and Peter Conway	1794	31
305	Robert Stringfellow	1794	29
306	Robert Stringfellow	1794	20
376	John Weaver	1794	6¼
377	James Smith	1794	182
587	John Winn Smith	1795	31
595	Daniel Bradford	1795	17

Book X.

23	Daniel Bradford	1795	17¼

25	Nathl. Dodd 1795	45
26	Claramond, Alice, Charles, Daniel Joanna and William Allen, heirs of Wm. Allen, decd. 1795	155
428	Thos. Homes, Sr. 1796	450
519	Jas. Thompson 1796	15½
541	John Blackwell 1797	18
598	Nicholas, Hannah Margaret, Isaac, Mary, Abraham, Wm., Eliz., and Sarah Wykoff, children and heirs of Nicholas Wykoff, decd. 1797	105
599	Same 1797	23

Book Y.

21	Jesse Brown 1798	62
59	Wm. Skinker 1798	34
90	Capt. John Kelley 1798	66
260	Alex. K. Marshall 1799	51
301	Benj. Crump 1799	13

(Continued)

ACCOMAC COUNTY.

Book No. 1.

Page	Name	Date	No. acres
56	Capt. Clement Dilke 1627		100
57	Hannah Savage 1627		50
49	Capt. Wm. Epes 1626		450
76	Clement Dilke 1626		20
81	John Webb, mariner 1627		50
85	Nicholas Hoskins, yeoman 1626		20
86	Robt. Browne, planter 1628		20
87	John Howe 1628		30
98	Roger Saunders 1628		50
100	Wm. Smith 1629		100
106	Robt. Saunders 1632		300
137	Thos. Savage, carpenter 1632		100

157	Nicholas Harwood	1634	50
182	Wm. Andrews	1635	200
181	Wm. Andrews	1635	100
183	Daniel Cugley	1635	400
189	Daniel Cugley	1635	400
270	Wm. Berriman	1635	150
275	Mrs. Hanna Savage, the relict of Ensyne Savage, a piece of land	1635	
286	Wm. Gany	1635	1250
322	Edmond Scarborough	1635	200
323	Edmond Scarborough	1635	200
364	Lewin Dinwood	1636	150
365	John Neale	1636	1500
365	John Neale	1636	500
366	James Berry	1636	350
366	John Forbush	1636	100
367	Thomas Smith	1636	150
367	Wm. Bibby	1636	400
375	Hy. Williams	1636	150
375	Wm. Roper	1636	150
376	Robert Drake	1636	200
376	Thos. Hunt	1636	50
376	Edwd. Drew	1636	300
377	John Harlowe	1636	300
377	Thos. Gaskins	1636	300
378	John Wilkins	1636	1300
406	Francis Stockeley	1636	50
409	Henry Wilson	1636	50
413	John Neale	1636	1500
417	Jno. Redman and Jno. Neale	1637	500
465	Jas. Berry	1637	350
465	John Neale, assignee of Edwd. Bestwicke	1637	200
466	Edwd. Bestwicke, assignee of Wm. Melling	1635	200
487	Capt. John Howe	1637	1000
490	Hy. Wilson	1637	50
493	Geo. Traveller	1637	500
495	Edwd. Stockdell	1637	400

496	Philip Taylor	1637	500
499	Thos. Salvage (Savage), decd., pce. of land	1637	
507	David Winley	1637	100
507	David Winley	1637	250
514	Stephen Charlton	1637	200
518	John Neale	1637	500
528	Stephen Charlton	1638	1000
539	John Wilkins	1637	500
568	Henry Walker	1638	175
571	Lineing Denwood	1638	50
595	Argoll Yeardly	1638	3700
614	Wm. Berryman	1638	350
614	Hy. Williams	1638	200
615	Wm. Cotton	1638	300
615	Edmund Scarborough	1638	400
623	Elias Hartree	1638	100
637	Christopher Thomas	1638	200
637	John Walton	1638	200
644	Alice Wilson	1639	200
651	Farmer Jones	1639	400
651	Jas. Perren	1639	100
652	Thos. Burbage	1638	1250
657	Wm. Burdett	1639	200
664	Hy. Bagwell	1639	400
670	John Vaughan	1639	30
676	Thos. Smith	1639	300
685	Edwd. Drew	1639	200
698	Christopher Kirke	1640	300
698	John Maior	1640	400
699	Elias Taylor	1640	150
699	Edmund Scarburgh	1640	600
700	George Traveller	1640	200
713	Wm. Burdett	1639	1050
725	Wm. Jones	1640	100
725	Francis Martin	1640	250
726	John Holloway	1640	550
782	John Browne	1642	200

783	Stephen Charleton	1641	500
786	Wm. Burdett	1641	300
789	George Smith	1642	200
790	John Harlow	1642	200
791	John Towlson	1642	450
794	John Waltham, Jr.	1642	300
817	Edmund Scarburgh	1642	350
947	Mr. Obedience Robins	1643	2000
3	John Blow	blank	150

Book 2.

108	Laurence or Leonard Pettock	1647	500

Book 3.

295	Luke Billington	1659	250
295	John Custis	1654	200

Book 4.

141	John Custis, Sr.	1657	200
224	Wm. Custis	1657	200
543	John, Sarah and Margaret Mitchell	1662	1000
544	John, Sarah and Margaret Mitchell	1662	200
581	Edmund Scarburgh	1663	1450
582	Nathl. Bradford	1664	1400
600	Edward Revel and Jonah Jackson	1663	1000
600	Fenlau Mackwilliam	1663	400
600	James Atkinson	1663	500
622	Mary Kendall, dau. of Lieut.-Col. Wm. Kendall	1663	300
625	John Prettiman	1664	200
625	Wm. Taylor	1664	600

Book 5.

70	John Stirgies	1663	200
71	Southey Littleton	1664	850
71	John Renny	1662	400
71	Dorothy Jordan	1664	450
71	Cornelius Watkinson	1664	450
72	Col. Edmund Scarburgh	1664	1000

72	Col. Edmund Scarburgh 1664	1000
72	Col. Edmund Scarburgh 1664	150
73	Col. Edmund Scarburgh 1664	3000
73	Col. Edmund Scarburgh 1663	2400
73	Col. Edmund Scarburgh 1664	2000
74	Col. Edmund Scarburgh 1664	1400
74	Wm. Onaughton and Teague Miskett 1664	400
75	John Dye 1664	450
75	Mr. John West 1664	1500
75	John Renny 1664	500
76	Miles Grey 1664	400
76	Richard Kellum 1664	900
76	Charles Ratcliffe 1664	600
77	Robert Hill 1664	400
77	Edmund Smith 1664	1250
77	Mr. John Stokeley 1664	2600
78	Tabitha Smart 1664	1000
78	Maj. John Tilney 1664	1000
78	Capt. Edmund Bowen 1664	1200
79	Jas. Grey and Alphonson Ball 1664	900
80	Law. Robinson 1664	800
80	Alex. Addison 1664	700
80	John Dolby 1664	1000
81	John Wallop 1664	400
81	Mr. Robert Pitt 1663	3000
82	Ann Toft 1664	500
83	Chas. Scarburgh, eldest son of Col. Edmund Scarburgh 1664	3050
118	Richard Hinman 1665	100
126	Robert Pitt 1662	1000
218	John Cary 1663	400
219	John Savage 1663	250

(Continued)

NORTHAMPTON COUNTY MARRIAGE BONDS.

Oct.   29, 1715. Francis Armistead, of Gloucester, and Sarah Smith.
Aug.   19, 1752. Jacob Andrews, of Accomac, and Margaret Joyne.
May   22, 1756. Arthur Addison and Tabitha, dau. of Edmund Joyne.
May   20, 1765. William, son of James Arbuckle, and Alathiel, dau. of John Hall.
May   4, 1768   Isaac Avery and Esther Preeson, widow.
Aug.   16, 1771. Samuel Attchison and Esther, dau. of John Respess.
Jan.   11, 1774. Maj. Andrews and Hannah Bell Powell, dau. of George Powell, decd.
Oct.   14, 1775. Thomas Addison and Margaret Walton, widow.
Feb.   28, 1775. Shadrach Ames and Matilda Christian.
Sept.   16, 1779. Ezekiel Abdell, son of Abel, and Sarah, dau. of Waterfield Dalby.
June   17, 1779. Abel Abdell and Nancy, dau. of Tilney Dixon, decd.
Jan.   11, 1780. Thomas Addison and Peggy, dau. of Nathaniel Savage.
April   5, 1785. Ellison Armistead and Susannah, dau. of Michael Christian .
April   26, 1781. Henry Abdell and Sarah, widow of John Tankred.
April   20, 1781. William Andrews and Bridget, dau. of Wm. Heath, Sr.
June   7, 1785. Isaac Avery and Margaret, dau. of Hillary Stringer.
April   11, 1786. William Abdell and Leviey Gooday.
March   8, 1786. Arthur Addison and Esther Cag.
July   23, 1787. William Andrews and Sarah Hunt.
June   26, 1787. Kendall Addison and Palmer Rogers.
Dec.   11, 1788. Robert Andrews and Betsy, dau. of Benj. Stratton, decd.

April	10, 1787.	Arthur Addison and Elizabeth Cook.
Dec.	11, 1789.	Thomas Allen and Elizabeth, dau. of Anne Massey.
June	20, 1791.	William Andrews and Sally Waterfield.
Dec.	29, 1791.	John Abdell and Elizabeth Kelly.
Aug.	14, 1792.	William Andrews and Adah Dennis.
Aug.	9, 1794.	Thomas Abdell and (woman's name not given).
April	25, 1794.	William Abdell and Amy Dettih.
April	8, 1794.	Matthew Anderson and Rosey Collins.
June	24, 1795.	Maj. Andrews and Nancy Custis.
July	30, 1796.	Preeson Abdell and Polly Key.
Dec.	20, 1795.	William Ames and Patsey Bool.
Oct.	1, 1796.	Henry Abdell and Hetty Stott.
May	21, 1800.	Thomas Ames and Sally Christian.
March	8, 1800.	Edmund Ayres and Cassa Johnston.
Sept.	21, 1710.	Moses Bow, mariner, and Margaret, dau. of Capt. Thomas Savage.
Dec.	25, 1721.	William Burton, Jr., and Elizabeth Eyre.
May	13, 1733.	Peter Bowdoin and Susannah Preeson.
May	3, 1748.	Ezekiel Bell and Ann Carpenter, widow.
Dec.	6, 1749.	Ralph Batson and Sarah Moor, widow.
Jan.	10, 1754.	John Bowdoin and Grace Stringer.
Jan.	8, 1753.	John Benthall and Elizabeth Goffigon, widow.
Feb.	19, 1759.	Preeson Bowdoin and Sarah, dau. of Littleton Eyre.
March	28, 1764.	Henry Bryant and Nancy Holland.
June	3, 1763.	Col. Robert Bolling, of Buckingham co., and Mary, dau. of William Burton.
March	15, 1763.	Abraham Boswell and Elishe, dau. of Esau Jacob.
Nov.	25, 1760.	Edward Belote and Mary, dau. of Jacob Nottingham, decd.
Jan.	29, 1765.	William Bishop, Jr., and Elizabeth, dau. of Wm. Graves.
Feb.	6, 1765.	Thomas Barlow and Jane Mapp, widow.

Nov. 27, 1766. Timothy Baker and Jane, dau. of John Wilkins, Sr.

Jan. 21, 1766. John Burton and Bridget, dau. of Thomas Dalby.

March 9, 1769. William Biggs and Elishe, dau. of John Smaw.

June 17, 1772. Robert Bell and Mary, dau. of William Jarvis.

Dec. 10, 1771. Levin Bunting and Ann, dau. of Solomon Bunting.

Jan. 14, 1772. Nathl. Burgess and Ann, dau. of Peter Goffigon, decd.

Jan. 22, 1772. John Blair and Mary, dau. of Benj. Darby, decd.

Nov. 12, 1771. Robert Bell and Abigail, dau. of Thomas Grice.

Aug.   6, 1770. Geo. Bunting and Elizabeth, dau. of Moses Johnson, decd.

Dec. 31, 1770. James Boswell and Margaret Jacob.

May 18, 1768. John Blair and Sarah, dau. of Samuel Mapp, decd.

Jan. 12, 1773. Thomas Bullock and Mary ———, widow.

March 31, 1773. John Biggs and Tabitha Goffigon, widow.

Aug. 19, 1774. Abraham Boswell and Mary Dixon, widow.

Oct. 11, 1774. Thomas Bullock and Athaliel Underhill.

Oct.   4, 1775. John Bishop and Anne, dau. of William Dixon, decd.

Dec. 26, 1775. John Barnes and Elizabeth, dau. of Esau Jacob, decd.

May   9, 1775. Thomas Barlow and Ann Stott.

March 18, 1775. Joshua Blake and Esther Warren, dau. of Devorax, decd.

May 30, 1776. Solomon Bunting and Polly Pitts, widow.

June 11, 1776. John Bool and Priscilla, dau. of Thomas Addison.

Feb. 19, 1778. Thomas Butler and Frances Costin.

Feb.   9, 1778. Nathl. Brown and Nanny Dillion, widow.

Jan.   6, 1779.   Reuben Beech and Mary, dau. of Patrick
                   Wilkins, decd.
May   21, 1779.   Caleb Benthall and Elizabeth, dau. of
                   Moses Stripe.
April 16, 1779.   William Belote and Sarah, dau. of John
                   Tankard, decd.
Jan.   24, 1780.   Alex. Boyd and Sally, dau. of Peter Gof-
                   figon.
Sept. 28, 1780.   Thomas Bell and Sarah Gascoyne.
Sept. 26, 1780.   Thomas Barlow and Elizabeth Roscoe.
Feb.   28, 1781.   Maj. Bool and Patience, widow of John
                   Turner.
Feb.   19, 1781.   William Barcraft and Elizabeth, dau. of
                   Thomas Speakman.
Nov.   21, 1781.   Geo. Brickhouse and Mary, dau. of Edward
                   Belote.
Dec.   2, 1782.   James Backurst and Bridgett Stott.
Dec.   10, 1783.   Richard Bool and Keziah Bool.
May   21, 1783.   James Bonwell and Mary Robins.
March 11, 1783.   Robert Brickhouse and Sarah Nottingham.
Dec.   29, 1784.   Ezra Bradford and Anne Smith.
——   —, 1785.   Elijah Baker (woman's name not given).
Feb.   19, 1785.   John Brickhouse and Susanna, dau. of
                   Thomas Nottingham, Sr.
Feb.   19, 1785.   Daniel Benthall and Adah Warren.
Aug.   31, 1785.   William Bain and Judith Stevenson.
Dec.   20, 1786.   Nathaniel Bell and Elizabeth Turpin.
Nov.   5, 1787.   Holloway Bunting and Priscilla, dau. of
                   John Furbush Turner.
May   31, 1787.   Richard Bool and Margaret Addison.
March   7, 1788.   Charles Bradford and Nancy Abdell.
March 14, 1788.   Brown Bradford and Peggy, dau. of Obe-
                   dience Johnson.

(Continued)

NORFOLK COUNTY MARRIAGE BONDS.

Oct. 5, 1706. John Browne and Elizabeth Ivy.
June —, 1711. George Burgis and Mary Butt.
Sept. 22, 1712. Charles Wood and Mary Catherine ——.
April 28, 1713. Walter Bayly and Mary Etheredge.
June 13, 1715. Richard Butt and Dinah Butt.
July 31, 1717. James Egerton, of Province of Maryland, and Mirium Tatem.
May 30, 1722. William Bell and Ellener Corprew.
Oct. 3, 1722. Nehemiah Jones and Edith Butt.
May 19, 1723. Rehodolphus Malbone and Mary Richardson.
Nov. 6, 1723. Jacob Walker and Mrs. Courtney Tucker.
Nov. 7, 1723. Robert Jackson and Elizabeth Brett.
Feb. 22, 1723. Thomas Nelson and Mrs. Frances Tucker.
July 20, 1724. James Wilson, Sr., and Grace Phillips.
July 28, 1724. John Ashely and Elizabeth Godfrey.
Aug. 13, 1724. Stephen Wright and Kathrine ——.
Aug. 13, 1724. John Ellegood and Abigail Mason.
Aug. 20, 1725. James Wilson and Dinah Nickason.
Aug. 15, 1727. Thomas Scott and Martha Smith.
Aug. 28, 1727. John Dale and Mary Cartwright, widow.
Nov. 17, 1727. James Avery and Mary McNary.
April 29, 1728. Nicholas Slack and Elizabeth Stewart.
June 7, 1728. Willis Wilson and Elizabeth Goodrich.
July 25, 1728. John Phripp and Charity Dison.
Nov. 11, 1728. Philip Dison and Susanna Phillippse.
Nov. 11, 1728. James Ivy and Mary Furlong.
Dec. —, 1728. Edward Bembowe and Elizabeth Falconar.
Dec. 13, 1728. Simon Holstead and Ann Mathias.
Feb. 14, 1728. Lazarus Sweeny and Elizabeth Wilson.
Feb. 22, 1728. John Edmunds and Sarah Russell.
April 2, 1729. John Spencer and Mary McDowell.
May 22, 1729. John Whiddon and Mrs. Abigail Cawson.
Sept. 25, 1729. James Libby and Sarah Wright.
May 1, 1731. John Hill and Margaret Wilson.
May 6, 1731. William Porter and Kezia Cawson.

May	24, 1731.	James Langley and Sarah Nickhalson.
July	29, 1731.	James Avery and Frances Brett.
Nov.	9, 1731.	Philip Mackduel and Sarah Drewry.
March	29, 1731.	Simon Hancock and Apphia Malbone.
April	3, 1732.	Richard Pool and Mrs. Ann Butt, widow.
May	22, 1732.	Nathl. Nichles and —— Matthias, widow.
June	9, 1732.	Robert Bramble and Mary Ewel.
July	22, 1732.	Gilbert McNary and Mary Wilson.
Aug.	9, 1732.	Revd. Moses Robertson and Mary Willoughby.
March	29, 1732.	Henry Miller and Elizabeth Godfrey.
Aug.	11, 1733.	Edward Archer and Mrs. Mary Anguish.
April	1, 1734.	James Tuell and Elizabeth Bax.
May	27, 1734.	John Sayer and Elizabeth Gwin.
Aug.	19, 1734.	William Gwinn and Elizabeth Sheals.
——	——, 1735.	Alexander Bayne and Margaret Connor.
Oct.	——, 1736.	William Dutton and Mary Edwards.
Nov.	16, 1736.	Paul Ballentine and Ann Cawson.
Jan.	17, 1736.	Henry Harbert and Abigail Cawson.
April	17, 1737.	Edward Magee and Ann Wise, widow.
Feb.	11, 1737.	John Thomas and Elizabeth Oagely.
——	——, 1738.	Caleb Wilson and Mrs. Ann Church.
April	11, 1738.	William Porter and Patience Wright.
July	4, 1738.	James O'Bryan and Mary Langley.
Aug.	11, 1741.	John Cooke and Mrs. Elizabeth Boush.
Feb.	13, 1741.	George Bevin and Miriam Godfrey.
June	26, 1742.	George Collins and Mary Phillips, widow.
Oct,	15, 1742.	Henry Jamason and Mary Stanley.
Dec.	29, 1742.	William Herbert and Janet Cawson.
Jan.	5, 1742.	John Portlock and Abiah Portlock.
Jan.	31, 1742.	Matthias Miller and Alif Ivy.
Feb.	9, 1742.	Duncan McNeill and Sarah Sparrow.
Nov.	7, 1743.	John Tatem and Anne Wright.
Dec.	13, 1743.	Nathl. Tatem and Prudence Wilson.
Dec.	16, 1743.	James Wilson, Jr., and Grace Duke.
Dec.	26, 1743.	John Willoughby and Mary Hutchings.
April	4, 1744.	Joshua Nicholson and Tabitha Lowery.

April   19, 1744. James Webb and Penelope Butt.
April   27, 1744. Thomas Tibbs and Martha Tomouth.
May   11, 1744. William Hodghon and Elizabeth Mesler.
May   26, 1744. William Baker and Rebecca Joel.
July   5, 1744. Robert Stewart and Abiah Church.
July   28, 1744. Capt. Maximilian Calvert and Mrs. Mary
                    Savage.
Sept.   24, 1744. Patrick Mcalroy and Mary Pilkington.
Oct.   6, 1744. Richard Jackson and Dinah Lewling.
Dec.   24, 1744. Joseph Stewart and Julian Church.
Jan.   12, 1744. Josiah Butt and Mary Boush.
Feb.   15, 1745. William Wright and Mary Butt.
April   19, 1746. Solomon Fife and Mary Drury.
May   21, 1746. Jeremiah Wilson and Jane ——.
May   28, 1746. Hillary Herbert and Elizabeth Veal.
June   4, 1748. Robert Ives and Cosiah Johnson.
Feb.   7, 1749. William Freeman and Tabitha Wilson.
Aug.   29, 1750. Robert Tucker and Elizabeth Cleeves.
Jan.   21, 1750. William Bradley and Mary Wilson.
Aug.   16, 1751. David Harper and Mary Manning.
Sept.   10, 1751. William Nimmo, Jr., and Anne Wilson.
Sept.   18, 1751. Leml. Willoughby and Martha Sweny.
Sept.   19, 1751. Shadrack Talbutt and Sarah Talbutt.
Oct.   18, 1751. John Lewis and Rachael Bingham.
Nov.   3, 1751. Horatio Stammers and Sarah Drury.
Dec.   14, 1751. Joseph Brown and Katherine Edmonds.
April   30, 1752. John Hamilton and Patience Rusell.
June   19, 1752. John Robe and Mary Fife.
June   26, 1752. Thomas Oldner and Sarah Wakefield.
June   28, 1752. Absalom Langley and Elizabeth Scady.
Sept.   30, 1752. John Streip and Mary Bready.
Nov.   1, 1752. James Ashley and Elizabeth Langley,
                    widow.
Nov.   14, 1752. William Smith and Ann Cleeves.
Dec.   2, 1752. Richard Scott and Rebecca Portlock.
Dec.   3, 1752   William Simmons and Sarah ——, widow.
Dec.   11, 1752. Thomas Wilson and Prudence Nicholson.
Jan.   18, 1753. Martain Bayne and Sarah Southerlin.

March 16, 1753. William Roberts and Ann Jennings.
March 17, 1753. Willis Bramble and Mary Ashley.
March 20, 1753. Lott Maund and Mary Wright.
April 5, 1753. Jorden Oast and Elizabeth Dial.
Aug. 17, 1753. Francis Weldon and Ruth Pertall.
Sept. 12, 1753. Christopher Wright and Mary Walke.
Sept. 23, 1753. Zachariah Hutchins and Dinah Inkson.
Sept. 29, 1753. James Holt and Ann Osheal.
Oct. 3, 1753. Lewis Hansford and Ann Taylor.
Oct. 5, 1753. William Murrey and Martha Lewelling.
Oct. 25, 1753. Joseph Church and Sarah Wilson.
Oct. 31, 1753. Roderick Conner and Margaret Scott.
Feb. 21, 1754. Stephen Hutchings and Sarah Portlock.
March 11, 1754. John Cleeves and Ann Silvester.
March 25, 1754. Thomas Nash, Jr., and Mary Portlock.
April 23, 1754. John Walsh and Patience Davis.
May 13, 1754. William Banks and Mary Collert.
June 5, 1754. George Snow and Mary Morrison.
June 12, 1754. Matthias Christian and Lydia Ashley.
Aug. 15, 1754. Thomas Thompson and Siphia Kinner.
Aug. 23, 1754. Charles Mayle and Dinah Bevan.
Aug. 27, 1754. Peter Dyes and Margaret Lewelling.
Aug. 29, 1754. Francis Hewlitt and Mary Hodges.
Sept. 13, 1754. John Hutton and Flora Hiley.
Sept. 19, 1754. Jonathan Portlock and Mary Bevan.
Oct. 8, 1754. Joel Jackson and Frances Lowery.
Nov. 27, 1754. Christian Moseley and Elizabeth Langley.
Dec. 12, 1754. William Kid and Hannah Duche.
Dec. 21, 1754. John Williams and Courtney Thelaball.
Jan. 14, 1755. Isaac Tolbutt and Elizabeth Langley.
Feb. 12, 1755. Nathl. Tatem and Dinah Nash.
April 1, 1755. John Williamson, Jr., and Mary Mathias, widow.
April 7, 1755. William Alexander and Sarah Dupree.
June 4, 1755. Francis Peart and Catherine Brown.
June 17, 1755. Joshua Connyer and Jane Davis.
June 19, 1755. Edward Pugh and Lucy Calvert.

June	21, 1755.	Thomas Bushnell and Max Murden.
July	7, 1755.	William Prata and Courtnay Edmunds.
Dec.	11, 1755.	Thomas Willoughby and Mary Portlock.
April	21, 1756.	Maj. John Willoughby and Sarah Abyvon.
May	3, 1756.	John Corprew and Euphan Wilson.
May	12, 1756.	Benjamin Guy and Jacamine Pead.
June	19, 1756.	Pavy Dison and Jane Ganmeony.
June	23, 1756.	Matt. Godfrey and Abigail Porter.
Sept.	7, 1756.	John Brown and Mary Hiley.
Sept.	7, 1756.	Joseph Nisbet and White Maye.

(Continued)

Vol. VI   JNUE, 1909   Part 2

𝔙𝔦𝔯𝔤𝔦𝔫𝔦𝔞

𝔆𝔬𝔲𝔫𝔱𝔶 𝔕𝔢𝔠𝔬𝔯𝔡𝔰

PUBLISHED QUARTERLY

EDITED BY

William Armstrong Crozier, F. R. S., F. G. S. A.

Published by
The Genealogical Association
211 West 101st Street
New York City

Virginia

County Records

PUBLISHED QUARTERLY

EDITED BY

William Armstrong Crozier

Published by
The Genealogical Association
511 West 102nd Street
New York City

Virginia County Records

Published Quarterly

CONTENTS

Virginia County Records

QUARTERLY MAGAZINE

| VOL. VI. | JUNE 1909 | No. 2 |

INDEX TO LAND GRANTS

ISLE OF WIGHT COUNTY

Book No. 5.

386	Edmond Palmer	1664	900
392	Nicholas Cobb	1663	202
397	John Naseworthy	1663	985
414	Robert Flack	1664	200
422	Wm. Westwary	1664	750
429	Anthony Fulgan	1664	1000
452	Nicholas Cobb	1664	900
460	Wm. Miles and Wm. Cooke, Sr.	1664	1100
462	Francis England	1664	2366
533	Robert Flack	1664	300
533	Same	1664	600
619	Wm. Richardson	1664	700
626	Doctr. Robt. Williamson	1666	3350
630	Christopher Wade	1665	300
637	Anthony Matthews	1666	1300
628	Capt. Joseph Bridger and Wm. Burgh..	1666	7800
639	Mrs. Ann Pitt	1665	150
640	Philip Huniford	1666	800
669	John Hardie	1666	1150

Book No. 6.

5	John Walton and Elizabeth, his wife...	1666	450
24	Mrs. Elizabeth Oudelant	1666	1500
45	Thomas Woodward, Jr.	1667	1100
69	Lt. Col. John George	1667	360
110	Robert Flack	blank	2400
110	John Wakefield and John Sherer	1688	1050
117	John King	1688	1000
124	Thomas Tooke	1667	1228
140	Thomas Bland, Mary, his wife and to the heirs of Mary	1668	750
151	Lt. Col. John George	1667	360
181	Robt. Coleman	1667	634
207	Capt. Jos. Bridger	1668	1000
215	Capt. Anthony Fulgham	1688	150
216	Thomas Woodward	1669	100
223	George Moore	1669	1400

224	Wm. Oldis and Robert Ruffin	1669	2050
232	Robert Flack	1666	2400
232	Robert Flack	1669	450
233	Wm. Richardson and Thomas Adkinson.	1669	230
233	Thomas Adkinson	1669	600
249	Mrs. Elizabeth Bouchier	1669	200
261	Edward Brantly	1669	675
285	James Ennis	1670	200
300	Thomas Moore	1670	2400
300	Tho. Blake	1670	400
306	John Wheatley	1670	100
306	Richard Madison	1670	200
307	John Gluderidge	1670	200
307	John Vicars, in behalf of James Benn, orphan	1670	200
307	Michael Fulgham in the right of his wife.	1670	100
308	Mistris Rebecca Izard, in the behalf of her two daughters, Mary and Martha Izard	1670	250
309	Col. Joseph Bridger	1674	800
443	Edmund Palmer	1672	2800
466	Jno. Portis and Hen. West	1673	900
467	Thomas Woodward, Jr.	1673	1600
497	Wm. Cooke	1670	800
506	Majr. Mich. Hill	1674	670
520	Gyles Driver	1674	930
520	Hen. Applewhaite	1674	300
521	John Hardie	1674	1390
521	John Portis	1674	376
527	Thomas Woodward, Sr.	1674	1300
536	Wm. Oldis and Robt. Ruffin	1674	2050
561	Thomas Joyner	1675	1300
606	James Bagnall	1675	300
605	Edward Jones	1675	680
609	Anthony Fulgham	1676	780
641	Hodges Councill	1677	941
643	Henry Applewhaite	1678	925

644	John Williams	1678	925
650	Col. Joseph Bridger	1678	850
651	John Lawrence	1678	530
653	Matthew Strickland	1678	902
683	Lt. Col. Arth. Smith	1679	2275
684	Richard Jordane	1679	363
684	Wm. Smelly	1679	480
684	Richard Reynolds	1679	566

ELIZABETH CITY COUNTY

Book No. 2.

9	Wm. Wilkinson, Minister	1644	100
23	Wm. Cock	1645	100
24	John Baker	1645	175
27	Marke Johnson	1645	198
35	Thomas Watts	1645	132
42	John Ingrame	1642	150
45	Ralph Barlowe	1642	150
64	Richard Grigson	1646	400
73	Elizabeth Ambrose	1646	100
81	Elizabeth Claiborne	1647	700
114	Thomas Hopkins	1647	300
114	Thomas Todd	1647	50
128	Maj. Richard Morrison	1648	110
138	John Howitt, carpenter	1648	204
138	Ralph Hunt	1645	300
138	John Houlder	1647	50
139	Wm. up Thomas	1648	335
140	John Ingram	1647	300
140	Edward Parish	1648	200
142	William Parry	1648	90
188	Lt. Wm. Warleich	1649	150
274	Thomas Preston	1650	100
288	Saml. Thorogood	1650	50
363	Capt. Leonard Yeo	1644	350
201	Thomas Coniers	1649	40

Book No. 3.

25	Symour Thorogood	1653	200
188	Richard Allen	1653	85
393	Richard Hull	1655	116

Book No. 4.

52	Wm. Parry	1656	100
59	Humphrey Tabb	1656	900
325	Robert Gray	1658	50
238	William up Thomas	1663	300
280	Richard Jones	1663	100A. 1R. 5P.
382	Thomas Spery	1664	100
389	Richard Pinner	1662	500
474	Richard Todd	1665	600
543.	Maj. Theophilus Hone	1663	1000
544	Same	1663	50

Book No. 6.

250	Capt. Charles Morryson	1669	350
251	Ann Wilson	1669	75 Acres
251	Wm. Morris	1669	50
408	Augustin Moore	1672	225
408	Thomas Tabb	1672	300
462	Rich. Jones	1673	240
611	Cap. Anthony Armestead	1676	928
614	Augustin Moore	1676	235

Book No. 7.

82	Henry Presson	1681	100
102	Richard Hurstly	1681	94
129	Anthony Armstead	1682	50
129	John Tilley	1682	50
129	John Symons	1682	50
217	Tho. Allamby	1682	184
229	Baldwin Sheppard	1682	360
396	Quintillian Gothrick	1684	200
435	Pasco Dunn	1685	146
712	Coleman Brough	1689	50

Book No. 8.

15	Richard Shewell	1689	115
33	Same	1690	115
214	John Lear and Rebecca his wife	1691	180
228	Xpher Copeland	1692	220
229	Jacob Walker and George Walker the younger	1692	125
229	Henry Copeland	1692	220
404	Capt. Anthony Armistead	1695	150
406	Walter Bayley	1695	106
106	John Archer	1695	375

NORTHUMBERLAND COUNTY.

Book No. 3.

Page	Name	Date	No. acres
62	William Hardidge	1653	1000
63	Nicholas Meriwether	1653	600
63	Thomas Ssoggin	1653	500
64	Colo. John Mottrom	1653	1000
64	Peter Knight	1653	1000
70	John Hillier	1653	920
71	John Hillier	1653	100
72	George Watts	1653	300
79	James Macgregory and Hugh Fouch	1653	450
80	Gervarse Dodson	1653	1300
85	Martin Coale	1653	400
87	Wm. Thomas	1653	400
91	John Shepperd	1652	1000
92	Lawrence Dameron	——	340
92	John Gresham	1652	520
96	Thomas Darrow	1652	100
99	John Chambers	1652	150
100	John Mottrom	1652	250
112	Thomas Wilsford	1652	50
124	John Howett	1652	650

126	John Wareham	1652	150
131	Edward Coles	1652	500
132	George Foster	1652	1200
133	Nicho. Morris	1652	182
134	John Earle	1652	200
134	Mrs. Mary Brent	1652	1644
134	Ralph Harsley	1652	495
139	Nicholas Sebrell	1652	100
147	Richard Nelmes	1652	400
169	Andrew Munrow	1652	440
171	Col. Thomas Pettus	1652	1000
184	Mrs. Jane Harmer	1652	2000
192	Cap. Giles Brent	1653	300
214	Samuel Taylor	1653	1050
218	Richard Budd	1653	400
218	Same	1653	150
219	Thomas Read	1653	300
220	Christopher Boyce	1653	602
234	Abraham Moon	1653	500
236	Thomas Hawkins	1653	2500
253	Robert Bradshaw	1653	345
266	Thomas Coniers	1653	550
267	John Hull	1653	500
272	Col. Wm. Claybourne	1653	750
277	John Rogers	1653	250
278	Matthw. Rhodum	1653	350
277	John Rogers	1653	50
278	Martin Coale	1653	300
279	Thomas Salisbury	1653	1100
288	Nich. Jernew	——	200
290	Peter Knight	1653	1200
299	Thos. Humphreys	1653	600
311	Roger Walters	1653	1000
320	Peter Ashton	1653	400
325	Peter Ransom	1653	950
329	John Williams	1655	550
344	Francis Clay	1655	400

345	Wm. Little	1655	100
346	Gervace Dodson	1655	1000
347	Wm. Nutt	1655	683
347	George Coltclough	1655	300
348	Thomas Broughton of Yeocomoco	1655	100
348	John Motley of Wicomoco, Carpenter	1655	600
350	John Johnson	1655	85
368	Nicholas Morris	1654	512
377	John Johnson	1655	227
378	Wm. Walker	1655	839
379	Richard Holder	1655	600
390	Hugh Lee	1656	388
390	Robert Horsley	1655	300
382	Wm. Walker	1655	839

Book No. 4.

3	John Hulet	1655	300
3	John Palmer	1655	300
17	Thomas Gerrard	1655	300
17	Thomas Hale	1655	79
20	Wm. Thomas of Yeocomo	1655	200
20	John Earle	1655	100
44	Richard Dennis	1656	400
49	John Mottrone	1655	300
56	Isaac Faxcraft	1656	2000
57	Lawrence Dameron	1656	342
58	George Mason	1656	900
58	Henry Smith, Jr.	1656	200
60	John Kent	1656	666
61	Capt. John Rogers	1656	300
61	Thomas Reade	1659	1000
62	Richard Holden	1656	100
62	Charles Ashton and Thomas Adams	1656	300
78	Peter Ranson	1656	950
83	Thomas Salsbury	1656	650
97	Richard Gible	1656	800
110	John Chandler	1656	1500

111	John Chandler	1656	350
111	Richard Rice	1656	400
120	Robert Wilson	1656	400
121	Thomas Coniers	1657	550
122	Wm. Reynolds	1657	650
122	Peter Knight	1657	500
123	Col. Richard Lee	1657	600
124	Miles Dixon	1656	500
124	Capt. Hugh Wilson	1656	500
138	Peter Knight	1657	1500
139	Same	1657	1200
151	Richard Spam	1657	350
154	David Kiffin	1657	650
160	John Hany	1657	200
161	John Hany	1657	600
187	Edmund Ayres	1657	500
193	Richard Flint	1657	150
195	Wm. Bacon	1657	250
199	Richard Holding	1657	525
204	Capt. John Rogers	1657	200
206	Peter Ashton	1657	550

WESTMORELAND COUNTY.

BOOK No. 5.

Page	Name	Date	No. acres
41	Robt. Alexander, John Alexander, Jr., and Christopher Alexander	1664	1460
41	George Weading	1664	212
42	Thomas Pope	1664	2454
49	John Washington	1664	300
45	Alexander Benum	1664	257
49	Maj. John Washington and Thomas Pope	1661	50
52	Ann Pope, alias Washington	1661	700
53	William Court and Robert Hutcheson	1662	660

54	John Washington and Thomas Pope...1661	1200
55	Dorothy Brooks alias Butler 1664	650
120	Robert Selfe 1665	300
129	Richard Griffin 1664	57
141	Vincent Coe 1665	400
142	John Rosier 1662	1450
148	William Tilt 1662	400
149	Giles Brent 1662	1000
151	Mary Pate 1662	300
153	Thomas Hunphries and Thomas Tupper 1662	547
154	Vincent Young 1662	200
154	James Harris 1662	60
158	John and Thomas Buckocks 1662	350
160	William Brown, Danl. White and Wm.	
	Baltrop 1662	745
169	Wm. and John Heaberd 1662	350
171	Richard Heaberd 1662	480
171	Henry Brookes 1662	1020
173	Sarah, Margaret, Judith and Elizabeth	
	Jones 1662	100
173	William Green 1662	250
174	John Drayton 1662	2000
214	Christopher Booze 1662	300
215	Wm. Heaberd and Wm. Horton.......1663	1600
220	John Butler 1663	350
224	Francis Gray 1663	374
224	Capt. John Ashton 1663	783
224	Same 1663	543
225	John Frissell 1663	104
227	Christopher Butler 1663	150
227	John Lord and Wm. Horton..........1663	2500
228	John Butler 1663	160
239	Lt. Col. Giles Brent 1662	1518
239	Daniel Wild, and Francis Kirkman....1663	2000
240	Margaret Brent 1662	700
244	Daniel White 1661	69
250	William Freeke 1662	600

260	Gerard Fowke	1662	3650
261	Col. Valentine Payton	1662	650
263	Andrew Pettigrew	1662	5200
265	John Matron	1662	3609
275	Richard Sturman	1664	2000
276	Henry Vincent	1664	400
290	Henry Payton	1664	1000
296	Samuel Hayward	1662	200
299	Robert Vauly	1662	6000
312	Isaac Watson and Samuel Mottershead.	1663	400
327	Thomas Wilsford	1662	50
353	Charles Wood	1663	268
373	James Pope	1662	1000
393	Thomas Dios	1664	500
394	Same	1664	1200
415	Thomas Phillpot	1664	500
421	William Horton	1663	600
440	John Bruerton	1664	1456
441	William Hardick	1664	1000
484	Wilkes Maunder	1665	1000
494	Col. Peter Ashton	1665	500
495	Edward Rogers	1665	600
498	Nicholas Jarnew	1665	178
499	Samuel Bonam	1665	99
521	Raleigh Traverse	1665	3659
523	James Harris	1665	60
525	Stephen Warman	1663	750
530	John Lord	1662	1200
531	Christopher Butler	1662	123¾
532	Wm. Horton	1665	100
545	John Lord	1664	100
578	John Whetstone	1665	250
578	Ralph and Thomas Blag	1665	209
579	Wm. Overett and George Browne	1665	400
579	Randolph Kirke	1665	1000
580	Wm. Basely and Ed. Haelly	1665	1000

580	James Green, Francis Lewis and Wm.		
	Baldrop	1665	1050
581	Richard Stereman	1665	2000
582	Wm. Overett	1665	590
583	Wm. Pearce	1665	1810
590	Robt. Alexander and George Weeding	1665	800
632	Thomas Greg	1662	450
645	Daniel Hutt	1666	875
645	Andrew Read	1666	400
646	Same	1666	400
652	Capt. Giles Brent	1666	1000
654	Robert Middleton	1665	700

Book No. 6.

1	(Blank)	1666	60
2	Richard Heaberd	1666	1500
11	Robert Middleton	1666	1120
12	Francis Clay	1666	1480
15	Richard Sturman	1666	1004
16	John Beard	1666	250
49	Maj. Wm. Perrie	1666	4310
50	Wm. Loyd and John Biddle	1667	4750
55	John Whetstone, Thomas Dyar, and		
	Patrick Spenson	1667	1050
56	John Whetstone	1667	2430
68	Vincent Coy	1667	665
75	Capt. John Lord	1667	1667
76	John Lord and Wm. Horton	1667	1544
76	Wm. Smith	1667	590
107	Ann Brett	1667	300
125	Henry Cossum	1668	450
152	James Hawley	1666	700
176	Thomas Beale and Randolph Kirke	1668	1500
156	Thomas Phillpot	1668	307
179	John Withers	1668	320
179	Gerard Fowke, Wm. Horton, Richard		
	Granger and Thomas Grigg	1661	2000

180	Wm. Webb	1668	400
187	Col. Nicholas Spencer	1668	1200
197	John Lee	1668	3100
227	Maj. Wm. Pierce	1669	3110
235	Richard Searles	1669	345
236	Same	1669	278
236	Thomas Yowell	1669	780
236	John Piper	1669	400
237	Peter Dunken	1669	140
237	Wm. Spence	1669	180
243	Wm. Browne and Wm. Baltrop	1669	744
264	Richard Coleman	1665	380
276	John Foxhall	1669	314
283	Philip Browne	1669	200
283	John Willis	1669	261
293	Mrs. Ann Barnet	1654	1000
296	John Butler	1670	597
307	Robert Nurse	1670	189
319	Nicholas Spencer	1670	900
322	John Boocock	1670	600
324	Robert Lovell	1670	500
325	John Berriman, Wm. Horton and John Palmer	1670	1227
327	Thomas Ludwell	1670	1432
328	Wm. Craddock	1670	560
330	Col. Nicholas Spencer	1670	3250
629	Elias Webb	1677	140
631	Originall Browne	1678	200
665	Malachi Peal	1678	843
671	John Quigley	1678	80
681	Adam Woffendall	1679	783
691	Daniel White	1679	60c
691	George Weedon and Daniel White	1679	483

YORK COUNTY.

Book No. 5.

Page	Name	Date	No. acres
1	Thomas Pinckman	1662	125
139	Gozen Delonie (alien)	1664	50
139	Thomas Iles	1664	225
168	Wm. Gantlett	1662	920
174	Robert Wesks	1662	50
203	John Horsington	1662	350
213	Lieut. Col. Wm. Barber	1662	596
215	Gabriel Jones	1664	300
256	Robt. Harrison	1662	389
295	Rebecca Jackson	1662	400
297	Thomas Flaunders	1663	50
309	Thomas Williams	1663	440
338	Capt. Wm. Hay	1663	1695
351	Edward Waad	1663	150
367	John Taylor	1663	50
381	Alexander Walker and Rice Jones	1662	94
387	Nicholas Sabrell	1663	200
418	Peter Plouvier	1663	196
424	Richard Page	1664	100
430	Peter Starley	1664	377
442	Richard Vardie	1664	850
529	Edward Wyatt	1663	850
534	Owen Morris	1664	130
535	Adam Miles	1663	300
536	Henry White	1663	100
541	Wm. Grimes	1663	100
541	John Lyman	1663	50
666	John Overstreet	1667	37A. 77chs.

Book No. 6.

Page	Name	Date	No. acres
6	Colo. Nathaniel Bacon	1666	25
6	Eliza. Meige	1666	50
31	Josias Modey	1667	300

38	Francis Hammond	1667	2000
43	Henrick Forsan Van Deavorack, Sr.	1666	214
123	Daniel Wild	1662	1484
209	John Overstreet 1667	37A. 77 ch. 69 Dec. parts	
238	John Clarke	1669	600
250	Thomas Roberts	1669	300
288	Edmond Chisman, Jr. or Sen...1670	202A. 60chs.	
443	Morris Price	1672	100
498	Robert Drapier	1673	50
507	Daniel Wylde	1674	100
653	Hen. Hayward	1678	216
655	Robt. Everett	—	147
670	Wm. Major	1678	130
670	Thomas Harwood	1678	206
670	Edward Mosse	1678	115
670	Thomas Chesman	1678	175
671	Same	1678	420

LANCASTER COUNTY.

Book No. 4.

Page	Name	Date	No. acres
16	John Bebey	1655	300
20	Cuthbert Potter	1655	1200
21	John Lawson	1655	500
22	Hugh Kinsey	1655	100
42	Bertram Obert	1656	773
46	Dennis Conniers	1656	1178
63	Wm. Thacker	1656	400
64	Enoch Hawker and Anthony Doney	1656	1000
66	Miles Dixon	1656	1000
69	Henry Chickley, Kt.	1656	800
99	Charles Grimes	1656	1000
99	Same, Clerk	1656	600
100	John Page	1656	2700
107	John Sharpe	1655	300

109	Henry Berry	1656	140
119	Gervace Dodson	1656	600
120	Edwin Conaway and Gervace Dodson	1656	1000
121	John Burton	1656	900
128	Robt. Thomas and Wm. Moss, Brothers	1656	800
136	Wm. Dudley	1657	2000
137	George Vezie and Nathaniel Browne	1657	250
143	Nicholas Heale	1657	500
152	Dominick Farriatt	1657	1600
164	Wm. Clapham	1657	500
165	John Edwards	1657	700
168	Same, Surgeon	1657	700
169	Vincent Stanford	1657	300
185	Chas. Grimes	1657	1000
185	Same, Clerk	1657	960
186	Same	1657	600
186	Same	1657	600
187	Chas. King	1657	40
193	Wm. Short	1657	400
195	Richard White	1657	500
201	John Robinson	1657	360
203	Thomas Pattison	1657	200
203	Same	1657	400
212	Henry Corbyn	1658	800
207	George Thompson	1657	400
216	Edwin Connaway and Hannah Mountney	1657	1650
218	Wm. Drew	1657	500
223	Thomas Powell	1658	700
251	Robert Chewning	1657	200
255	Edwin Connaway	——	2500
257	Vincent Stanford	1657	300
276	Cuthbert Potter	1658	600
278	Richard Lewis	1658	500
278	Robert Young	1657	200
281	John Curtis	1657	1200
296	John Nicholls	1657	900

297	John Nicholls	1657	900
300	Vincent Stanford	1657	1000
299	John Edwards	1657	118
314	Thomas Willis and John Middleton	1658	600
317	Wm. Butcher	1658	300
318	John Wortham	1658	400
329	Robt. Woolestone	1658	128
333	John Cossens and Thomas Steed	1658	600
343	John Woodington	1658	27
348	John Gore	1658	150
348	Robert Middleton	1658	250
349	Richard Lewis	1658	500
349	Same	1658	500
349	Same	1658	200
350	Peter Montague	1658	200
353	Col. Augustus Warner	1658	3000
350	Col. Wm. Bernard	1657	800
379	Cuthbert Potter	1659	5380
382	Col. Robt. Smith	1661	1299
404	John Harris	1661	500
405	Abya Bonyson	1661	1300
411	John Bebey	1661	700
419	Samuel Parry	1661	1250
420	David Thomas and Richd. Macubins	1662	100
421	Wm. Thatcher and Thomas Chetwood	1662	800
422	Thomas Chetwood	1662	300
422	John Ashly	1662	240
425	John Simpson	1662	600
426	Richard Davis	1662	420
427	George Whale	1662	1400
428	John Cox	1662	1150
438	Richd. Parrott	1662	800
442	John Newman	1662	400
473	John Appleton	1661	1000
480	Wm. Blaze	1662	250
481	Same	1663	350
482	David Fox	1663	510

483	Nich. and Maurice Cock	1663	600
484	Matthew Kemp and Peter Jennings	1663	1000
509	Col. John Carter	1661	450
564	Richard Lewis	1662	190
596	Thomas Paine	1662	600
597	Edward Sanders	1662	2900
609	Edward Boswell	1663	200
616	Thomas Kidd	1664	194
626	John Appleton	1664	400
627	Robert Jones	1664	400
627	Wm. Thatcher and Wm. Hutcheson	1662	500
628	Hugh Brent and Toby Horton	1664	200
629	John Wells	1662	200
629	Wm. Cooke, John Potter, Edward King and Saml. Gough	1663	450
630	John Chinn	1664	100
631	Wm. Thomas, Sr.	1664	150
630	Wm. Thomas, Sr.	1664	100
631	John Rayney	1662	271
631	John Cable	1664	250
632	Thomas Harris	1662	600
633	Richard Hawker or Hacker	1663	200
633	Hugh Brent	1662	200
634	Charles Hill	1663	590
634	John Taylour	1662	100
635	Same	1662	400
635	Same	1662	450
635	Wm. Ironmonger	1663	700
636	John Appleton	1661	1000
636	Tobias Horton	1662	1200
637	Wm. Michaell	1663	50
637	Jos. Smith and Humphrey Jones	1663	300
638	Eppy Bonnyson	1664	400
638	Oliver Segar and Francis Brown	1662	200
639	Daniel Welch	1663	600
640	John Beauford and Francis Braughton	1663	300

641	John Simpson	1662	600
642	John Appleton	1664	1000
643	George Vesey and Nathaniel Browne...	1663	300

HENRICO COUNTY.

BooK No. 6.

Page	Name	Date	No. acres
5	Wm. Baugh	1668	577
52	Thomas Taylor	1667	631
52	Solomon Knibb	1667	710
53	Francis Perce and Wm. Perce	1667	100
84	Robert Bowman, Jr.	1667	215
135	George Worsnam	1668	399
170	George Browning	1668	189
188	Maj. Wm. Ferrer and Lt. Col. Thos. Ligon	1668	300
189	John Browne	1668	110
211	John Beachampe	1668	82
211	Godfrey Ragsdale	1668	450
216	Thomas Webster	1669	115
231	Gilbert Elam	1671	867A. 3R. 24p.
224	Henry Randolph	1666	961
233	Rowland Place	1669	1228
241	Francis Redford	1659	250
260	Robert Bullington	1669	100
260	George Archer	1671	784
272	Thomas Stegg	1669	2773
279	Richard Parker	1669	350
287	Robert Woodson	1670	1192
387	Henry Randolph	1671	1254
387	Bartholomew Chandler	1671	1238
388	Essex Bevill and Anne, his wife	1671	600
399	Robert Bowman, Jr.	1671	557
409	Francis Radford	1671	629
425	Col. Thomas Liggon	1672	1468A. 1R. 28p.

426	John Davis	1672	500
427	John Baugh	1672	200
427	Parish of Henrico	1672	198A. 3R. 16P.
437	Col. Thomas Stegg	1669	2773A. 32P.
454	Edward Mathews	1673	1536
454	James Adkin and Richard Womack	1673	335
480	Francis Epes	1673	927
445	Richard Perrin	1672	740
446	John Stuard	1672	600
447	Richard Womack	1672	450
447	Thomas Ligon, senior	1672	340
414	Charles Fetherston	1672	700
451	Francis Radford	1673	93A. 2R. 8po.
420	Thos. Wells	1672	560A. 2R. 24po.
483	Thos. Webster	1673	754A. 1R. 3po.
484	Timothy Allen	1673	681A. 3R. 24po.
487	George Archer	1673	1395A. 3R. 2po.
485	John Fowler	1673	398
486	Capt. Wm. Bird	1673	1280
495	Henry Trent	1673	200
495	Henry Shereman	1673	228
496	Abel Gower	1673	501A. 1R. 24po.
496	Maj. Wm. Harris	1671	1202A. 2R. 4po.
497	John Rogers and John Lewis	1673	400
509	Thomas Batts	1674	1862A. 1R. 32po.
529	Wm. Hatcher	1674	227
530	Nicholas Perkins	1674	537A. 3R. 20po.
530	Henry Lowne	1674	516
534	Wm. Randolph	1674	591A. 2R. 20po
534	Eusebius King	1674	507A. 2R. 8po.
564	Thomas Cock	1675	3087A. 3R. 24po.
568	Robert Huson	1675	200
570	Edward Hatcher	1675	1300
570	Robert Huson	1675	126
604	Capt. Wm. Bird	1675	7351
632	John Wattson	1677	478A. 3R. 1po.
632	Thomas Wells	1677	296A. 3R. 19po.

642 Robert Bullington 1678   244A. 1R. 4po.
653 Rebecca Gyles 1678   162A. 2R.
663 John Greenbaugh 1678   446
687 Benjamin Hatcher and John Milner....
                                  1679   350A. 2R. 14po.

BOOK No. 7.

11 Francis Warren 1679   647
12 Henry Wyatt 1679   900
12 John Pleasants and John Halddellsey.
                                  1679   548A. 20po.
17 Hen. Watkinson 1679   170
24 Wm. Randolph, Fra: Epps, Jos. Royall..1680   580
44 Thomas Burton 1680   350
75 George Browning 1681   37A. 2R. 8po.
84 Lyonell Morris 1681   860A. 20po.
86 Mrs. Francis Izard 1681   1036A. 5po.
86 Henry Turner 1681   712A. 1R. 24po.
102 Robert Woodson, John Woodson, Thom-
      as East, Robert Clarke and Wm.
      Porter 1681   531A. 1R. 4po.
108 Wm. Giles 1681   100
127 Col. Wm. Bird 1682   4250
200 Wm. Pucket and Thomas Pucket.......1682   757
226 Eusebius King 1682   731
250 Jos. Tanner and Richard Wamocke
                                  1683   260A. 1R. 20po.
278 Evan Baker, als. Belange, and Robert
      Mann 1683   89A. OR. 8po.
318 James Baugh 1683   119A. 1R. 30po.
356 Evan Bellange 1684   83A. 1R. 32po.
362 Wm. Byrd 1684   300
387 John Piggot 1684   374
389 Wm. Greenfield 1684   119
433 Wm. Porter, Sr. 1685   315
435 Wm. Porter, Jr. Nicholas Amoss and
      Richard Ferres 1685   459

450	John Stewart, Sr. 1685	670
454	Thomas Osborne 1685	85
454	Lemon Childres 1685	406
455	Wm. Clarke 1685	124
489	Thomas Branch, Sr. 1685	760
508	Samuel Bridgewater 1686	333
508	Abel Gower and Ed. Statton 1686	487
534	Francis Cater 1686	622
547	Wm. Byrd 1687	5075
548	Same 1687	956
459	Same 1687	1820
551	Samuel Newman 1687	559
667	Abraham Bayly 1688	142
668	Thomas Cock, Sr. 1688	1650
713	Daniel Johnson 1689	391
716	Thomas Cardwell 1689	550
691	Alexander Mackenny .... 1688 296A. 3R. 19po.	
556	Thomas Cock, Jr. 1687	671
557	Thomas Cock .... 1687 296A. 3R. 19po.	
560	John Bayley 1687	736
560	Samuel Bridgewater 1687	404
561	Richard Bland 1687	1254
562	Gilly Groomeren 1687	539
569	Henry Pruett and John Fiels 1687	440
570	Michael Turpin 1687	215
590	Francis Redford 1687	775
596	John Everett .... 1687 162A. 2R.	
562	James Lyle 1687	156
601	Robert Woodson, Richard Ferres, Giles Carter, Wm. Ferris and Roger Cummins 1687	1780
602	Robt. Woodson, Sr., John Woodson, Sr., Wm. Lewis and Thomas Charles..... 1687	470
605	Joshua Stapp 1687	277
610	Peter Field 1687	483
611	Samuel Fowler 1687	750
633	Thomas Taylor, of Harahadoa 1687	1053

636	Robert Thompson	1688	390
637	Henry Pewe	1688	411
638	John Woodson, Sr.	1688	1850
655	Wm. Dodson and James Frankling	1688	360
666	Thomas Peren	1688	140
666	Nicholas Marsh	1688	528

ACCOMAC COUNTY.

Book No. 5.

Page	Name	Date	No. acres
220	Elias Hartree	1663	600
221	Thos. Crily	1663	600
221	Richard Hill	1663	1000
222	Alex. Massy	1663	400
222	Laurence Robinson	1663	500
222	Wm. Gowers	1663	600
223	John Lewis	1663	1000
223	John Renny	1663	400
362	Arthur Upshott	1664	2000
366	Richard Hill	1663	200
410	Mary Lewis	1664	400
411	John Savage	1664	350
413	Richd. Hill, Jr.	1664	650
418	Gilbert Henderson	1664	500
421	Col. Wm. Waters	1664	1350
460	Richd. Bundock	1664	1400
522	Col. Edmund Scarborough	1664	1000
522	Littleton Scarborough	1664	1000
592	John Williams	1666	100
592	Major John Tilney	1666	100
599	Thomas Rideing	1666	1000
599	Tobias Selvey	1666	600
600	Barth. Meares	1666	300
600	John Smith	1666	300
601	Mr. John Fawcett	1666	937

601	Wm. Chase	1666	650
602	John Michaell	1666	500
602	Robt. Houstone	1666	500
602	Richd. Robinson	1666	150
603	Nicholas Layter	1666	200
603	James Taylor	1666	200
603	William Aylworth	1666	400
604	John Williams	1666	500
604	Thomas Davis	1666	400
604	John Prettiman	1666	200
605	Jas. Henderson	1666	400
605	Robt. Richardson	1666	500
606	Dorman Sullivant	1666	450
606	Timothy Coe	1666	1000
606	John Wallop alias Wadlow	1666	1700
609	Charles Ratcliff	1666	500
609	John Williams	1666	500
610	Robt. Johnson	1666	600
610	Jno. Wallop alias Wadlow	1666	300
610	John Davis	1666	700
611	David Williamson	1666	6000
612	Eliz. Sarah and Margt. Dye, children of John Dye, decd.	1666	600
613	Laurence Robinson	1666	1200
613	Saml. Taylor	1666	950
614	Henry Smith	1666	1700

LOUDOUN COUNTY.

Book No. I.

Page	Name	Date	No. acres
18	Joshua Dunkin	1757	72
53	Alex. and Mary Coleclough	1760	325
60	Benj. Sebastian	1761	350
61	John Hough	1761	265
62	Same	1761	250
63	George Gregg	1761	55
64	John Moss, Jr.	1761	232
66	Jonathan Palmer	1761	100
67	Dan'l Jones	1761	410
68	Robert Adams	1761	70
77	Jonas Potts, blacksmith	1761	521
84	John Little	1762	408
86	Wm. Jones	1762	136
96	John Ethell	1763	120
97	Thos. Dent	1763	223
98	John Hough	1763	200
99	Anthony Russell	1763	180
103	Wm. Robinson	1763	223
107	Joseph Hough	1764	125
109	Henry Rector	1764	237
110	Wm. Lane	1764	202
111	Chas. Lewis	1764	341
112	John Piles	1764	30
113	Same	1764	308
120	Jas. Hamilton and Aeneas Campbell	1764	80
121	Jas Hamilton	1764	41
122	Wm. Saunders, Jr.	1764	180
127	Stephen Roszel	1765	253
130	Lee Massey	1765	10
131	Craven Peyton	1765	51
132	Joseph West	1765	80
133	Edwd. Snicker	1765	352

135	Wm. Barr	1765	265
139	John Hough	1765	2248
140	John Hague	1765	34½
141	Saml. Mead	1765	195
142	Eneas Campbell	1765	107
146	Eliz. Hough	1766	405
152	Wm. West	1766	230

DINWIDDIE COUNTY.

Book No. 31.

Page	Name	Date	No. acres
171	Wm. Poythress	1752	531
250	Robt. Whitehall	1752	228
332	Wm. Raines	1753	336
588	Chas. Butterworth	1755	371
589	John Hardaway	1755	170
620	Wm. Cryer	1755	400
622	Joseph Tucker and Stephen Evans	1755	430
630	Robert Walker	1755	90
631	John Ellington	1755	48
639	Wm. Pritchard	1755	62
640	Geo. White	1755	49
713	Richd. Taylor	1755	400

Book No. 32.

7	Thos. Dickinson	1752	250
48	Geo. Burras	1753	31
60	John Jones	1753	1494
225	Matt. Coleman	1753	200
378	Thos. Eggleston	1754	884
422	Chas. Williams	1754	604
429	Wm. Clayton	1754	200
578	Robt. Jones	1755	47
579	John Jennings	1755	90
582	John Jones	1755	82

595	Stephen Evans	1755	59
598	David Smith	1755	51
614	Isham Eppes	1755	200
668	Abraham Wells	1756	200
687	David Walker	1756	28
696	Ussery Hitchcock	1756	504
117	John Ferguson	1753	580
535	Thos. Williams	1755	564

BOOK NO. 33.

230	Wm. Cryer	1756	73
244	Roger Reece, Jr.	1756	400
351	Geo. White	1757	304
358	Chas. Pistol	1757	179
477	Wm. Butler	1758	43

GOOCHLAND COUNTY.

BOOK NO. 13.

Page	Name	Date	No. acres
317	Edward Scott	1728	250
324	Amos Lad	1728	400
325	Same	1728	400
325	Edward Scott, John Scott and Stephen Hughes	1728	4000
330	Jas. Holman	1728	400
330	Same	1728	400
340	Patrick Mullin	1728	350
374	Richard Wade	1728	400
379	Charles Massie	1729	400
381	John Macon	1729	400
385	Barth. Stovall and Thos. Walker	1729	400
386	Nicholas Cox	1729	400
387	Marmaduke Hicks and Wm. Moss	1729	400
387	Ashford Hughes and Daniel Price	1729	400
393	Daniel Stoner	1729	3800

396	Ebenezer Adams	1729	400
396	Same	1729	400
396	Same	1729	400
397	Same	1729	400
397	Same	1729	250
397	Same	1729	350
398	Same	1729	185
398	Same	1729	400
398	Thos. Randolph	1729	800
406	Jas. Nevil	1729	400
407	Howell Burton	1729	400
407	Geo. Payne	1729	400
407	John Martin	1729	400
407	James Nevil	1729	400
408	Ashford Hughes and Joseph Thomas	1729	400
409	Same	1729	400
410	Anthony Morgan	1729	50
420	Dan'l. Wilmore	1729	400
423	Henry Cary	1729	3942
424	Geo. Nicholas	1729	2600
427	James Holman	1730	100
433	Josiah Woodson and Stephen Woodson	1729	110
435	Tobias Lafeet and Nicholas Sulie	1728	400
443	Chas. Christian	1728	400
444	John Sailes	1730	400
446	Henry Anderson	1730	1500
452	Arthur Moseley, Jr.	1730	1200
463	John Owen	1730	400
464	Philip Thomas	1730	400
464	Stephen Chastain	1730	400
465	Same	1730	400
465	Geo. Hudspith	1730	400
478	John Carter, Esq.	1730	9350
479	Edward Scot	1730	400
481	John Syme	1730	3400
482	Ralph Hudspith	1730	400
482	Francis Epes	1730	2400
485	Same	1730	6500

NORTHAMPTON COUNTY.

Book No. 1.

Page	Name	Date	No. acres
823	John Holloway	1642	1300
851	John Harlowe	1642	200
852	Christopher Kirke	1642	400
854	James Pereene	1642	400
909	Pharoe Young	1643	100
935	Philip Taylor	1643	1000
847	John Foster	1643	300
947	John Major	1640	200
948	John Wilkins	1640	600
948	Wm. Berryman	1640	800
948	John Major	1643	400

Book No. 2.

16	Eliz. Harmer, dau. and sole heir of Charles Harmer	1644	1200
17	Edwin Conaway (clerk)	1644	500
29	Wm. Jones	1645	450
30	John Severne	1645	500
44	Peter Walker	——	150
67	John Brown	1646	200
68	Wm. Shrimpton, one of the exrs. of Dame Eliz. Dale, decd., the relict and sole exr. of Sir Thomas Dale	1645	1000
68	Sir Thos. Dale's bill of adventure	1610	——
69	Thomas Johnson	1646	600
69	John Rosyer	1646	200
76	Thomas Johnson	1647	1000
75	John Brown	1646	100
75	Michael Williams	1646	250
77	James Bruse	1645	500
77	Roger Johns	1645	250
77	Richard Jacob	1645	300

91	Eliz. and Rachael Robbins, orphans of Edward Robbins, decd.	1646	350
109	Wm. Whitington	1647	450
109	Stephen Hawsey and Nicho. Waddelow.	1646	100
110	Edmond Scarbrough	1646	100
110	Nicholas Granger	1647	350
110	John Little	1647	100
112	Jonathan Gills	1647	450
113	Francis Martin	1645	300
115	John Ellis, Jas. Jones and John Taylor.	1648	500
118	Henry Pedenden	1646	550
119	Thomas Savage	1646	500
131	Wm. Many	1647	150
134	John Robbins	1645	100
134	Chas. Scarbrough	1647	550
135	John ———————	——	450
159	John Baldwin	1648	300
167	Wm. Shrimpton, one of the exrs. of Dame Eliz. Dale	1649	2000
177	John Walthams	1649	450
177	Nicholas Waddelow	1649	300
178	Same	1649	400
178	Edmond Scarburgh, Jr.	1649	2000
179	Richard Vaughan	1649	300
179	Richard Bayly	1649	700

HALIFAX COUNTY.

Book No. 31.

Page	Name	Date	No. acres
426	Wm. Finney	1753	4485
436	Thos. Estes	1754	394
439	John Roberts	1754	4200
442	Edmond Pendleton and Edmond Taylor.	1754	4750
475	Redmon Follin	1754	1080
476	James Wood and John Tilpot	1754	600

480	James Machan	1754	270
481	Same	1754	240
532	David Hailey	1755	137
603	Wm. Irby, Jr.	1755	165
604	Edward Owen	1755	240
635	David Hailey	1755	30
637	Same	1755	40
637	Joseph Minor	1755	46
711	Robert Hodges	1755	388

Book No. 32.

80	James Hunt	1753	370
95	Chas. Barrett and John Lewis	1753	1800
120	John Martin	1753	1616
238	Thos. Harbour	1753	354
242	Same	1753	204
244	Same	1753	144
246	Same	1753	115
248	Joice Thornwell	1753	92
250	Thos. Harbour	1753	150
252	Same	1753	140
254	Same	1753	318
347	John Adams	1754	250
349	Burgess Wall	1754	390
357	Robert Barrett	1754	860
363	Nicholas Edmunds	1754	2435
358	Peter Fontaine	1754	1213
377	Clement Reade	1754	360
383	Wm. Maclin	1754	400
398	Daniel Daly	1754	400
437	Sam'l Powell	1755	200
514	James Terry	1755	354
515	James Terry	1755	2950
546	John Chiswell	1755	200
547	Same	1755	400
551	Peter Fontaine, Jr.	1755	404
551	Same	1755	800

558	Hugh Miller	1755	3320
560	Matt. Talbott, Jr.	1755	100
602	Abraham Ardin	1755	90
616	James Machan	1755	100
642	John Hawkins	1755	745
643	John Owen	1755	362
651	Thos. Comer	1755	450
662	John Dyer	1755	400
662	Edward Coleman	1755	400
663	Erasmus Weathers Allen	1755	400
666	Wm. Gill	1755	400
697	Jas. Shepperd	1756	400

RAPPAHANNOCK COUNTY WILLS

Doughty, Enoch. 27 Feb., 1675—9 May, 1677. To my children; overseers Francis Doughty and James Phillips; witnesses John Simpton, Hugh Mane.

Mott, John, Sittingbourne Parish. 8 Oct., 1675—17 Jan., 1677-8. Brother George Mott; my four nieces Elizabeth, Margaret, Anne and Ellen Mott; Ellen Pigg; nephew John Vickers to be executor; witnesses Richard Wallace, William Winn.

Hawkins, Thomas, Sittingbourne Parish. 8 Feb., 1675—20 Jan., 1677. Sons Thomas and John; my former wife's ring; daughter Elizabeth Hawkins; daughter Hannah Hawkins; wife Frances and my Brother Samuel Bloomfield to be executors; witnesses John Graves, Abraham Raw, William Saile.

Curtis, John. 29 Nov., 1677————. Dr. Peter Hopegood and Randall Peters to be executors; witnesses Simon Gray, John White, Thomas Graham.

Clark, Richard. 30 Jan., 1676—2 Jan., 1677-8. Edmond Paget; friend Theophilus Whale to be executor; witnesses Anthony North, Edmond Paget.

Nangle, George, City of Dublin, Ireland, merchant. 4 Jan., 1675—4 July, 1677. William Smith and Robert Akins, merchants of the City of Dublin; Gerrard Nangle, my brother, and Judith Nangle, my niece, in Dublin, to have all estate in Dublin and Virginia; Mary Evans; Thomas Gouldman; Col. William Travers; Col. Thomas Goodrich and Thomas Gouldman to be executors; witnesses George Morris, Jacob Lumken.

Turner, Hezekiah, Farnham Parish. 25 Dec., 1677—25 Jan., 1677. Wife Elizabeth; son Hezekiah; daughter Michell; neighbor James Samford; grandchild Anne Chissell; Mr. John Saffen; witnesses James Samford, Roger Bagwell.

Stephens, John. 5 March, 1661—6 Feb., 1677. To John Fulcher, son-in-law to Richard Webley, gent; Alexander, son of Richard Dudley; witnesses Clement Herberts, Thomas Luddle.

Gibson, William. 4 May, 1676—7 Feb., 1677-8. Daughter Elizabeth; James Bartlett; Thomas Bartlett; wife Mary executrix; witnesses Law. Rochefort, John Patterson.

Jones, Rice. 23 Nov., 1676—26 Feb. 1677-8. Son John; son Rice; daughter Ann; daughter Mary, wife of John Brocke; grandchildren Barbary and Margaret Brocke; friend Edward Thomas; son and daughter-in-law Henry and Jane Creighton; friends Humphrey Jones, Nicholas Cock, Henry Williams, Richard Symms; sons John and Rice to be executors; witnesses Peter Hopegood, John Powell.

Hopkins, Robert. 10 March, 1677—6 March, 1679. Wife Katherine executrix; three sons Thomas, Robert and George; friends William Moss and John Fennell; witnesses John Hubbard, Frances Donner.

Barber, Richard. 4 May, 1676—6 March, 1677. Sons Richard and John; wife Mary executrix; witnesses Lawrence Rochefort, Francis Dawkins.

Godfrey, John. ————30 April, 1678. To friend ———— all my estate.

Fullerton, James. 21 March, 1677-8—2 May, 1678. Daughters Hannah and Mary; son James and friend Thomas Gaines executors; my wife; witnesses Thomas Edmundson, Thos. Wheeler, James Baughan.

Drenn, Edward. 4 March, 1677-8—2 May, 1678. To the children of Richard West, viz.: Elizabeth, Mary and Ellen; Andrew Boughan; David Samson; Richard West executor; witnesses Lawrence Rochefort, David Jamison.

Curtis, John. 29 Nov., 1677—7 Feb., 1677. Friends Dt. Peter Hopegood and Randall Peters to be executors; witnesses Simon Gray, John White, Thomas Graham.

Whitlock, Thomas. 23 Nov., 1677—5 June, 1678. Father Thomas Whitlock, deceased; sisters Sarah Rowzie, Elizabeth Rowzie and Katherine Rowzie; brother Edward Rowzie; brother Lodowick Rowzie; brother John Rowzie; Uncle Robert Gullock and Robert Pley executors; witnesses Thomas Roberts, Jonathan Batho.

Willcocks, Matthew. 26 Feb., 1677—23 March, 1678. Wife Rebecca; godson Zachariah Nicholls; kinsman William Nutt; witnesses Daniel Hawkins, Thomas Chittie, John Alloway, William Barber.

Moss, Thomas. 31 March, 1678—13 Jan., 1678-9. Wife Elizabeth executrix; daughters Elizabeth and Frances; witnesses Abraham Stapp, Henry Muncaster.

Talbutt, William. 6 March, 1676-7—28 Jan., 1678-9. Wife Mary executrix; son Thomas; wife's father John Sharp, deceased; witnesses Henry Mandsley, Thomas Harware.

Peterson, Neale. 20 Nov., 1672. Son John; daughters Mary and Anne; wife executrix; witnesses William Johnson, Henry Jorden.

Fullerton, Joane. 14 April, 1678—22 July, 1678. Elizabeth Meade; John Topp, Jr.; Robert Doewell, Samuel Parry, Jr.; witnesses Samuel Parrt, Humphrey Perkin.

Gregory, John. 18 Dec., 1677—4 Sept., 1678. Sister Mary Gregory; Katherine Armstrong; sister Elizabeth; brother Richard Gregory executor; witnesses Thomas Games, James Fugett.

Clark, Henry. 18 April, 1678—6 Jan., 1678-9. Son John; son-in-law Francis Gore; daughter Elizabeth, wife of Angell Jacobus; wife Joane executrix; witnesses John Sampson, John Taverner.

Dike, John, Sr. 24 March, 1677-8—29 Jan., 1678. Son John executor; witnesses Henry Mandsley, Daniel Fautes.

Butler, Amory. 21 Aug., 1678—29 Jan., 1678-9. My books and sermon notes to my brother Mr. William Butler, minister of Washington Parish; brother John Butler; Valentine Allen; godson William Pannell; nephew John Underwood; brother William Underwood; Daniel Gaines executor; witnesses Samuel Bloomfield, Lawrence Rochefort.

Bucksome, Annanias. 23 March, 1678-9—3 April, 1679. Wife Jane Willson sole heir and executrix; witnesses Col. John Stone, Sarah Bowyer.

Goodrich, Thomas. 15 March, 1678-9—10 April, 1679. Sons Benjamin, Joseph and Charles; daughter Anne; son Peter; daughter Katherine; wife Alice; eldest son Benjamin to be executor; witnesses Chris. Hargill, Dennis Conners, Thomas Edmundson.

English, John. 16 Sept., 1677—21 May, 1679. Henry Johnson; Thomas Elvert; Richard Rice; William Barber; wife Elizabeth executrix; witnesses Peter Ellis, Thomas Naylor.

Robinson, John, Farnham Parish. 25 March, 1679—22 May, 1679. My mother to be executrix; brother Samuel Bayley; cousin Joice Bayley; father-in-law William Thornbury; witnesses John Stratton, Samuel Bayley.

Hopegood, Peter. 28 May, 1678—21 May, 1679. Daughters-in-law Frances and Elizabeth Godson to be executrixes; Thomas Roberts; uncles Paul Allentree and John Hopegood to look after my daughters-in-law; friends Henry Smith, William Young and Thomas Roberts to be overseers; witnesses Thomas Graham, Alex. Wetherstone.

Everest, John. 22 April, 1679—7 May, 1679. Cousin Margaret Everest; witnesses Thomas Everest, William Cresswell.

Taylor, Richard. 22 March, 1678-9—21 May, 1679. Sons Richard and Simon; daughter Constance; wife Sarah; friends John English, Peter Ellis and Edward Friar; Col. Leroy Griffin executor; witnesses John English, Elizabeth Wood, Elizabeth English.

Bowler, Thomas, Esq. 17 March, 1678-9—28 July, 1679. Son James; daughter Elizabeth Bowler; daughter Anne; wife Tabitha executrix; friends Col. Nicholas Spencer and Capt. Thomas Gouldman overseers; witnesses Robert Barrett; Nicholas Franklin.

Hudson, Thomas. 12 June, 1679—5 Nov., 1679. Daughter Mary Yates and son-in-law Elias Yates, latter to be executor; wife Mary; witnesses Richard Glover, William Thornton.

Walker, Sarah. 28 Jan., 1668-9—22 Dec., 1679. To Col. William Walker's six daughters, Anne Paine, Frances Walker, Elizabeth Walker, Sarah Walker, Esther Walker and Jane Walker; son Henry; daughter Mary Burden; witnesses Francis Setle, Richard Fox.

Lunn, William. 1 March, 1678—7 May, 1679. Son Roger; daughter Mary; wife Alicia; Giles, son of John Webb; witnesses Thomas Taylor, Edward Jones.

Smith, Thomas. 20 Nov., 1678—21 Jan., 1679. Sons John and Thomas; daughters Elizabeth and Sarah; my wife; John Cheney overseer; witnesses Richard Brooks, Frances Stafford.

Wiere, Walter. 3 Sept., 1673—5 May, 1680. Wife Mary to be sole executrix; witnesses Thomas Erwin, William Sargent.

Waight, John, planter. 3 March, 1679—3 Sept., 1679. Daughter Mary; Elizabeth Vickers; sons Robert and John; John Vickers and William Griffin overseers; witnesses George Lodge, Stephen Ferrell.

Jones, Richard. 3 March, 1674—12 May, 1680. Eldest son John; son Richard; daughter Jane; wife Avis executrix; George Morriss and Thomas Cooper overseers; witnesses John Price, John Soper.

Hollister, William. 18 May, 1680—3 Sept., 1680. Elizabeth Bayley, Jr.; Robert Bayley, Jr., to be executor; brother Thomas Hollister, living in Temple Parish in Bristol; witnesses Giles Webb, Thomas Taylor.

Love, James (Nuncupative will). 4 April, 1681—6 April, 1681. To John More, Parish of St. James, city of Bristol, commander of the ship "Alexander"; Richard Farrington of Wiccocomocoe; John Hawkins of Deep Creek in Rappahannock River.

NORTHAMPTON COUNTY WILLS.

ORDER BOOK No. 12.

Flint, John, tailor, Northampton Co. 15 Aug., 1704—29 March, 1706. Godson John Stratton, son of Benj. Stratton; friend Matthew Short; witnesses Benj. Stratton and Matthew Short.

Green, John, Northampton Co. 5 March, 1706-7—(No date of probate). Son Joseph; daughter Ann; daughter Sarah; daughter Mary; son George; son John; daughter Elizabeth, wife of John Procter; wife Alice Green executrix; witnesses John Walker and Sarah Beer.

Clay, Leveret, planter, Northampton Co. 18 March, 1706-7—8 May, 1707. Son John; daughter Ann Clay; wife Elizabeth and the child she now goes with; brother-in-law Benj. Griffith; brother John Clay; son John to remain with his mother until 18 years of age; witnesses Jerome Griffith and Eliz. Bandling.

ORDER BOOK No. 14.

Gascoigne, Henry. 26 Feb., 1698—30 May, 1699. Brother Thomas Gascoigne; nephew Robert Gascoigne, my plantation which was formerly my godfather Wm. Gascoigne's;

brother William when he comes of age; my godfather
Captain Philip Fisher; witnesses Daniel Mackenny,
Michael Halsherd, Aaron Westerhouse, Jr.

Poulden, Morgan, Northampton Co. 23 Feb., 1699—28
March, 1700. Daughter Ann Rice; grandson Henry
Rice; granddaughter Mary Rice; Elizabeth Clegg, daughter of John Clegg; daughter Ann Rice to be executrix;
witnesses William Dunton, John Clegg, John Walker.

Roberts, Sarah, widow, Northampton Co. 9 May, 1700—28
May, 1700. Servant Thomas Dane; grandson Nathl.
Kellam; grandson William Kellam; daughter Sarah Kel-
lam; son John White executor; witnesses Luke Taylor,
Francis Poole, Sarah Adkinson.

Baker, William, Northampton Co. 12 Aug., 1700—(No date
of probate). Sons John and William Baker; my wife
Mary, who is now with child; daughter Elizabeth; my
wife's sister, Ann Carpenter; granddaughter Ann Eves;
witnesses Thomas Leonard, Michael Underhill, Jacob
Bishop, Leverett Clay.

Dowell, Morgan, Northampton Co. 21 Feb., 1698-9—28 Jan.,
1700. To Elizabeth Teague; Sophia Teague; Abigail
Teague; John Abdell; Ann Stott; William Abdell;
Thomas Abdell; Thomas Teague's children; William and
Thomas Abdell executors; witnesses William Prosser,
John Smith.

Tilney, John, Nassawaddox, Northampton Co. 6 April, 1700
—28 May, 1701. Daughter Susannah, wife of Michael
Dixon; daughter Ann, wife of Richard Drumond; son
John Tilney; daughter Margaret, wife of John Moore;
daughters Mary and Martha Tilney; son-in-law John
Moore executor; witnesses Richard Ariss, Francis Cassin,
John Swindall.

Stratton, Thomas, Northampton Co. 1 Oct., 1700—28 May,
1701. My father; brother Benjamin Stratton; brother
Nathaniel Stratton; sisters Agnes and Ann Stratton; witnesses William Rue, Nathl. Capell, Hannah Capell.

Hunt, Thomas, Northampton Co. 15 Jan., 1700—28 May, 1701. Sons John, Thomas and Gawdon Hunt; wife Ann; daughter Ann Pigott; witnesses Ralph Pigott, Daniel Benthall, Margaret Nelson

Knight, John, Sr., planter, Northampton Co. 4 April, 1701—29 Sept., 1701. Sons John and Dixon Knight; my wife Elizabeth; witnesses John Nelson, Hannah Capell, Nathl. Capell.

Foxcroft, Isaac, Northampton Co. 7 June, 1698—28 Nov., 1702. Wife Bridget; Michael Underhill, son of Michael Underhill; witnesses Michael Underhill, John Harper, Margaret Cope.

Harmanson, Thomas, Sr., gentleman, Northampton Co. 26 March, 1696—28 Nov., 1702. Wife Elizabeth; son-in-law William Waters and my daughter Isabel, his wife; sons Benjamin, George and Thomas; grandson Thomas, son of my son Thomas; granddaughter Elizabeth, daughter of my son Thomas; my sons William, John and Henry; friend Capt. Hillary Stringer; daughter Elishe, wife of Mr. Thomas Savage; grandson Jacob, son of Thomas Clay and Margaret, his wife; friend Major John Custis; my wife and six sons executors; witnesses Wm. Shepheard, Argoll Wilkins, Matthew Moore, Nathl. Littleton, William Waters. Codicil dated 19 Oct., 1700.

Powell, John, Northampton Co. 6 Dec., 1700—28 Dec., 1702. Sons Nicholas and Nathaniel; my wife Frances; friend Col. John Custis; brother Benj. Stratton; wife to be executrix; witness Thomas Bayley, Agnes Stratton, Benj. Stratton.

Littleton, Nathaniel, Northampton Co. 25 Jan., 1702-3—1 March, 1702. Son Southey; daughter Sarah Custis Littleton; daughter Esther Littleton; my wife Susanna to be executrix; witness Leverett Clay, John Clay, Mary Baker, Daniel Neech.

Fisher, Phillip, gentleman, Northampton Co. 9 Dec., 1701—1 March, 1702. Son John; daughters Tamar Hunt and Anne Gascoigne; son Thomas; daughters Mary Smith

and Rebecca Fisher; daughters Bridget Bradford and
Sarah Michael; son Phillip; grandsons Thomas Smith and
Harman Gascoigne; wife Elizabeth executrix; witnesses
Jacob Johnson, Alex. Bagwell, Peter Grice.

Duparkes, Thomas, Northampton Co. 3 Dec., 1702—1 March,
1702. Son Thomas; daughters Ann and Sarah; son William Jarvis and his wife; son Thomas Goffigon and my
daughter, his wife; grandchildren Thomas and Rose Goffigon and Thomas Jarvis; son William Spady and my
daughter, his wife; wife Elizabeth to be executrix; witnesses John Tatum, Harman Firkettle.

Shepheard, John, Northampton Co. 7 Jan., 1702—1 March,
1702. Sons Thomas and John; my father Thomas Shepheard; sons Jacob and Joseph; my sister Esther Shepheard; witnesses George Corben, John Savage, Robert
Hamilton.

Shepheard, William, Northampton Co. 2 Jan., 1702—I
March, 1702. My son William and the rest of my chil-
dren; wife Esther to be executrix; witnesses Charles
Gelding, Thomas Hayes, Thomas Shore.

Higginson, Samuel, Chirurgeon, Northampton Co. 10 March,
1702—28 April, 1703. To Francis Page; James Waters;
Thomas Maddox, Jr., and his daughter Margaret Maddox residuary legatees; witnesses Thomas Savage, Geo.
Marshall, Obedience Johnson.

Haward, James, Northampton Co. 9 March, 1702—28 April,
1702. My estate to be equally divided between Samuel
Haward, Jonah Jackson and John Watts; witnesses Jacob
Johnson, Jacob Dewey, George Dewey.

Norly, Thomas, Northampton Co. ——— 1702—4 June, 1703.
Sons-in-law William Ellegood and Peter Norly; grandchildren Mary, Norly, Susanna and Sarah Cripps; wife
Esther; daughter Esther; Richard Cripps; wife to be executrix; witnesses Nathl. Littleton, Michael Dixon, Susanna Dixon.

Waterson, Frances, widow, Northampton Co. 13 Dec., 1702
—4 June, 1703. Grandson John, son of William Water-

son; Frances, daughter of Richard Waterson, my son; Bridget Waterson; Elisheba Frank; son William executor; witnesses John Knight, Thomas Nelson, John Frank, Ralph Pigott.

Hamilton, Robert, Northampton Co. 5 Feb., 1701-2—4 June, 1703. Sons Robert and Isaac and daughter Mary Hamilton; Benj. Foster; wife Mary executrix; witnesses Thomas Savage, Grace Banks, Eliz. Hardnedge.

James, David, Northampton Co. 19 April, 1703—28 Aug., 1703. Sons David, William, John, Robert and Thomas; my wife Joan; daughters Sarah and Elizabeth James; daughters Mary Badger and Ann Taylor; my wife and son David executors; witnesses Luke Taylor, John Eshom, Robert Briggs.

Noock, Daniel, Northampton Co. 16 April, 1703—28 Sept., 1703. To Agnes Somers; godson Daniel Underhill; to my sister in England; Noock Eyre; my wife Margaret executrix; witnesses Edward Garrit, John Eyres.

Jacob, Esau, Northampton Co. 1 Sept., 1702—28 Sept., 1703. Sister Ann and her husband Thomas Dolby; my sister Amyah Stott; the children of my mother Stott; Jonathan Stott my brother-in-law; Richard Smith and Robert Scott; my cousin Risdon Jacob; Angus Campbell; William Dunton; Abraham Jacob; my mother to be executrix; witnesses Robert Scott, Angus Campbell, Risdon Jacob.

Walter, Benjamin, Northampton Co. 8 July, 1702—28 Jan., 1703. All estate to wife Elizabeth; witnesses William Waterfield, Thomas Ward.

Foxcroft, Bridget, widow. 13 Jan., 1703-4—28 March, 1704. My deceased husband; kinsman Isaac Waterhouse of Halifax in ye kingdom of England, dyer; ——— Eyre; my kinswoman Elizabeth, wife of John Stanhope; Bridget Lathbury; Isaac Luks; kinsman Isaac Charlton; kinswomen Elizabeth Lathbury and Susanna, daughter of John Luke; Thomas Chick; witnesses John Luke, Thomas Lucas, John Harper.

Marshall, Thomas. 5 Jan., 1703-4—30 May, 1704. To Mary and Anne, daughters of my son Thomas; sons John and George to be executors; witnesses Obedience Johnson, Jacob Johnson, Arthur Roscoe.

Batson, John, Northampton Co. 13 Sept., 1704—28 Sept., 1704. Sons Francis and William; wife Grace to be executrix; witnesses Richard Carvy, Alice Sanders, Benj. Nottingham.

Pettite, Mary, widow, Northampton Co. 5 Nov., 1704—29 Jan., 1704. Sons John, Justinian and Bartholomew; daughter Margaret Pettite; daughter Mary Evans; grandson William Pettite; granddaughter Mary Pettite; grandson Justinian Evans; son Thomas to be executor; witnesses John Hamby, Thomas Frost.

Clegg, John, Northampton Co. 24 Feb., 1704-5—28 March, 1705. Son ——— Clegg; sons John and Peter; daughter Elizabeth; wife Joan executor; witnesses Benj. Nottingham, William Dunton, Henry Marsh.

Johnson, Thomas, Northampton Co. 10 Feb., 1704—30 Feb., 1705. Sons Thomas and Luke; daughter Ann; wife Mary executrix; witnesses John White, Robert James.

Brown, Thomas, Northampton Co. 2 Nov., 1704—29 May, 1705. Daughter Elizabeth; grandson ——— Pearson; daughters Sarah and Anne; daughter Mary; wife Susanna and four daughters to be executrixes; witnesses Samuel French, Andrew Hamilton.

Griffith, Jerome, Northampton Co. 14 March, 1707-8—28 May, 1708. Sons Jerome, James, Jonah, Luke, Josias, Benjamin and Thomas Griffith; daughter Frances Hull (Hall?); daughter Ellen; daughter Dorothy Hays; daughter Eliza; wife Elizabeth executrix; witnesses Nicholas Eyre, Henry Harmanson.

EARLY SETTLERS IN VIRGINIA.

(Continued from page 26).

Walton, John, tr. by John Drayton, Westmoreland Co., 25 Nov., 1654.

Gerrall, Katherine, tr. by Wm. Hatcher, Sr., Henrico Co., 2 May, 1705.

Strange, John, tr. by Abraham Willary and Dorothy, his wife, King William Co., 2 May, 1705.

Thevenos, James, tr. by John Ralls, Nansemond Co., 25 Oct., 1695.

Redcross, Abraham, tr. by Richard Jordan, Surry Co., 20 Oct., 1689.

Chote, Thomas, tr. by Peirce Lennon, 5 Nov., 1635.

Jening, William, tr. by Wm. Woolritch, Elizabeth City, 17 June, 1635.

Blake, Edward, tr. by Capt. Adam Thorogood, 18 Dec., 1635.

Everett, Christopher, tr. by Lieut. John Cheesman, Charles River, 21 Nov. 1635.

Ackerman, Robert, tr. by Sergt. Thos. Crompe, 28 Sept., 1635.

Melton, Thos., tr. by Capt. Adam Thorogood in "Hopewell" in 1628.

Evans, Jones, tr. by David Mansell, 22 July, 1635.

Brattaine, Robert, tr. by Capt. Wm. Peirce, 22 June, 1635.

Bussy, Ann, tr. by Richard Bennett, 26 June, 1635.

Connagrave, Thomas (servant), tr. by Wm. Stone, Accomac Co., 4 June, 1635.

Moore, William, tr. by Rev. George White, 3 June, 1635.

Heyley, William, tr. by David Mansell, 22 July, 1635.

Cole, Thomas (servant), tr. by Erasmus Carter, 10 July, 1635.

Davis, Rice, tr. by John Brewer, 11 June, 1635.

Foster, Zachariah, tr. by Doctoris Christmas, Elizabeth City, 21 Nov., 1635.

Fowler, James, tr. by Hugh Cox, 6 Dec., 1634.

Greene, Judith, tr. by Wm. Swan, James City, 5 Nov., 1635.

Jones, William, tr. by Thomas Harris, Henrico Co., 11 Nov., 1635.

Johnson, John, tr. by Rev. Wm. Wilkinson, 20 Nov., 1635.

Holdin, John (servant), tr. by Wm. Spencer, 19 June, 1635.

Huggons, Nathl., tr. by Augustine Smith, Essex Co., 2 May, 1705.

Myson, Andrew, tr. by Charles Wilks, Nansemond Co., 25 Oct., 1695.

Elliott, John, tr. by Richard Jordan, Surry Co., 20 Oct., 1689.

Hallcock, Roger, tr. by Rev. Willis Heyley of Mulbery Island, 8 Dec., 1635.

Farr, John (servant), tr. by Wm. Stafford, 12 Nov., 1635.

Gannil, Robert, tr. in "John and Dorothy" 1634, by Capt. Adam Thorogood.

Newton, Richard (servant, tr. by Charles Harmar, 4 July, 1635.

Johnston, Robert, tr. by John Brewer, 11 June, 1635.

Newman, John, tr. by Elizabeth Parker, Henrico Co., 12 Feb., 1635.

Long, James (servant), tr. by Capt. Francis Epes, 26 Aug., 1635.

Long, John (servant), tr. by Capt. Francis Epes, 26 Aug., 1635.

Long, Ann, tr. in "Africa" by Capt. Adam Thorogood, 24 June, 1635.

Gaines, Alexander, tr. by Richard Bennett, 26 June, 1635.

Dryhurst, Thomas, tr. in "Neptune" 1618, by Saml. Matthews, Esq.

Cupperwhaite, Thomas, tr. by George Keith, 29 July, 1635.

Bradford, John, tr. in "Temperance" 1621, by Lieut. Thomas Flint.

Flood, John, tr. by Richard Bennett, 26 June, 1635.

Hankinson, William (servant), tr. by Wm. Stone, Accomac Co., 4 June, 1635.

Mahoney, Dennis, tr. by John Brewer, 22 June, 1635.

Moore, Sara, tr. by Richard Jordan, Surry Co., 20 Oct., 1689.

Burke, Tobie, tr. by David Jones, Charles City, 4 July, 1635.

Wise, William, tr. by John Ralls, Nansemond Co., 25 Oct., 1695.

Burt, William, tr. by Ensign John Utie, 1624.

Hether, John (servant), tr. by William Gany, Accomac Co., 17 Sept., 1635.

Dugg, Robert, tr. by John Sparkes, 3 June, 1635.

Boy, Thomas, tr. by John Moone, 21 Oct., 1635.

Atwood, Ann, tr. by Richard Bennett, 26 June, 1635.

Asley, John, tr. by John Russell, 1634.

Palmer, Edward, tr. by Capt. Adam Thorogood in "Friendship," 1629.

Jennings, John, tr. by Francis Fowler of James City Co., 1635.

Goodwin, Alexander, tr. by William Barker, 26 Nov., 1635.

Thomas, Samuel, tr. by John Ralls, Nansemond Co., 25 Oct., 1695.

Goodwin, John, tr. by Rev. William Wilkinson, 20 Nov., 1635.

Lee, Elizabeth, tr. by Augustine Smith, Essex Co., 2 May, 1705.

Hall, Edward, tr. by Allenson Clarke and Charles Russell, Henrico Co., 2 May, 1705.

Yates, Jonathan, tr. by Abraham Willary and Dorothy, his wife, of St. John's Parish, King William Co., 2 May, 1705.

Gorving, John, tr. by Sergt. Thomas Campe, 28 Sept., 1635.

Keith, George, headright, York Co., 29 July, 1635.

Keith, John, son of George Keith, headright, York Co., 29 July, 1635.

Moone, Susan, tr. by her husband, John Moone of Warwick Co., 21 Oct., 1635.

Deaxter, Thomas (servant), came in the "Mary Providence," 1623.

Creasor, Thomas, tr. by Capt. Adam Thorogood, in "John and Dorothy," 1634.

Ball, William, tr. by Allenson Clarke and Charles Russell,. Henrico Co., 2 May, 1705.

Burt, Edward (servant), tr. by Wm. Stone, Accomac Co., 4 June, 1635.

Adams, Elizabeth, tr. by Capt. Wm. Peirce, 22 June, 1635.

Gallopin, William, tr. by John Sparkes, 3 June, 1635.

Galloway, William, tr. in the "Anne" in 1623, by Capt. William Epes, Accomac Co.

Grace, Robert, tr. by Francis Fowler, James City Co., 1635.

Clement, Edy, wife of Mr. Jeremiah Clement, headright, 11 June, 1635.

IMMIGRANTS TO VIRGINIA.

The Immigrant Lists to Virginia are taken from MSS. on file in the State Paper Department, Public Record Office, London. They were published by John C. Hotten in 1874, but the volume has been out of print for many years, and can only be found in the larger Libraries and Historical Societies. A comparison of the names in these lists with the similar names printed in the list of "Headrights," will furnish important clues to the genealogical searcher.

LICENSES TO GO BEYOND THE SEAS.

Post festum Natalis Christi 1634, usqr. ad festum Nat. Christi 1635.

Secundo Januarii, 1634.

Theis under written are to be transported to Virginia, imbarqued in ye Mercht. "BONAVENTURE," James Riccoste, Mr., bound thither, have taken the oath of allegiance.

Name.	Years.	Name.	Years
William Sayer	58	Henry Irish	16
Robert Percy	40	Henry Quinton	20
Edward Clark	30	Robert Payton	25
Richard Hargrave	20	Michaell Browne	35
Francis Spencer	23	John Edmonds	16
Richard Hughes	19	John Wise	28
William Guy	18	Symon Kenneday	20
James Redding	19	Thomas James	20
Andrew Jefferies	24	Emanuell Bomer	18
Arthur Howell	20	James Lickburrowe	20
James Moyser	28	Jesper Withy	21
William Smith	20	Jo. Spemgall	18
Miles Riley	20	James Perkyns	42
Peter Dole	20	William Hutton	24
Jo. Underwood	23	Hugh Garland	20
John Wood	26	Humphrey Topsall	24

Bazill Brooke	20	John Bamford	28
Chas. Hilliard	22	Jo. Cooke	47
John Ogell	18	Tho. Parson	30
John Anderson	20	William Surgisson	25
John Lewes	23	Robert Fisher	34
John Clerk	19	Jo. Atkinson	24
John Burd	18	Joseph Washborn	22
Richard Cooper	18	Edward Mawr	19
William Munday	22	Henry Aunne	16
Jo. Abby	22	William Ridgell	24
Matthew Marshall	30	Jo. Feildhouse	19
Garrett Riley	24	Jo. Grimscroft	27
William Burch	19	John Lee	17
James Metcalf	22	Jo. Mosely	18
Robert Luck	25	Richard Ast	30
Walter Morgan	23	Richard Glaister	31
George Greene	20	John Towse	26
Jo. Bryan	25	Thos. Goodman	25
Thomas Symons	27	Launcelot Pryce	21
John Hodges	37	Thomazine Pryce (uxor).	18
Garrett Pownder	19	John Dunn	26
Henry Dunnell	23	Thos. Anderson	18
Tho. Hyet	22	Jo. Baggley	14
Jo. Sotterfoyth	24	Thos. Smith	14
Leonard Wetherfield	17	Thomas Townsend	14
Tho. Smyer	18	Mary Saunders	26
Robert Kersley	22	Margaret Muddock	21
Tho. Jessopp	18	John Wigg	24
Daniel Green	24	Andrew Dunton	38
John Wilkinson	19	William Hudson	32
Richard Spicer	18	John Hill	50
Tho. Stanton	20	Robert Smithson	23
Jo. Watson	28	James Graston	22
John Fountaine	18	Reginoll Harris	25
Loughton Bostock	16	Jo. Hutchinson	22
Thomas Ridgeley	23	Richard Harman	20
William Mason	19	Elizabeth Jackson	17

Mary Ashley 24
Margaret Huntley 20
Thomas Perry 34
Dorothy Perry (uxor).. 26
Ben. Perry 4
Richard Champion 18
Abram Silvester 14
Jo. Atkinson 30
Ralph Nicholson 20
Joan Nubold 20
Tho. Murfie 20
Henry Redding 22
John Russell 19
Robert Harris 19
Victor Derrick 23
Geo. Session 40
Thomas Tomason 26
Michell Hopkinson 27
Edward Fisher 35
Richard Ellis 29
Jo. Hickcombottom 24
Richard Pitt 19
Jo. Futror 18
Ellen Jones 18
Christopher Carnoll 23
Tho. Taylor 19
Jesper Meston 27
John Skorie 16
Jerremy Redding 18
John Rolinson 26
Alice Protherock 24

Richard Cave 28
Phillip Conner 21
Kat. Yate 19
Averyn Cowper 20
Leonard Evans 22
Edward Cranfield 24
Ann Cranfield (uxor)... 18
William Weston 30
Edward Davies 25
Jane Chambers 23
Roger Sturdevant 21
John Greenwood 16
John Wise 30
Tho. Edenburrow 37
Henry Rogers 30
Nicholas Harvy 30
Daniel Daniell 18
Geo. Burlingham 20
James Grund 17
Sam. Ashley 19
Sara Turner 20
Margaret Furbredd 20
Richard Doll 25
Mary Carlton 23
Abram Silvester 40
Tho. Bolton 18
Richard Champion 19
Elizabeth Nunick 20
Richard Hore 24
Robert More 19
Thomas Hebden 20

(To be continued)

SURRY COUNTY RECORDS.

6 Sept., 1654. Bond of John Dibdall, clk., Richard Dibdall, planter, Lieut. Catt and Thomas Swann, Esq., relative to the estate of John Fisher, decd., and his children, viz.: Mary and Joseph Fisher. Wit.: William Cockerham, Robert Stanton, Sack. Brewster.

6 Sept., 1654. Bond of John Dibdall, clk., and Richard Dibdall, planter, to William Fisher, son of John Fisher, decd. Wit.: William Cockerham, Sack. Brewster, Robert Stanton.

7 Sept., 1654. Letter to Mr. Cockerham, signed "yr. loveing sister Elizabeth Shepard."

2 Sept., 1654. Indenture between William Canfield, planter, and Henry Bannister and Karbye Kigan, all of Surry. "Mentions children Robert and Elizabeth Canfield and wife Dorcas Canfield. Wit.: John Board, Sack. Brewster.

6 Sept., 1654. Confession of judgment by Thomas Calmer to John Spilltimber.

7 Sept., 1654. Bond from John Dobbs to George Burcher.

23 Sept., 1654. Indenture between Mr. Thomas Warren, gent., and Mrs. Elizabeth Sheppard, widow, both of Surry as to a marriage to be solemnized between them. "Mentions children by a former marriage, viz.: Anne, John, Robert, Wiliam, Priscilla and Susanna Sheppard." Wit.: Edward Ffolliott, William Cockerham.

9 Oct., 1654. Deposition of William Gasing, aged 50 years or thereabouts.

9 Nov., 1654. Lease dated 6 April, 1643, between Capt. Henry Brown of the "Four Mile Tree," Esq., to Peter Adams. Wit.: William Harman, George Jordan.

6 Dec., 1654. Deed from Richard Tyas to Daniel Massingall. Wit.: Matthew Battell, John Rawlins.

6 Dec., 1654. Bond from Edward Hurlstone, Parish of Lawnes Creek, carpenter, to Richard Garrett of same place. Wit.: Robert Warren, Walter Starte.

7 March, 1654. Bond of Foulke Jones to Mr. Lawrence Baker. Wit.: George Jordan, John Jennings.

9 March, 1654. Power of Attorney to Richard Merydale from William Powell of Parish of St. Mary Oneryes, alias St. Saviours, near the Borough of Southwarke, Co. Surry, baker, brother and heir to Capt. William Powell. George Powell of this Colony and his nephew Richard Powell and Mary Powell, daughter of said Richard, make claim to the plantation now in occupation of John Bishop, near Crouches Creek in Co. Surry.

7 March, 1654. Deed from Francis Jordan to William Jennings.

14 Aug., 1653. Deed from Major Robert Shepard to Henry Medhouse. "Recorded by me, Thomas Warringe, who married the relict of said Shepard, 7 March, 1654."

7 March, 1654. Indenture of Peter Garrett, tarmaker to Mr. Thomas Warringe. Wit.: Foulke Jones, Thomas Hart.

1 May, 1655. Conveyance from William Morrell to Thos. Stagge.

22 April, 1655. Intention of marriage between Thomas, alias Sackford Brewster of Sackford Hall, Co. Suffolk, gent., and Elizabeth Watkins. Ceremony performed 23 April, 1655, by Mr. Thomas Luke, minister. Wit.: John Corker, Robert Stanton.

1 May, 1655. Conveyance from Thomas Woodhouse of James City to Robert Hubbard of same place.

27 Jan., 1653. Deed from John Blackborne to Samuel Swanne. Wit.: Jone Blackborne, William Stevens, Sackford Brewster. Acknowledged in Court by Jone Blackborne, relict of John Blackborne, and recorded 1 May, 1655.

23 April, 1655. Indenture between Thomas, alias Sackford Brewster, gent., and Elizabeth Watkins, his espoused and admx. of John Watkins, decd., for the benefit of her three children.

23 Jan., 1653. Conveyance from John Blackborne to William Norwood. Recorded 1 May, 1655.

20 June 1655. Appraisement and inventory of the estate of
Mr. James Taylor, decd.

30 July, 1655. Power of Attorney from William Collins of
London, merchant, to Robert Stanton.

3 July, 1655. Deposition of Richard Warrener, aged 20 or
thereabouts. "That the first of September last, Mr. Richard Gossage departed this life in the house of Mr. Peter
Green, and that he died in the presence of this deponent
and Eliza Sawyer, and that he did tell Peter Green that
all he (sd. Gossage) had he did give to said Peter Green.

3 July, 1655. Deposition of Elizabeth Sawyer, aged 24 years
or thereabouts, in re. above.

4 July, 1655. Petition of Elizabeth, the admx. of John Watkins, decd., now wife to Thomas, alias Sackford Brewster.

4 July, 1655. Discharge by Col. Richard Meredith to Mr.
Peter Green of all debts due. Wit.: Francis Slaughter

4 July, 1655. Petition of Thomas Burns that Mrs. Elizabeth
Mason, wife of Mr. James Mason, hath defamed in a
vile manner, Martha, ye wife of ye petitioner.

4 July, 1655. Deposition of John Board that Mr. Banister
did in the hearing of George Donnigo and "myself" give
unto his daughter Clara, 2 suites of her mother's linen.

4 July, 1655. Letter to Thomas Gray from John Cogan to
pay to John Corker 100 lbs. of tobacco.

14 Aug., 1655. Bond of Lieut.-Col. Thomas Swann relative to
the death of one Elizabeth Burke.

6 Oct., 1655. Bond of Giles Brent, Esq., attorney of William Bretton and Temperance, his wife, regarding land
sold to Thomas Binns and John Bishop.

7 Oct., 1655. Conveyance from Samuel Herbys of Lawnes
Creek, planter, to William Batt of same place. Certain
head of cattle.

6 Oct., 1655. Indenture made 1 Dec., 1654, between Robert
Warren and Humphrey, the Indian. Wit.: Charles Barecroft, George Seaton.

10 June, 1655. Discharge of Mr. Francis Slaughter of all
debts, etc., in relation to the estate of James Taylor, decd.

18 Dec., 1655. Deed from Alice Carter, widow, reciting that Edward Pettaway married Elizabeth, relict of William Carter, son-in-law to me Alice Carter, and that there was a parcel of land bequeathed to said William Carter, Jr., by his father William Carter, Sr., husband to said Alice, and it is agreed that the said Edward Pettaway shall have the said land, etc., etc. Wit.: Nich. Perry, Richard Blunt.

"Robert Webb, the sonne of Stephen Webb, was borne ye 16th day of Nov., 1636. William Webb was borne ye 15th day of Feb., 1645. Being founde in an old Bible and subscribed by their Father's owne hand." Recorded in Surry Court 3 Jan., 1655.

3 Jan., 1655. Indenture made 25 Nov., 1655, between John Corker of Co. Surry and Dorothie, his wife, and Capt. Richard Webster of James City. Wit.: George Jordan, Henry Soane.

—— Jan., 1655. Indenture made 20 May, 1655, between Arthur Jordan, Southwark Parish, Surry, planter, and Robert Stanton of same county, in reference to Elizabeth Hutton, orphan of Daniel Hutton, who is now in charge of said Jordan. Wit.: Richard Hill, John Flood.

3 Jan., 1655. Record of debts due from John Spilltimber to John Bradye.

2 Jan., 1655. Conveyance from John Dibdall, clerk, to Mr. Richard Hill of all interest in patent of land in Co. Surry, except 500 acres which is due to Benjamin Harrison, orphan.

1 Jan., 1655. Conveyance from William Rose to Mary Crafton. Wit.: William Browne, John Fitch.

3 Jan., 1655. Power of attorney from Henry Clarke to Edward Muntford.

17 Jan., 1655. Whereas there being a difference between Robert Stanton and John Dibdall concerning the land which Mr. John Fisher by will gave to his children, and which for non-payment was repossed by said Dibdall, yet for the composure of the said difference he hath in Surry Court offered to give to the children of said Fisher (one

of whom, I, the said Stanton, hath married), the sum of
3,500 lbs. of tobacco and caske, and I, the said Stanton,
do accept the same. Recorded 1 Feb., 1655. Wit.:
George Jordan, John King, Roger Potter.

1 Nov., 1656. Power of attorney from Thomas Strong to
Robert Stanton to acknowledge in Court a bill due from
me to Mr. John Holmewood.

1 Feb., 1655. Summons for Court of Surry to Elizabeth
Bannister, Robert Hill and Charles Barecroft in regard
to the bond of said Elizabeth as guardian to Robert Webb.

15 Jan., 1655. Know all by these presents, that I, Abraham
Sheares, Jr., lawful attorney for my mother Mrs. Elizabeth Sheares, the administratrix of the estate of Mr.
Abraham Sheares my father, decd., do acknowledge to
have received out of the said estate, 23,000 lbs. of tobacco for the use of my mother and by her order. Wit.:
Thomas Taberner.

GOOCHLAND COUNTY MARRIAGE BONDS.

Dec.   11, 1780. David M. Randolph and Mary Randolph.
Thomas M. Randolph consents to dau.'s
marriage and that David M. Randolph
was 21, in March, 1780.

Jan.   23, 1781. James Davenport and Mary, dau. of William Rutherford.

March 21, 1785. John Thompson and Sarah Strong.

Nov.   21, 1785. Jesse Redd and Mary Woodson.

Aug.   18, 1788. William Johnson and Susanna Holland.

Dec.   23, 1785. Benjamin Watkins and Anna Riddle.

Oct.   11, 1781. Pleasant Turner and Agnes Woodson.

Dec.   27, 1781. John Farrar and Sarah Harris.

Jan.   11, 1788. Rowling Pointer and Rebecca Walker.

Dec.   4, 1781. Larner Bradshaw and Ann Bradshaw.

Sept.   17, 1784. Isham Railey, of Chesterfield County, and
Susanna, dau. of John Woodson.

April   8. 1785. Richard Johnson and Milly Walker.

Aug.	19, 1782.	Isaac Pleasants and Jane Pleasants.
Sept.	15. 1788.	Reuben Cosby and Lucy Alvis.
Dec.	20, 1784.	Stephen Southall and Martha Wood.
Dec.	20, 1784.	Archibald Riddle and Frances Massie.
Dec.	30, 1780.	Nathaniel Moss and Joanna Johnson.
June	16, 1788.	David Hudson and Mary Clopton.
Dec.	24, 1785.	William Brown and Isabel Herndon.
Feb.	17, 1783.	Charles Johnson, Jr., and Mary Ann Farrar.
March	25, 1789.	Newton Curd and Elizabeth, dau. of Thomas Hatcher.
Oct.	21, 1788.	Benjamin Colvard and Mary George.
June	16. 1788.	Peter Johnson and Mary Wood.
Feb.	4, 1783.	Stephen Mayo and Ann Isbell.
March	18, 1789.	Turner Clarke, Jr., and Eliza Ann Cragball.
Nov.	25, 1785.	Peter Walker and Elizabeth Ellis.
April	21, 1783.	Patrick Vaughan and Mary Smith.
Nov.	25, 1785.	Thomas Pankey and Martha Cannon.
March	8, 1785.	Thomas Poor and Frances Matthews.
Jan.	12, 1788.	Charles F. Payne and Polly, dau. of Thomas Adams.
Oct.	29, 1784.	William Stark and Elizabeth Kernear.
May	16, 1785.	Samuel Proffit and Molly Massie.
Nov.	5, 1783.	Abraham Pruett and Ann Davison.
Oct.	25, 1785.	John Davis and Nancy Walmack.
Oct.	15, 1784.	Robert Pleasant, Jr., and Elizabeth, dau. of Thomas M. Randolph.
Dec.	11, 1785.	Obediah Pruett and Frances Jarrett.
Nov.	12, 1783.	Hughes Bowles and Mary Shipp.
Nov.	15, 1783.	John Kesher and Sarah Parrish.
Dec.	20, 1784.	Benjamin Johnson and Rachael Pace.
Dec.	27, 1784.	Shadrach Alvis and Judith Hancock.
Feb.	15, 1785.	Charles Rodes and Jane Hopkins.
Aug.	19, 1782.	Robert Farrar and Fanny Woodson.
Oct.	11, 1785.	John Saunders and Anne Cawthorn.
July	22, 1789.	Joseph Walker and Susannah, dau. of Ellender Willis.

July   31, 1787. George Walker and Eliza Green.
July   19, 1784. Perrin Redford and Susanna Woodson.
Dec.   24, 1784. Martin Palmer and Elizabeth, dau. of William Powers.
Oct.   23, 1785. Edward Hutchens and Nancy Clements.
Aug.   15, 1785. William Poore and Judith Sampson.
July   4, 1788. William Hatcher and Jane L. Mayo.
Oct.   17, 1783. William Redford and Susanna Ellis.
Dec.   18, 1782. Matthew Nightingale and Judith Perkins.
April   16, 1784. Howell Lewis to Anne, dau. of John Bolling.
Aug.   30, 1781. David Mullins and Rosanna Herndon.
March   17, 1782. David Mitchell and Betsy Cosby.
Sept.   28, 1785. Joseph Green and Lydia Wood.
Oct.   17, 1784. David Nowlin and Ann, dau. of William Powell.
Feb.   19, 1786. John, son of Randall Rountree, and Lucy, dau. of John Gordon.
Feb.   7, 1787. Robert Poor and Eliza. Mimms.
May   29, 1787. Isaac Robinson and Elizabeth Wingfield.
Oct.   30, 1787. Robert Scott and Tabitha Hopper.
Sept.   23, 1786. William Anderson and Martha Hancock.
Aug.   21, 1786. Daniel Trabue and Elizabeth Farrar.
May   10, 1786. Robert Lewis, Jr., and Mary G., dau. of Archibald Brice.
Sept.   29, 1786. Nathaniel Parrish and Martha Clarkson.
June   18, 1787. William Martin and Ann Green.
Dec.   18, 1786. Meredith Parrish and Eliza Curtis.
Nov.   17, 1786. Jesse Holbrook and Susanna Meanley.
May   7, 1787. William Richards and Judith Martin.
June   15, 1786. Gwathney Dabney and Elizabeth, dau. of James Maddox.
Jan.   10, 1786. Burwell Baugh and Betsy Neves.
Dec.   12, 1786. Thomas Railey and Martha Woodson.
July   8, 1786. George Dromwright and Eliza Riddle.
Oct.   2, 1786. Mitchell Martin and Jennie Clark.
Nov.   27, 1787. David Carroll and Sally Carroll.

Oct.	24, 1787.	Matthew Johnson and Mary Mantle.
May	14, 1787.	Smith Payne and Margaret B. Payne.
June	9, 1787.	Francis Blankenship and Polly Woolbanks.
May	7, 1787.	Richard McCary and Nancy Martin.
Aug.	16, 1786.	Nicholas Crutchfield and Sarah Williams.
July	4, 1786.	Moses Hicks and Eliza Johnson.
Dec.	17, 1787.	Stephen Mallory and Mary Banks.
Jan.	30, 1787.	Jesse Clark and Lucy Willis.
Oct.	9, 1787.	Daniel McCoy and Jane Parrish.
Dec.	13, 1787.	Thomas Bernard and Elizabeth, dau. of John Laprade.
Dec.	8, 1785.	Robert Bradshaw and Mary Bradshaw.
Jan.	23, 1785.	John Smither and Agatha, dau. of Agatha Payne.
Dec.	15, 1783.	William Saunders and Sally Crow.
Nov.	15, 1784.	Lewis Shandoin and Kitty Mimms.
Sept.	26, 1780.	William Lee of Northumberland and Jane, dau. of John Payne.
March	17, 1782.	Nathaniel Harris and Mary Howard.
Oct.	16, 1780.	Anderson Peers and Judith, dau. of John Laprade.
July	3, 1788.	John Lee and Jane Tuggle.
Oct.	26, 1785.	William Williams and Canadace Meeks.
April	28, 1780.	Howell Lewis, son of Howell Lewis, of Granville Co., No. Carolina, who certifies him to be 21 years 2 April, 1780, and Betsy Coleman.
Dec.	18, 1788.	Edward Willis and Susanna Smith.
April	8, 1783.	Peter Walker and Elenor Clarke.
April	15, 1785.	Johnson Hodges and Eliza, dau. of Willoughby Mulles.
Dec.	18, 1780.	David Jarratt and Anna Wade.
Nov.	21, 1785.	Baxter Folkes and Susanna Weber.

NORFOLK COUNTY MARRIAGE BONDS.

Dec.	7,	1756.	Ashbury Sutton and Mary Burdess.
Jan.	5,	1757.	Doctor John Ramsay and Mary Hutchings.
Jan.	13,	1757.	Saunders Calvert and Frances Tucker.
Jan.	20,	1757.	Willis Dyson and Mary Conner.
April	27,	1757.	Colonel Edwd. Hack Moseley and Frances Wyllie.
Sept.	3,	1757.	Captain John Marnex and Jemima Garroway.
Oct.	11,	1757.	Charles Roff Gardner and Elizabeth Rothery.
Nov.	13,	1757.	John Sheales Gwin and Elizabeth Lowry.
Jan.	19,	1758.	Hillarey Herbert and Jane Miles.
Jan.	19,	1758.	William Chisholm and Sarah Kinner.
Feb.	4,	1758.	Nathl. Fife and Elizabeth Richards.
Feb.	14,	1758.	John Whiddon and Mary Corprew.
Feb.	25,	1758.	James Esthor and Elizabeth Hiley.
April	8,	1758.	Samuel Bacon and Mary Dale.
April	11,	1758.	Lancaster Fentress and Mary Etheredge.
May	7,	1758.	Arch. Taylor and Louisa Richards.
June	1,	1758.	Nathl. Newton Mason and Ann Snale.
June	3,	1758.	Robert Waller and Mazias Wilson.
June	14,	1758.	John Morehouse and Edith Moseley.
June	29,	1758.	Anthony Lawson and Mary Calvert.
July	6,	1758.	Samuel Galt and Sarah Jefferies.
July	22,	1758.	William Kays and Elizabeth Dale.
Aug.	21,	1758.	William Moore and Betsy Bird.
Sept.	18.	1758.	Francis Williamson and Martha Mathias.
Sept.	29,	1758.	James Murphree and Elizabeth Bratt.
Oct.	12,	1758.	Nathl. Godfrey and Elizabeth Wakefield.
Dec.	15,	1758.	William Scott and Prudence Dale.
Jan.	7,	1759.	Butts Roberts and Sarah Church.
Jan.	20,	1759.	John Sutherland and Eliz., dau. of Thomas Herbert.
Jan.	20,	1759.	Henry Smith and Sarah Miller.
Jan.	25,	1759.	Goodrich Boush and Mary Wilson.
Feb.	22,	1759.	John Milliner and Jane Robinson.

March	29, 1759.	James Robe and Elizabeth Gordon.
April	11, 1759.	Malcom Bowie and Barbara Munro.
April	13, 1759.	Thos. Claiborne and Uphan, dau. of Charles Sweny.
April	23, 1759.	William Evens and Mary Keaton.
April	28, 1759.	Samuel Denbey and Monica Williams.
May	7, 1759.	John Hurt and Mary Ivy.
July	14, 1759.	Captain George Gordon and Martha Moseley.
Aug.	16, 1759.	John Cheshire, Jr., and Mary Miller.
Oct.	4, 1759.	Captain John Kelso and Margaret Williamson.
Oct.	11, 1759.	Josiah Smith and Frances Wilson.
Oct.	18, 1759.	George Webb and Frances Ashley.
Oct.	20, 1759.	Paul Watlington and Jane Bickerdick.
Dec.	30, 1759.	Captain Samuel Southerland and Ann Watkins.
Dec.	31, 1759.	James Hall and Mary Robe.
Jan.	3, 1760.	John Williamson and Prudence Williamson.
Jan.	4, 1760.	Josias Slack and Mary Warden.
Jan.	8, 1760.	Severn Eyre and Margaret Taylor.
Jan.	29, 1760.	William Nicholson and Mary, dau. of W. Shields.
Feb.	2, 1760.	Abram Wormington and Mary Portlock.
Feb.	9, 1760.	Daniel Rothery and Ann Rothery.
April	10, 1760.	Joseph Hodges, Jr., and Ann Balentine.
April	15, 1760.	Joshua White and Lydia, dau. of Patrick White.
April	27, 1760.	Samuel Happer and Mary Porter.
May	22, 1760.	William Jones and Mary Dades.
May	31, 1760.	John Woodside and Jane Bird.
June	4, 1760.	John Ivy, Jr., and Elizabeth Nash.
June	14, 1760.	John Emerson and Dinah Williams.
June	29, 1760.	John Hodges and Lydia Thomas.
July	15, 1760.	William Calvert and Ann Barlow.
July	16, 1760.	John Runsberg and Rebecca Pearson.

Aug.	29, 1760.	Jonathan Dison and Sarah, dau. of William Talbot.
Sept.	12, 1760.	Thos. Simpson and Ann, dau. of Daniel Dale.
Oct.	19, 1760.	Samuel Langley and Elizabeth Lewelling.
Nov.	29, 1760.	Nathl. Denby and Elizabeth Langley.
Dec.	4, 1760.	John Dunn and Sarah Weatheradge.
Dec.	4, 1760.	Joseph Hutchings and Sarah Smith.
Dec.	29, 1760.	John Wilson and Mary Happer.
Dec.	29, 1760.	Thomas Burges and Amy White.
March	19, 1761.	Stephen Wright and Ann Phripp.
April	15, 1761.	Jacob Taylor and Alice Smith.
April	24, 1761.	Jacob Nimmo and Frances White.
May	10, 1761.	Thomas Carter and Mary Carter.
May	15, 1761.	Jacob Acworth and Susannah Hensley.
May	17, 1761.	George Logan and Isabella Campbell.
May	20, 1761.	John Lindsay and Jane Drummond.
May	23, 1761.	Captain Anthony Moseley and Dinah Scott.
June	4, 1761.	George Veale, Jr., and Mary Morgan.
July	1, 1761.	Thomas Applewhaite and Mary Archer.
July	24, 1761.	Francis Williamson and Kezia Mathias.
Aug.	31, 1761.	Thomas Phillips and Margaret Hughs.
Sept.	5, 1761.	Edward Archer and Dinah Belgrove.
Sept.	8, 1761.	Neil Jamieson and Fernelia Ellegood.
Sept.	10, 1761.	Richard Cheshire and Dinah Miller.
Sept.	23, 1761.	James Rae and Abigail Conner, dau. of Wm. Conner.
Sept.	26, 1761.	John Hutton and Margaret Boyd.
Oct.	29, 1761.	James Ramsay and Ann Ballard.
Dec.	8, 1761.	Peter Edwards and Mary Portlock.
Dec.	19, 1761.	Peter Nolley Ellegood and Mary Thelaball.
Dec.	20, 1761.	Robert Bignall and Peggy Parrish.
Feb.	13, 1762.	Alexander Bruce and Elizabeth Curle, widow.
March	12, 1762.	Alexander Kincaid and Martha Brodie.
April	17, 1762.	Charles Smith and Elizabeth, dau. of Richard Joliff.

April	22, 1762.	Joshua Wilkins and Lydia, dau. of Philip Northern.
April	26, 1762.	John Godfrey and Ruth Weldon.
May	8, 1762.	Christopher Thompson and Margaret Ritch, widow.
May	13, 1762.	John Smith and Penelope Talbutt.
May	20, 1762.	Richard Gurley and Mary Hamilton.
June	1, 1762.	Captain Hugh Brown and Rhodah Morgan.
June	12, 1762.	Florence McNamara and Sarah Brodie.
July	26, 1762.	Southward Simmons and Martha, dau. of John Wallis.
July	29, 1762.	James Ashley and Mary Calvert.
Aug.	4, 1762.	John, son of James Pasteur, and Abi Ballentine.
Aug.	27, 1762.	Joshua Nicholson and Patience Porter.
Sept.	2, 1762.	Philip Carbery and Sarah Galt.
Oct.	27, 1762.	Christopher Calvert and Peggy Boush.
Nov.	4, 1762.	Solomon Smith and Prudence Wilson.
Nov.	12, 1762.	Moses Manning and Lydia Smith.
Nov.	17, 1762.	Gawin Corbin and Joanna, dau. of Robert Tucker.
Nov.	26, 1762.	Thomas Knight and Ann ————.
Dec.	6, 1762.	George Lathbury and ———— Baker.
Dec.	16, 1762.	Ebrander Thomson and Mary Ross.
Jan.	10, 1763.	Samuel Wise and Mary, dau. of Margaret McNeil and John Blackburn.
Jan.	13, 1763.	Christopher Bustin and Elizabeth Dunn.
Jan.	20, 1763.	Saunders Colley and Honour McCloud, widow.
Jan.	20, 1763.	———— Thompson and Prudence Scott, widow.
Feb.	7, 1763.	Captain John Sutherland and Celia Brickell.
Feb.	8, 1763.	Arthur Boush and Ann Sweny, dau. of Charles Sweny.
Feb.	27, 1763.	Daniel Gwyn and Mary Janes, widow.
March	19, 1763.	John Johnson and Frances Lewelling.
April	2, 1763.	Andrew Lush and Sarah Cooper, widow.

April	4, 1763.	Matthew Rothery and Mary, dau. of William Orange.
April	18, 1763.	Charles Butler and Jane Dison.
April	23, 1763.	William Copeland and Maren Porter.
April	23, 1763.	John Connor and Elizabeth Jening.
April	28, 1763.	Alexander Taylor and Elizabeth Sparrow.
April	28, 1763.	John Ashley and Margaret Williamson.
May	2, 1763.	James Bird and Diana Saunders.
June	8, 1763.	Robert Thompson and Isabel Franks.
Aug.	4, 1763.	Edward Good and Ann Avery, born March 4, 1742, dau. of James and Mary Avery.
Aug.	4, 1763.	John McCarthy and Mary, dau. of James and Mary Avery, born Aug. 11, 1740.
Sept.	14, 1763.	Captain Thomas Snale and Elizabeth, dau. of Wm. Ivy, Sr.
Nov.	13, 1763.	Daniel Leech and Ann Rogers.
Nov.	15, 1763.	Captain Thomas Veale and Bathiah Edwards.
Dec.	3, 1763.	William Lane and Courtney Prata.
Jan.	24, 1764.	John Wills and Ann Childers.
Jan.	26, 1764.	John Ardis and Louisa Taylor, widow.
Feb.	11, 1764.	William M. Caa and Sarah Brough.
March	29, 1764.	Samuel Meade and Elizabeth McCurdy.
April	7, 1764.	John Corprew and Sarah Smith.
April	9, 1764.	Irby Bressie and Ann Ivy.
May	2, 1764.	James Brown and Mary Walker.
May	5, 1764.	Doctor Alexander Gordon and Sarah Alexander.
May	24, 1764.	John Streip and Margaret Kingston.
June	14, 1764.	Henry Rothery and Mrs. Mary Godfrey.
June	21, 1764,	Robert Dallas and Mrs. Sarah Camack.
June	27, 1764.	Anthony Fleming and Mary Portlock.
July	4, 1764.	Samuel Calvert, son of Cornelius Calvert, decd., and Peggy Ross.

ORANGE COUNTY MARRIAGE BONDS.

June 4, 1778. William Watts and Elizabeth Beazley. Security—John Beazley.

Dec. 12, 1775. Ambrose Medley and Frankey Burton. Security—May Burton, Jr.

Jan. 9, 1779. Thomas Stapp and Betsey Burbage. Security—Joel Stodghill.

June 9, 1775. William Strother and Anne Kavenah, widow. Security—William Cave.

Aug. 14, 1775. George Stubblefield and Sarah Morrison. Consent of Richard and Catherine Reynolds to marriage of their daughter. Security—Joseph Spencer.

Aug. 24, 1778. Richard Reynolds and Ann Roach, widow. Security—Thomas Farish.

Oct. 13, 1778. Rodes Thomson and Sally Vivian. Consent of her father John Vivian. Security—Nathl. Mills.

April 3, 1778. William Thomas and Elizabeth Woolfork. Consent of her father John Woolfork. Security—Robert Thomas.

Sept. 3, 1779. William Quarles and Frances Vivian, Consent of father John Vivian. Security—Nathl. Mills.

May 9, 1778. Thomas Gilbert and Ann Farneyho. Consent of her father Thomas Farneyho. Security—James Taylor.

July 25, 1776. John Daniel and Lucy Mary Marshall. Security—Thomas Bell.

Jan. 28, 1779. James Chiles and Jennie Saied. Security—John Leather.

Nov. 20, 1776. John Conner and Lucy Daniel, dau. of Reuben Daniel. Security—James Taylor, Jr.

Jan. 19, 1779. James Burton and Mary White. Consent of her father Jeremiah White; witnessed by John and Richard White. Security—Francis Taylor.

Nov.   8, 1779.   Garland Burnley and Frances Taylor. Security—Robt. Taylor.

Feb.   9, 1778.   John Adkins and Ann Burras. Consent of father Edmond Burras. Security—Joseph Adkins.

March 29, 1781.   William Young and Mildred Douglas. Security—Edmund Massey.

March 22, 1781.   Joseph Woods and Margaret Bell, consent of mother Mary Bell. Security—James Taylor.

April 20, 1781.   Moses Willis and Elizabeth Thomas. Consent of father Joseph Thomas. Security—Joseph Boston.

Oct.   25, 1781.   Absolom Smith and Lester Chandler. Consent of father Joseph Chandler. Security—Edward Dean.

Feb.   13, 1781.   Reuben Scott and Margaret Cope. Security—Lewis Cope.

April 17, 1780.   Richard Parker and Hannah Cave, dau. of William Cave. Security — Rowland Thomas.

Aug.   24, 1781.   James Olive and Susannah Minor. Security—Nathl. Mothershead.

Aug.   11, 1781.   Nathaniel Mothershead and Ruthey Birt. Consent of father Moses Birt.

April 10, 1781.   William Moore and Betsey Johnson Grymes. Security—Ludwell Grymes.

Dec.   24, 1781.   Henry Mallory and Lucy Long, widow. Security—John Dear.

Dec.   18, 1781.   John Lee (Major) and Elizabeth Bell, dau. of Thos. Bell. Security—Ambrose Madison.

April 19, 1781.   John Herndon and Elizabeth Wright. Consent of father John Wright. Security—Wm. Wright.

March 22, 1781. John Gully and Mary Laud. Consent of father John Laud. Security—Enoch Gully.

June 28, 1781. Thomas Coleman and Susannah Hawkins. Security—James Taylor.

May 24, 1781. Edward Collins and Ann Collins. Security —James Coleman.

April 7, 1781. Benjamin Adams and Nelly Coleman. Security—Lau. Egbert.

May 16, 1780. Henry Wood and Mary Weatherspoon. Security—James Taylor, Jr.

June 28, 1780. John Tomlinson and Mildred White. Consent of father John White. Security—Wm. White, son of John.

Nov. 23, 1780. William Terrell and Ann Daniel. Security —James Taylor.

Oct. 31, 1781. Nicholas Taliaferro and Ann Taliaferro. Consent of Ann Taliaferro. Security—Francis Taliaferro.

April 27, 1780. John Rucker and Betsey Tinsley. Consent of father John Tinsley. Security—James Rucker.

April 27, 1780. Thomas Loyd and Sally Gresham, widow. Security—John Loyd.

Nov. 20, 1780. William Linney and Ann Burras, widow. Security—William Luke.

Oct. 3, 1781. William Lindsey and Nancy Shepherd. Security—Wm. Crickman.

Nov. 2, 1780. Robert Lancester and Lucy Dean. Consent of father John Dean. Security—John Dean, Jr.

Aug. 21, 1780. Spencer James and Frances Davis. Security—Philemon Davis.

—— — —— Azariah King and Mary Abell. Security— Caleb Abell.

Dec.   4, 1780.   John Hinshaw and Patty Newman. Consent of father Jas. Newman. Security—William Newman.

Oct.   28, 1780.   John Hawkins and Mary Gaines, widow. Security—Aurelia Hawkins.

Nov.   15, 1780.   Thomas Garnet and Sukey Brockman. Consent of father Daniel Brockman. Security—Adam Linsay.

Nov.   1, 1780.   James Davis and Mary Johnson. Security —John Bell.

Jan.   25, 1780.   Edmund Adkins and Frankey Wisdom. Security—Jos. Adkins.

Nov.   9, 1779.   Major Brockman and Mary Paterson. Consent of parents Turner and Susannah Paterson. Security—Sam. Brockman.

Dec.   27, 1779.   Julius Gibbs and Aggy Davis. Consent of father Joseph Davis. Security—James Davis.

Oct.   30, 1780.   John Blakey and Sarah Cowherd. Consent of father Jonathan Cowherd. Security—James Cowherd.

April   14, 1780.   James Coleman and Sarah Taylor. Security—Moses Hayes.

May   16, 1782.   James Adams and Mary Chambers. Consent of father Thomas Chambers. Security—Geo. Bledsoe.

Feb.   6, 1782.   John Cox and Mary Bryson. Security— John Ball.

March 13, 1782.   Francis Dade and Sarah Taliaferro. Consent of father Lawrence Taliaferro. Security—Hay Taliaferro.

March 23, 1782.   Philip Eastin and Elizabeth Henderson. Consent of Alexander Henderson, the father. Security—William Timkins.

Dec.   5, 1782.   Jacob Furnis and Mary Page. Consent of father John Page. Security—William Glass.

VIRGINIA REVOLUTIONARY SOLDIERS.

(Cont'd from page 61)

Royal, Francis, Private, State Artillery, 3 years' service.

Hunney, Calis, Private, Va. Cavalry, 3 years' service.

Eubank, Royal, Private, Va. Cavalry, 3 years' service.

Lightfoot, Philip, Corporal, State Line, 3 years' service.

Mead, Richard Kidder, Lieut.-Col., Va. Line, 3 years' service.

Spence, Hy., Private, Contl. Line, 3 years' service.

Brown, Thos., Drum Major, Contl. Line, 7 years ending 17 Feb., 1783.

Daugherty, Patk., Private, Contl. Line, 3 years ending 26 Feb., 1783.

French, Thos., Private, Contl. Line, 3 years ending Dec., 1781.

Williams, Geo., Private, Contl. Line, 3 years ending Oct. 1779.

Glass, Isaac, Private, Contl. Line, 3 years ending March, 1783.

Farrell, John, Drummer, Contl. Line, 3 years ending Sept., 1781.

Williams, John, Sgt., Contl. Line, 3 years ending March, 1783.

Brent, John, Private, Contl. Line, 3 years ending Aug., 1779.

Headen, Anthony, Private, Contl. Line, 3 years ending Feb., 1782.

Warner, John, Musician, Contl. Line, 3 years ending Feb., 1783.

Marshall, Hy., Sgt., Contl. Line, 3 years ending April 1, 1782.

Campbell, Archibald, Private, Contl. Line, 3 years ending Sept., 1781.

Mahoney, Joseph, Private, Contl. Line, 3 years ending May, 1780.

Anderson, Jas., Private, Contl. Line, 3 years ending March, 1783.

Sublett, Benj., Sgt., Contl. Line, 3 years' service.

Merryman, Francis, Private, Contl. Line, 3 years' service.

Andrews, Claiborne, Private, Contl. Line, 3 years' service.

Cumbo Danl., Private, Contl. Line, 3 years' service.

Powell, Robt., Capt., Contl. Line, 3 years' service.

Pearson, Thos., Lieut., Contl. Line, 3 years' service.

Ball, Bengers, Lieut.-Col., military service 10 Feb., 1776, to
May, 1783.
Halfpenny, John, Private, Contl. Line, 3 years' service.
Stokes, Robert, Private, Contl. Line, 3 years' service.
Sparks, Saml., Private, Contl. Line, 3 years' service.
Buckley, Joshua, Private, Contl. Line, 3 years' service.
Death, Wm., Sgt.-Major, Contl. Line, 3 years' service.
Dean, Michael, Private, Contl. Line, 3 years' service.
Dean, Joseph, Private, Contl. Line, 3 years' service.
Gassaway, Jas., Private, Contl. Line, 3 years' service.
Stotherd, Thos., Private, Contl. Line, 3 years' service.
Clavenger, Edwin, Private, Contl. Line, 3 years' service.
Green, John, Private, Contl. Line, 3 years' service.
Veal, Solomon, Sgt., Contl. Line, 3 years' service.
Flaugherty, Jas., Sgt., Contl. Line, 3 years' service.
Jenkins, Wm., Sgt., Contl. Line, 3 years' service.
McNolly, Michel, Private, Contl. Line, 3 years' service.
Tapp, Venet, Private, Contl. Line, 3 years' service.
Kelly, John, Private, Contl. Line, 3 years' service.
Jacobs, Roley, Private, Contl. Line, 3 years' service.
Beeks, Christopher, Private, Contl. Line, 3 years' service.
Tolin, Elias, Sgt., Contl. Line, 3 years' service.
Chapman, Thos., Private, Contl. Line, 3 years' service.
Bell, John, Private, Contl. Line, 3 years' service.
Knight, Jas., Private, Contl. Line, 3 years' service.
Buckley, Abraham, Private, Contl. Line, 3 years' service.
Smith, Geo., Private, Contl. Line, 3 years' service.
Brown, Absolom, Private, Contl. Line, 3 years' service.
Casell, Wm., Private, Contl. Line, 3 years' service.
Stump, Michell, Private, Contl. Line, 3 years' service.
Mead, John, Private, Contl. Line, 3 years' service.
Jacobs, Wm., Private, Contl. Line, 3 years' service.
Glass, Hugh, Private, Contl. Line, 3 years' service.
Nevill, John, Col., served in army from August, 1775, to June
25, 1783.
Vance, Joseph, Private, Contl. Line, 3 years' service.
Thompson, Jas., Private, Contl. Line, 3 years' service.

Mardis, Wm., Private, Contl. Line, 3 years' service.
Hicks, Wm., Private, Contl. Line, 3 years' service.
Hall, Thos., Sgt., Contl. Line, 3 years' service.
Ray, David, Private, Contl. Line, 3 years' service.
France, Peter, Private, Contl. Line, 3 years' service.
Brown, Isaac, Sgt., Contl. Line, 3 years' service.
Black, Geo., Private, Contl. Line, 3 years' service.
Botts, Archibald, Sgt., Contl. Line, 3 years' service.
Bogert, Cornelius, Private, Contl. Line, 3 years' service.
Kingore, Wm., Private, Contl. Line, 3 years' service.
Sollers, Wm., Private, Contl. Line, 3 years' service.
Cosse, Wm., Private, Contl. Line, 3 years' service.
Wafield, Geo., Private, Contl. Line, 3 years' service.
Crawford, John, Sgt., Contl. Line, 3 years' service.
Smith, John, Private, Contl. Line, 3 years' service.
Dollar, Wm., Private, Contl. Line, 3 years' service.
Johnson Moses, Private, Contl. Line, 3 years' service.
Gassaway, John, Private, Contl. Line, 3 years' service.
Haines, Peter, Private, Contl. Line, 3 years' service.
Ashby, Thos., Private, Contl. Line, 3 years' service.
Demsey, John, Private, Contl. Line, 3 years' service.
Lahaw, Jeremiah, Private, Contl. Line, 3 years' service.
Blair, Robert, Private, Contl. Line, 3 years' service. .
Grove, Anthony, Private, Contl. Line, 3 years' service.
Tomlin, Jno., Private, Contl. Line, 3 years' service.
Anderson, Danl., Private, Contl. Line, 3 years' service.
Boush, Dennis, Private, Contl. Line, 3 years' service.
Drake, Andw., Private, Contl. Line, 3 years' service.
Berkley, Wm., Private, Contl. Line, 3 years' service.
Musgrove, Wm., Private, Contl. Line, 3 years' service.
Anderson, John, Private, Contl. Line, 3 years' service.
Gray, Benj., Private, Contl. Line, 3 years' service.
Lahaw, David, Private, Contl. Line, 3 years' service.
Johnston, John, Private, Contl. Line, 3 years' service.
Murdock, Joseph, Private, Contl. Line, 3 years' service.
Ginoman, Hy., Private, Contl. Line, 3 years' service.
Bushop, Solomon, Private, Contl. Line, 3 years' service.

McKnight, Wm., Private, Contl. Line, 3 years' service.
Ragor, Barth., Private, Contl. Line, 3 years' service.
Rumage, David, Private, Contl. Line, 3 years' service.
France, Lewis, Private, Contl. Line, 3 years' service.
Oram, Hy., Private, Contl. Line, 3 years' service.
Finley, Archibald, Private, Contl. Line, 3 years' service.
Waller, Wm., Private, Contl. Line, 3 years' service.
Polock, Thos., Private, Contl. Line, 3 years' service.
Gibbs, Wm., Private, Contl. Line, 3 years' service.
Hartford, Wm., Sgt., Contl. Line, 3 years' service.
Giles, Jas., Private, Contl. Line 3 years' service.
Musgrove, Wm., Corporal, Contl. Line, 3 years' service.
Powle, Wm., Private, Va. Artillery, 3 years' service.
Cary, Saul, Lieut., State Line, 3 years' service.
Brooks, Walter, Commodore, Va. State Navy, 3 years' service.
Smith, Francis, Fifer, State Line, 3 years' service.
Dodd, Wm., Private, State Line, 3 years' service.
Casey, Robt., Private, State Artillery, 3 years' service.
Cropper, John, Lieut.-Col., State Line, 3 years' service.
Stribling, Sigismund, Capt., Contl. Line, 7 years ending Aug.,
    1782.
Howard, Robt., Private, Contl. Line, 3 years' service.
Solloman, Geo., Private, Contl. Line, 3 years' service.
Mitchel, Thos., Private, Contl. Line, 3 years' service.
Morgan, Brig.-Gen., additional quantity of land for 8 years'
    service, June 21, 1783.
Fautz, Valentine, Private, Contl. Line, 3 years' service.
Simmons, Bryan, Private, Contl. Line, 3 years' service.
Waggoner, Andrew, Major, Contl. Line, July, 1775, to May,
    1783.
Wallace, Jas., Dr., Surgeon, Contl. Line, 3 years ending Aug.,
    1779.
Grayson, Wm., Col., Contl. Line, 3 years' service.
Mallory, John, Sgt., decd., Contl. Line; warrant to Peter
    Mallory.
Crittenden, John, Lieut., Contl. Line, 3 years' service.
Hood, John, Private, Va. Cavalry, 3 years' service.

Russell, Jas., Sgt., Va. Artillery, 3 years' service.
Bouton, Richd., Corporal, Va. Artillery, 3 years' service.
Lawson, Andw., Private, State Line, 3 years' service.
Taylor, Benj., Midshipman, State Navy, 3 years' service.
Parker, Wm. Harvey, Lieut., State Navy, 3 years' service.
Dunbar, Jas., Sgt., Contl. Line, 3 years' service.
Murphy, John, Private, Contl. Line, 3 years' service.
Wright, Thos., Private, Contl. Line, 3 years' service.
Murphy, Owen, Private, Contl. Line, 3 years' service.
Parsons, Thos., Private, Contl. Line, 3 years' service.
McKenny, John, Private, Contl. Line, 3 years' service.
Young, Nathan, Sgt., Contl. Line, 3 years' service.
Anderson, Hy., Private, Contl. Line, 3 years' service.
Shores, Thos., Private, Contl. Line, 3 years' service.
Smock, Jacob, Sgt., Contl. Line, 3 years' service.
Crawford, John, Private, Contl. Line, 3 years' service.
Shannon, P'tk., Sgt., Contl. Line, 3 years' service.
McMeans, Wm., Private, Contl. Line, 3 years' service.
Chinworth, John, Private, Contl. Line, 3 years' service.
Lindsey, Hezekiah, Private, Contl. Line, 3 years' service.
Bruce, John, Sgt., Contl. Line, 3 years' service.
Edmondson, Wm., Sgt., Contl. Line, 3 years' service.
Bowen, Hy., Sgt., Contl. Line, 3 years' service.
Porter, Elisha, Private, Contl. Line, 3 years' service.
Willis, Hy., Capt., Va. Cavalry, 3 years' service.
Brough, Wm., sailor, State Navy.

Return of Capt. Springers Co., in the Va. Line, Who
Listed During the War.

Wood, Thos., Sgt. Major	Coxon, Wm., Fifer
Williams, John, Sgt.	Hend (or Hinds) Fifer
Tannehill, Thos., Sgt.	Crawford, Robert, Private
Harfield, Thos., Sgt.	Lockhart, John, Private
Adams, Jas., Corporal	Cavernear, Garret, Private
Hagerly, Nich., Corporal	Fennegan, Pat, Private
Smith, John, Drummer	Gowrin, Benj., Private

Barry, Wm., Private
Britton, Jno., Private
Hainey, Michael, Private
Young, John, Private
Herbert, Wm., Private
Roach, Richd., Private
Phelps, Geo., Private
Carter, Rich., Private
Smith, Wm., Private
Reynolds, Jas., Private
Maines, Francis, Private
Cunningham, Jas., Private
McClean, Laughlin, Private
McDonald, Edwd., Private
Smith, Jas., Private
Moore, Thos., Private
McIntosh, Alex., Private
Henthorn, Philip, Private
Paul, Edwd., Private
Smith, Saml., Private
Saveall, Jas., Private
Conrad, Jacob, Private
Carter, Nich., Private

McKay, Eneas, Private
Vann, Hy., Private
Osburn, Saml., Private
Craig, Thos., Private
Duffey, Jas., Private
Gosset, John, Private
Brooks, Chas., Private
Kairns, Michael, Private
Sharrow, Rich., Private
Smith, Michael, Private
Carpenter, Christopher, Private
Finney, John, Private
McCartney, Peter, Private
Hurley, Matt., Private
Hansford, Wm., Private
Earlywine, Danl., Private
Craig, Wm., Private
Brooks, Benj., Private
Kulling, Jas., Private
Haley, Thos., Private
Bready, Jno., Private.
Brandon, Peter, Private

The above named Non-Com. officers and privates of the Va. Contl. Line enlisted for the war and served upwards of 3 years. Warrants issued June 24, 1783.

Ret. of Non-Com. Officers and Privates of Capt. Biggs Co., Va Line, Fort Pitt, in actual service.

Jas Lane, Q. M. Sgt.
Hull, John, Sgt.
Fazer, Alex., Sgt.
Ware, Moses, Sgt.
McElwin, Thos., Drummer
Overlin, Wm., Private
Barnett, Jno., Private
Riley, Jno., Private

Johnson, Jas., Private
Brute, Thos., Private
Violett, Jno., Private
Rooke, Jno., Private
English, Jno., Private
Phillips, Jno., Private
Robinson, Jno., Private
Orish, Jas., Private

Berry, Jno., Private

Bacon, Robt., Private

Fowler, Jos., Private

Doeherty, Jno., Private

Rucker, Jacob, Private

Sheat, (or Shea), John Private

Lennon, Saml., Private

Gillehan, Jno., Private

Parlen, Jas., Private

Cloyd, Wm., Private

Woods, Wm., Private

Beham, Jas., Private

Thornton, Pat, Private

Walker,—E., Private

Low, Jas., Private

Woodman, Jno., Private

Jackson, Thos., Private

Morgan, Chas., Private

Cordones, Jno., Private

Abbit, Reuben, Private

Brazen, Wm., Private

Robinson, Chas., Private

Conally, Wm., Private

Brumingham, Wm., Private

Jones, Thos., Private

Halfpenny, Isaac, Private

Stackpole, Jas., Private

Brean, Jno., Private

Winters, Stephen, Private

Morrison, Jno., Private

Guthrey, Jno., Private

Shephard, Edw., Private

Skinner, Hy., Private

Clark, David, Private

McCord, Saml., Private

Anderson, Jas., Private

Carr, Jas., Private

Cruswell, Saml., Private

Dennison, Joseph, Private

Welch, Jonathan, Private

Wood, Joseph, Private

Martin, Wm., Private

Murphy, Michael, Private

Adams, Jacob, Private

Crafford, Chas., Private

Richeson, John, Private

Devere, Jas., Private

The above named Non-Com. Officers and Privates of Va. Contl. Line having enlisted for the war and served upwards of three years are entitled to warrants of land for such service. June 24, 1783.

Draper, Geo. Dr., Reg. Surgeon, Contl. Line, 3 years' service.

Mercer, Hugh, Brig.-Genl., decd., 3 years' service. Warrant to Wm. Mercer, his heir, June 24, 1783.

Snead, Smith, Major, Contl. Line, 7 years' service.

Kerney, Jno., Capt., State Line, 3 years' service.

Greer, Chas., Surgeon, Va. Line, 3 years' service.

Dudley, Robt., Lieut., Contl. Line, 3 years' service.

Booker, Richeson, Sgt., Contl. Line, 3 years' service.
Hackett, John, Private, Contl. Line, 3 years' service.
Stubblefield, Geo., Ensign, decd., Contl. line, 3 years' ser--
vice. Benj. Stubblefield, his heir at law.
Atkins, Lewis, Private, Contl. Line., 7 years' service.
Barbour, Jas., Lieut., decd., Contl. Line, 3 years' service.
Mordecai Barbour, heir at law.
Massey, Thos., Major, Contl. Line, 3 years' service.
Gloucester, Jas., Private, Contl. Line, enlisted for the war.
Spruce, John, Private, Contl. Line, 3 years' service.
Cabbell, Saml. I., Lieut.-Col., Contl. Line, 7 years' service.
Jones, Zach., Private, Contl. Line, 3 years' service.
Aaron, Wm., Private, Contl. Line, 3 years' service.
Toler, Wm. Corporal, Va. Artillery, 3 years' service.
Carrick, Patk., Private, Contl. Line, enlisted for the war.
Guille, John, Private, Contl. Line, 3 years' service.
McLardy, Alex., Corporal, Contl. Line, 3 years' service.
Hurt, West, Private, Va. Cavalry, 3 years' service.
Merritt, Archelaus, Private, State Line, 3 years' service.
Coleman, Whitehead, Capt., Contl. Line, 3 years' service.
Miles, Wm., Private, Contl. Line, 3 years' service.
Kendrick, Danl., Private, Contl. Line, 3 years service.
McCue, Hy., Private, Contl. Line, 3 years' service.
Ballenger, John, Private, Contl. Line, 3 years' service.
Hutson, Wm., Private, Contl. Line, 3 years' service.
Mitchell, Mark, Private, Contl. Line, 3 years' service.
Carter, Hy., Private, Contl. Line, 3 years' service.
Button, Harmon, Private, Contl. Line, 3 years' service.
Miles, Jno., Private, Contl. Line, 3 years' service.
Pelham, John, Private, Contl. Line, 3 years' service.
Coons, Fdk., Private, Contl. Line, 3 years' service.
Catlett, Thos., Capt., Contl. Line, 3 years' service.
Lindsay, Wm. Capt., Va. Cavalry, 3 years' service.
Jones, Lewis, Lieut., State Navy, 3 years' service.
Jones, Lewis, Master's Mate, State Navy, 3 years' service.
Lightburn, Richd., Lieut., State Navy, 3 years' service.

Stubblefield, Beverly, Capt., Contl. Line, Feb. 10, 1776—
Jan. 1783.
Mitchell, Reaps, Sgt., Va. Line, 3 years' service.
Timberlake, Joseph, Private, Va. Line, 7 years' service.
Straughan, John, Private, Contl. Line, 3 years' service.
Arrington, Wm., Private, Va. Line, 3 years' service.
Brumley, Robt., Private, Va. Cavalry, 3 years' service.
Barbee, Jno., Corporal, Contl. Line., 3 years' service.
Barbee, Francis, Corporal, Contl. Line, 3 years' service.
Robion, Green, Private, State Line, 3 years' service.
Dulany, Thos., Private, State Line, 3 years' service.
Dyer, Saml., Private, Contl. Line, 3 years' service.
Carr, Wm., Private, State Line, 3 years' service.
Drury, Saml., Private, Contl. Line, 3 years' service.
Carrol, Joseph, Private, State Line, 3 years' service.
Murray, Wm., Private, State Line, 3 years' service.
Barron, Fielding, Private, Va. Artillery, 3 years' service.
Lyle, Chas., Private, Contl. Line, 3 years' service.
Britt, Jno., Private, State Line, 3 years' service.

Vol. VI   SEPTEMBER, 1909   Part 3

Virginia
County Records

PUBLISHED QUARTERLY

EDITED BY

William Armstrong Crozier, F. R. S., F. G. S. A.

Published by
The Genealogical Association
Hasbrouck Heights
New Jersey

Virginia County Records

Published Quarterly

CONTENTS

Virginia County Records

QUARTERLY MAGAZINE

VOL. VI.   SEPTEMBER 1909   No. 3

INDEX TO LAND GRANTS

CUMBERLAND COUNTY

Book No. 31.

Page	Name	Date	No. acres
11	Peter Jefferson and Thos. Turpin	1751	528
44	Geo. Wright	1751	1200
45	John Stevenson	1751	74
55	Philemon Childers, Jr.	1751	150
153	John Retterford	1752	237
300	Wm. Harrison	1752	787
302	Ezekiel Slaughter	1752	400
339	Wm. Megginson	1753	251
595	Ambrose Ransone	1755	120
623	Alex. Spiers	1755	195
731	James Anderson	1755	800
469	Creed Haskins	1755	400

Book No. 32.

Page	Name	Date	No. acres
374	Francis Dickens	1754	400
380	Wm. Mouat	1754	400
516	Orlando Hughes	1755	800
527	Micajah Mosby	1755	99
528	John Burton	1755	64
539	Thomas Davenport	1755	256
651	Richard Scruggs	1755	230
675	John Wayles	1756	500

675	John Wayles	1756	1000
709	Henry Harmon	1756	147

BOOK NO. 33.

13	Thomas Harris	1756	400
233	James Rea	1756	99
254	Charles Macceney	1756	124
350	Wm. Parry	1757	200
353	John Woodson	1757	250
573	John Ganaway	1759	1023
576	John Wayles	1759	3713
577	Wm. Duguid	1759	400
655	Benj. Sims	1759	233
739	Richd. Murray	1760	400
740	Richd. Murray	1760	400
831	Wm. Holland	1760	140
869	Thomas Williams	1760	535
899	Richard Bandy	1760	48
937	Wm. Daniel	1760	400
981	Francis Amos	1761	47
982	George Carrington	1761	89
1054	John Wayles	1761	400
1069	John Robinson	1761	290
1072	William Gates	1761	200
371	John Wayles	1757	254
692	William Dillon	1760	250

BOOK NO. 34

23	Robert Kent	1756	263
45	Wm. Arnold	1756	194
196	Robert Hudgens	1757	400
425	Joseph Hughes	1759	400
772	John Stevenson	1760	90
935	Thos. Davenport	1761	125
1049	Martin Burk	1762	100

BOOK NO. 35.

195.	John Bernard	1763	46

Book No. 36.

612	Wm. Edwards	1764	400
880	Gideon Patison	1765	200
1048	Joseph Calland	1767	68

Book No. 37.

204	Hamstead Ransone	1767	118
205	Hamstead Ransone	1767	125
217	Peter Field Trent	1767	400
319	Nicholas Davies	1768	100

Book No. 38.

728	Thomas Davenport, Jr.	1769	58
850	John Wright	1769	99

Book No. 39.

57	Samuel Pleasants	1770	60
399	Benj. Mosby	1771	400

Book No. 40.

652	John Chatwin	1772	22
673	Drury Woodson	1772	50

Book No. 41.

451	Zachariah Brown	1773	96

Book No. 42.

597	Wm. Davenport	1774	300
674	Jacob Michaux	1774	7½

Book A.

490	John Jefferson	1780	53
665	Richard Randolph	1780	34

Book L.

80	Abraham Daniel	1784	25¾

Book R.

483	John Woodson	1785	17

Book No. 16.

105	Francis Cox	1787	36

Book No. 28.

139   John W. Baird 1792   466

Book No. 35.

119   Mayo Carrington 1796   5

Book No. 39.

49   Henry Guthrey 1796   71 8-10

PRINCE GEORGE COUNTY

Book No. 9.

Page	Name	Date	No. acres
663	Benj. Evans	1705	300
676	Adam Heath	1705	681
705	Lewis Green	1705	97
711	Richd. Bland	1705	1254
714	Robt. Bolling	1706	1973
714	Robt. Mumford	1706	351
715	Jno. Anderson and Robt. Mumford......	1706	405
718	Richd. Bland	1706	43
740	Benj. Harrison, Jr.	1706	4583

Book No. 10.

40   John Sadler, citizen and grocer of London, and
    Rev. Joshua Richardson, clerk, husband of
    Ellinor Richardson, ex'crs. of Thos.
    Quincy 1711   2208

40	Same	1711	5037
51	Chas. Williams	1711	347
51	Wm. Rives	1711	422
52	Thos. Parrum	1711	153
66	Edwd. Goodrich	1712	100
77	Wm. Stainback	1712	200
125	Jas. Binford	1714	261
144	Jno. Scott	1714	221

157	Thos. Anderson	1714	105
178	John Nickells	1714	423
197	Robt. Rives	1714	219
198	Richd. Hudson	1714	401
198	Wm. Maise	16 Dec., 1714	401
198	Jno. Nicholls	16 Dec., 1714	217
198	Thos. Burge	16 Dec., 1714	196
199	Mrs. Frances Wynne	16 Dec., 1714	142
221	Jno. Evans	16 Dec., 1714	1001
222	Jno. Eaton	16 Dec., 1714	429
239	Nicholas Overly	16 Dec., 1714	964
241	Benj. Evins	1715	81
299	Jno. Leadbeter	1715	100
304	Joshua Prichard	1715	147
304	Wm. Gibbs	1715	82
309	Thos. Simmons	1715	299
309	Peter Wynne	1715	355
309	Nathl. Tatum, Sr.	1715	321
309	Danl. Malone	1715	99
315	John Freeman	1717	431
316	Abraham Heath	1717	151
319	Peter Lee	1717	112
320	Edwd. Woodlief	1717	80
320	Saml. Lee	1717	172
322	Nathl. Tatum, Jr.	1717	321
335	Richd. Dearden	1717	100
335	Jno. Stroud	1717	46
335	Robt. Abernathy	1717	100
335	Richd. Smith, Sr.	1717	370
336	Wm. Davis	1717	100
336	David Williams	1717	100
336	Thos. Wood	1717	199½
336	Hy. Michell, Jr.	1717	327
337	Thos. Hobbey	1717	198½
337	Thompson Stapley	1717	200
337	Thomas Parrum	1717	54
337	Richard Tally	1717	181

337	Thos. Clay	1717	100
338	Chas. Williams, Jr.	1717	197
338	Jno. Tucker	1717	200
338	Thos. Jones	1717	200
338	Thos. Jones	1717	247
338	Wm. Pettypoole	1717	65
338	Francis Coleman, Sr.	1717	333
339	John Ellington	1717	200
339	Wm. Coleman, Sr.	1717	100
339	Francis Tucker, Sr.	1717	289
339	Richard Smith, Sr.	1717	83
340	Robert Tucker	1717	141
340	Wm. Rives	1717	206
340	Jno. Tally	1717	300
341	Jno. Fountain and Robt. Wynn	1717	221
342	Wm. Caleb	1717	119
348	Shanes Raynes	1717	230
348	Thos. Michell	1717	250
349	Wm. Raines	1717	400
363	Jas. Baugh, Jr. and Henry Mayes	1717	284
366	Geo. Passmore and John Peterson	1717	225
367	Capt. John Evans	1717	175
400	Christopher Roberson	1718	115
401	Abraham Jones	1718	141
401	John Davis	1718	400
401	Wm. Anderson	1718	299
402	Wm. Westbrooke	1718	100
402	Matthew Mayes	1718	398½
402	Henry Mayes	1718	200
402	Joseph Tucker	1718	403
403	John Lewis	1718	251
403	Robt. Mumford	1718	592
403	Peter Michell, Jr.	1718	142
446	Robert Mumford	1718	390
446	Wm. Tucker	1718	143

(Continued)

RAPPAHANNOCK COUNTY

BOOK No. 4.

Page	Name	Date	No. acres
130	Chas. Snead	1657	883
155	Toby Smith	1657	1350
166	Clement Herbert	1657	500
167	Jas. Yeates	1657	600
182	Lt. Col. Hy. Fleete	1657	2000
226	Leonard Joanes	1657	200
232	Geo. Bryer	1657	400
233	Francis Brown	1657	370
235	Jno. Sherlock	1657	210
260	Jas. Baughan	1658	250
261	Francis Brown	1658	1100
267	Jno. Cox	1657	600
267	Robt. Young	1658	710
273	Anthony Haynes	1658	1000
275	Thos. Joanes	1658	1000
303	Jno. Stephens	1657	1000
332	Jas. Kenneygan and Jas. Foullerton	1658	458
344	Wm. Underwood	1658	882
344	Wm. Underwood, son of sd. Wm. Underwood	1658	2784
345	Robert Armstrong	1658	650
346	Robt. Linnee	1658	200
362	Thos. Robison, Francis Gower, Robert Sessen and Jno. Deyoung	1658	172
364	Anthony Stephens	1658	650
364	Jno. Williams	1658	1800
374	Jno. Barrow	1658	200
378	Rice Jones and Anthony Jackman	1658	1040
380	Geo. Morris and Wm. Lane	1662	2500
381	Henry Corbin	1662	4000
385	Leonard Jones	1662	200
386	Wm. Killman	1661	164
393	Robt. Thomas and Wm. Moss	1660	800

408	John Frumpton	1662	800
409	Saml. Griffin	1662	2200
412	Robt. Bayly	1661	300
413	Humphrey Booth	1661	1000
425	Margt. Brent	1662	1000
464	Walter Granger	1661	2000
472	Saml. Griffin	1660	1155
482	Thos. Payne and John Chinley	1663	3100
488	Thos. and Anthony Stephens	1662	1800
546	Alex. Fleming	1662	650
546	Jno. Catlett	1662	1850
548	Jno. Catlett	1662	792
572	Aug. Heath or Horth	1662	350
572	Wm. Harper	1662	150
573	Wm. Harper	1662	230
598	Wm. Underwood, son and heir of Col. Wm. Underwood, decd.	1662	2561½
597	Margt. and May Williamson	1662	882
601	John Sharpe	1664	840
602	John Miles	1663	500
604	Robert Davies	1664	448
604	John Smith	1663	473
606	Thos. Rason	1663	518
610	Geo. Marish	1664	420
612	Robt. Bayley	1663	250
615	Jas. Samford	1663-4	400
615	Miles Riley	1663	200
624	Jno. Cannida	1663	200
626	David Fox	1662	800
641	Rice Jones	1664	700

Book No. 5.

8	Paul Woodbridge	1664	800
8	Rich. Bridger	1664	400
10	Wm. Williamson	1663	200
11	Geo. Bryer and Richd. Lawson	1663	1300
10	Thos. Griffith	1664	350
11	John Chinley	1664	200

13	Geo. Broyer	1664	320
15	Wm. Denby	1663	400
16	Jno. Ingram and Wm. Barber	1664	506
17	Jno. Gibbs	1664	250
18	Jno. Green	1664	200
19	Jno. Hull	1664	650
20	Wm. Barber and Jno. Ingram	1664	464
26	Jas. Allyson	1662	360
29	Wm. Pierce	1663	4054
94	Thos. Bryar	1663	300
96	Saml. Griffin	1664	260
133	Michael Hugill	1664	591
137	Michael Hugill	1662	664
137	Thos. Meader	1663	320
138	Geo. Bryer and Richd. Laurence	1663	3000
141	Wm. Moseley and Jno Hull	1662	5798
143	Thos. Hobson	1663	500
149	Thos. Robinson and Edward Lewis	1662	1140
156	Geo. Marsh	1662	750
161	Geo. Bryer and Richd. Laurence	1664	1000
162	Geo. Bryer	1662	500
163	John Killman	1663	150
182	Thos. Prickett	1665	137
184	Evan Davis and Jno. Cole	1665	356
191	Anthony Jackman	1664	700
192	Hy. Awberry	1664	1050
192	Roger Overton and Jno. Lary	1663	100
192	Luke Bullington	1663	250
198	Richd. Laurence and Geo. Bryer	1664	1000
199	Evan Davis and Thos. Williamson	1663	900
201	Richd. Laurence and Wm. Baldwin	1663	300
201	Jno. Pate	1662	1000
216	Jno. Walker	1662	238
217	Jno. Martyn	1663	268
231	James Samford	1662	736
232	Capt. John Weir	1663	200
234	Capt. John Weir and Thomas Erwin	1663	251

235	David Mansfield and Robt. Fristow......1664	654
235	John Newman 1664	600
242	Edwd. Lewis 1663	498
271	Robt. Tomlin and Wm. Moss 1663	600
307	Thos. Robinson 1663	700
310	Thos. Pattison and Wm. Denby 1663	504
324	Anthony North 1662	200
329	Henry Wilson 1664	450
332	Dennis Sullivant 1663	1446
337	Robt. Bedwell 1662	640
353	John Shurlocke 1663	410
355	John Pigg 1662	365
357	Luke Bullington and James Tune 1663	656
371	Robert Ballis 1663	150
372	Geo. Pley 1662	225
383	Neale Peterson 1663	220
391	Miles Hugill 1663	277
404	John Deyoung 1664	450
414	Wm. Mosse 1664	500
419	Richd. White 1664	300
422	Lt. Col. Thos. Goodrich 1664	2000
436	Hugh Nevett 1664	1800
436	Thos. Robinson and Quintain Sherman...1664	800
446	Paul Woodbridge 1664	600
456	Nicholas Copland and Wm. West........1665	1589
457	Robert Davis 1665	2580
459	Francis Overton and Wm. Charlton......1663	410
465	John Tabott and John Cheney 1665	265
466	John Lacy 1665	28
466	Richard King 1665	32
468	Jno. Williams 1665	600
470	Jas. Coghill 1664	246
470	Geo. Bryer and Richd. Laurence.........1663	3000
471	Richd. Laurence, Evan Davis and Thos. Williamson 1663	900
477	John Catlett 1663	500
478	Daniel Gaines 1663	400

483	Richd. White	1665	1500
487	Miles Reily	1665	1100
492	Jno. Sharp	1665	800
497	Richd. Brainham	1665	240
498	Jas. Browne	1664	346
504	Mary Fantleroy, widow	1665	2600
529	John Cox	1664	737
575	Hy. Creighton	1665	321
576	Richd. Bridgar, Robt. Hill and Jno. Mayhew		
		1665	1200
577	Jas. Samford	1665	800
587	Robt. Tallifer and Law. Smith	1666	6300
621	Jno. Weire	1666	2502
623	Danl. Gaines and Nich. Willard	1665	1376
624	Peter Cornehill	1665	947
634	Eliz. Hampshire	1666	100
634	Harman Kelderman	1666	800
639	Thomas Butten	1666	3650
655	John Maddison	1663	280
659	John Bowen	1666	550
660	Charles Snead	1666	1933
662	Philip Wadding	1666	300
662	Nathl. Baxter	1666	500
665	Edwd. Hudson	1666	356
666	Evan Davids	1666	861

Book No. 6.

3	Wm. Grey and Christopher Blackburne	1666	775
7	John Paine	1666	542
8	Lt. Col. Thos. Goodrich	1666	200
12	Wm. Lane	1666	164
12	Col. Jno. Catlett	1666	150
13	Major John Weire	1666	1770
14	Major John Weire	1666	1800
15	Wm. Moseley	1666	520
16	Thos. Ballard	1666	800
23	Peter Pett	1666	600

27	Capt. John Hull	1666	7110
28	John Meders and Henry Peters	1667	4200
29	Francis Triplett	1666	1050
37	Thos. Pells	1670	400
48	Thos. Games	1665	1030
48	Jas. Boughan	1665	150
48	Wm. Aires	1665	592
49	Thos. Harper and Robt. Clemends	1667	700
61	Jas. Coghill	1667	1050
62	Alex. Fleming	1667	2750
63	Silvester Tacker	1667	150
63	Jas. Coghill	1667	600
64	Pekethtern Gilson, Jr.	1667	1050
65	Col. John Walker	1667	900
66	John Catlett	1667	4506
68	Wm. Ball and Thos. Chetwood	1667	1600
73	Henry Corbin	1667	350
77	Major John Weir	1667	150
77	Richd. Laurence	1665	2000
87	Wm. Fogg	1666	650
105	Miles and Richd. Lewis, orphans of Richd. Lewis	1667	400
105	Thos. Goldman	1667	1200
106	Thos. Button	1667	404
116	Major Genl. Robert Smith	1667	1900
117	Henry Corbyn	1667	5776
118	Wm. Loyd	1668	1300
121	Philip Ludwell	1667	200
121	Christopher Wormly	1668	800
121	Peter Wells	1668	490
122	Francis Haile	1668	1865
122	James Yates	1668	300
122	Mathew Barratt	1668	300
124	Jno. Bowen and Geo. Soones	1668	689
127	Robert Payne	1668	3141
138	Jno. Newman and Wm. Fitzharbett	1668	320
139	Capt. Josias Pickns	1667	420

140	John Lacy	1667	370
141	John Cale	1667	287
146	Jas. Gaynes	1667	519
147	Col. John Walker	1668	1030
149	Thos. Edmondson	1667	513
155	Thos. Fogg and Henry Lucas	1666	397
155	Wm. Blaike	1668	97
156	Wm. Hoskins	1668	350
156	Jas. Fullerton	1667	700
175	Wm. Hodgson	1668	25
177	Capt. John Hull	1668	1400
181	Wm. Grey and Christopher Blackburn	1668	1138
182	Thos. Chetwood and Jno. Prosser	1667	5275
182	Thos. Page, Wm. Hodgson and Saml. Wielding	1667	3075
183	Capt. Alex. Fleming	1667	560
183	Thos. Page	1667	783
192	Capt. John Hull	1668	1200
205	Thos. Harwarr and Nick Cox	1668	922
209	John and George Mott	1668	3700
217	Arthur Etty	1669	491

(To be continued.)

SUSSEX COUNTY

Book No. 31.

Page	Name	Date	No. acres
483	Jarvis Windfield	1755	30
484	Wm. Moor	1755	75
485	Jas. Cain, Jr.	1755	28
487	Thos. Heath	1755	98
504	Wm. Parham	1755	90
515	Robert Petway	1755	28
516	Wm. Allen	1755	50
519	David Hind	1755	83
589	Thos. Atkins	1755	136

596	Mary Browne	1755	477
597	Joshua Rowland	1755	829
625	David Hunter	1755	200
625	John Edmonds	1755	142
627	James Bass	1755	130
627	Richard Cocke	1755	336
628	Henry Meecham	1755	100
629	David Hunter	1755	175
630	Thomas Renn	1755	64
633	Major Tiller	1755	39
637	John Gilbert	1755	100
640	Wm. Hutchings	1755	78
691	Richard Hill	1755	102
691	David Hunter	1755	214
710	Wm. Rowland	1755	265
741	James Chappel	1755	636

Book No. 32.

406	John Hargrove	1754	175
471	Wm. Bank	1755	60
487	Philip Bailey	1755	71
490	Thomas Clary	1755	67
506	John Irby	1755	1516
508	John Edmonds	1755	1832
521	Robert Jones	1755	10
530	Benj. Hancock	1755	154
537	Thos. Gresswith	1755	304
583	John King	1755	32
641	Robert Jones	1755	213
667	Robert Jones, Jr.	1756	791
671	Travis Griffis	1756	146
704	Elizabeth Bellema	1756	133
706	John Rachel	1756	154

Book No. 33.

226	Eppes Moore	1756	92
239	Wm. Thompson	1756	40
241	Thos. Renn, Jr.	1756	48

245	Wm. Spain	1756	354
250	Benford Pleasants	1756	370
252	Edward Pettway	1756	143
257	James Nicholson	1756	93
258	Benj. Ellis	1756	199
264	Nathl. Feltz, Jr.	1756	450
290	John Sills	1756	333
302	Thos. Hersie	1756	104
321	John Judkin, Sr.	1756	200
329	Jacob Jones	1756	164
332	James Horn, Jr.	1756	254
334	John Hancock	1756	199
341	Sloman Wynne	1756	168
389	Wm. Cooper	1757	250
486	John Morgan	1758	75
498	David Clanton	1758	80
506	Mathew Parham, Jr.	1758	39
509	John Thomlinson	1758	150
552	Jacob Newsum	1759	193
603	Willut Roberts	1759	465
660	Peter Green	1759	1100
663	John Mason	1759	445
726	Jesse Jones	1760	244
812	Valentine Williamson	1760	456
813	Henry Tyler	1760	1454
814	Henry Freeman	1760	230
842	Charles Partin	1760	170
843	David Pennington	1760	250
879	Richard Northcross	1760	158
890	Sampson Newsum	1760	180
891	James Chappel, Jr.	1760	150
892	Thos. Davis	1760	240

Book No. 34.

29	Thomas Atkinson	1756	200
32	Abraham Brown	1756	344
33	Wm. Knight	1756	214

35	Walter Lashly, Jr.	1756	158
36	Thos. Newsum	1756	92
44	John Watkins	1756	235
52	Matthew Whitehead	1756	140
149	Robert Bolling	1756	1436
165	David Hunter	1757	211
193	John King	1757	176
254	Thomas Avens	1759	193
266	Richd. Jones	1759	175
266	Thomas Mitchell	1759	113
277	Benj. Richardson	1759	138
340	Shelly Booth	1759	193
403	Richard Jones	1759	902
422	John Hood	1759	175
547	Joseph Wren	1760	160
601	Henry Blow	1760	495
621	Willut Roberts	1760	680
633	Saml. Cornwell	1760	165
717	Isaac Mason	1760	264
755	Morris Dunn	1760	190
784	Charles Baker	1761	100
933	Thomas Man	1761	145
941	James Stewart	1761	440
781	David Mason	1760	1167
788	Henry Sharpe	1761	200
789	Henry Sharpe	1761	150
820	Thomas Vaughan	1761	100

(Continued.)

FINCASTLE COUNTY

Book No. 41.

69	Geo. Washington	1772	10,990
80	Geo. Mercer, Esq.	1772	13,532
83	James Craik	1772	4232
88	John Fry	1772	4149
90	John Fry	1772	1525

91	John Fry 1772	2034
94	John Savage and others 1772	28,627

Book No. 42.

505	John Connolly 1773	2000
507	Chas. Warmstrof 1773	2000
511	Wm. Edmiston 1774	1000
514	Wm. Ingles 1774	1000
522	Mitchell Clay 1774	803
524	Wm. Edmiston 1774	1000

Book B.

304	John Campbell 1780	200

Book D.

714	Griffin Pearl 1781	2000

Book F.

56	James Hickman 1781	2000
423	Hugh Inness 1782	2000

Book G.

34	Saml. Edmiston 1782	200

Book K.

598	John and James Bell, devisees of David Bell, decd. 1784	2000

Book L.

682	George Washington 1784	10,990

Book No. 22.

578	Robert Sanders 1790	750
580	Matthew French 1790	226

Book No. 23.

310	James Ogle 1790	78
314	Martin Kimberlaine 1790	87
315	George Keasler 1790	190

317	Abraham Stelly	1790	152
318	Jarvas Smith	1790	173
447	John Hambleton	1791	1000

GOOCHLAND COUNTY
Book No. 13.

493	Geo. Southerland	1730	400
493	Gideon Jambon	1730	40½
494	Drury Vanderhood	1730	400
494	Jas. Holeman	1730	183
494	Stephen Chastain	1730	400
495	Peter Jefferson	1730	322
495	Wm. Barnes	1730	400
496	Peter Legran	1730	400
496	Thos. Turpin	1730	283
504	Wm. Randolph, Esq.	1730	577
505	Dudley Digges	1730	3650
507	Peter Dep	1730	400
512	Henry Wood	1730	110
513	Michael Holland	1730	400
513	Michael Holland and Wm. Ford	1730	400
514	Wm. Rent	1730	270
537	Hutchinson Burton	1730	400
538	Benj. Woodson	1730	400
538	John Woodson	1730	1250
539	John Lavillian	1730	170

Book No. 14.

7	Wm. Allen	1730	400
42	Anthony Rapean	1730	274
43	Nathl. Maxe	1730	400
44	Amos Lad	1730	400
44	Wm. Maxe	1730	400
45	Nathl. Maxe	1730	400
48	Thos. Locket	1730	400
48	Henry Cox	1730	400
49	Geo. Cox	1730	400

49	Hutchinson Burton	1730	400
50	Wm. Cannon	1730	300
50	Fred'k Cox	1730	400
51	Josias Paine	1730	400
56	Allen Howard	1730	400
59	Alex. Marshall	1730	3000
60	Timothy Rich	1730	400
61	Thos. Locket	1730	900
115	Seth Ward	1730	220
116	Same	1730	880
129	Henry Breazeale	1730	400
133	David Patterson	1730	400
133	John Lane	1730	400
134	Chas. Christian	1730	400
134	Marmaduke Hix	1730	400
135	David Patterson	1730	400
135	Henry Atkinson	1730	400
136	John Merryman	1730	400
137	Stephen Woodson	1730	358
138	Wm. Mayo	1730	9350
141	Hutchinson Burton	1730	400
142	Thos. Watkins	1730	300
142	David Patterson	1730	342
143	Wm. Salle	1730	64
143	Anthony Hoggatt	1730	107
144	Thos. Carter, Jr.	1730	200
145	Capt. Danl. Stoner	1730	500
145	John Sanders	1730	400
146	Francis Coley	1730	400
146	Thos. Murrell	1730	400
147	Richard Kirby	1730	400
148	Richard Barker	1730	350
149	Richard Oglesby	1730	600
151	Michael Holland	1731	400
159	Stephen Lacy	1731	400
165	Thos. Edwards	1731	400
172	Matthew Cox	1731	400

175	Martin King	1731	400
174	Thomas Walton	1731	400
175	Joseph Mayo	1731	400
176	John Merryman	1731	400
177	Richard Parker ...	1731	400
179	Robert Hughes	1731	1200
181	Thos. Prosser	1731	400
185	Robert Spear	1731	400
187	Bowler Cocke	1731	2400
195	James Akin	1731	1000
256	Ashford Hughs	1731	400
257	Charles Hudson	1731	540
258	Benj. Harris	1731	400
259	Adam Butry	1731	120
260	Stephen Lacy	1731	400
261	Benj. Woodson	1731	200
261	Chas. Rayley	1731	394
262	Jas. Cunningham	1731	400
263	Alex. Logan	1731	400
264	Robt. Adams	1731	400
265	Richard Moseby	1731	400
191	Charles Hudson	1730	2000
267	Henry Bailey	1731	400
267	Abraham Wamack, Jr.	1731	400
268	Thomas Friend	1731	400
269	Saml. Nuckles	1731	400
271	Michael Holland	1731	400
271	Henry Wood	1731	268
273	Nathl. Bassett	1731	400
274	Wm. Mayo	1731	2850
275	John Bernard	1731	154
316	Wm. Chamberlayn	1731	400
329	Robert Horsley	1731	400
329	Rev. Wm. Swift	1731	400
330	Wm. Walton	1731	400
330	Merry Webb	1731	800
331	John Taylor	1731	400

331	Robert Horsley	1731	400
332	John Max	1731	250
333	Josias Payn	1731	400
333	John Wit, Jr.	1731	400
334	Henry Turner	1731	300
334	Geo. Payn	1731	400
340	Mathew Ligon	1731	1100
366	John Simkin	1731	300
367	Joseph Jackson	1731	400
367	Thos. Tanner, Jr.	1731	200
368	Joel Chandler	1731	400
369	Joseph Baugh	1731	400
375	Charles Lewis	1731	1200
389	Thos. Goolsby	1732	400
390	Same	1732	400
391	Same	1732	400
392	Francis James	1732	250
393	Wm. Chamberlayne	1732	1400
394	Nathl. Maxey	1732	200
396	Robert Adams	1732	400
398	Benj. Johnson	1732	400
403	Ashford Hughes and Danl. Price	1732	400
404	Jacob Winfree	1732	400
406	Robert Adams	1732	400
407	Wm. Mills	1732	400
408	Jacob Winfree	1731	400
408	John Walker, Jr.	1732	400
420	Stephen Cox	1732	800
421	Henry Webb	1732	400
422	Danl. Pero	1732	200
423	John Woodson	1732	1000
423	Same	1732	1500
424	Henry Webb	1732	400
427	Henry Runalds	1732	400
428	Danl Guairant	1732	400
429	Mary Ann Ditway	1732	400
431	Benj. Mossby	1732	200

431	Robt Adams	1732	400
435	Thos. Tindall	1732	173
436	Thos. Williamson	1732	400
437	Michael Holland	1732	400
439	John Johnson	1732	400
440	Wm. Woodson, Benj. Woodson, Jr., Joseph Woodson, Jr., John Woodson, Jr., Robert Woodson, Jr.	1732	1500
441	John Pleasant	1732	400
442	Thos. Wooldridge and Edward Wooldridge	1732	400
443	Arthur Hopkins	1732	400
444	Wm. Swift	1732	400
446	Gideon Chamboon	1732	59
447	Agnes Noland	1732	354
448	Edward Scott	1732	619
461	Arthur Hopkins	1732	400
461	Giles Allegree	1732	328
462	John Spear	1732	200
463	James Nevil	1732	700
463	Henry Hatcher	1732	400
463	Barth. Stoval	1732	250
464	John Bolling	1732	400
464	Barth. Stoval and John Stoval	1732	200
465	David Liles	1732	800
465	Edward Scott	1732	67
465	Same	1732	350
466	Abraham Michaux	1732	400
466	Charles Johnson	1732	77
467	Joseph Chandler	1732	400
467	John Robinson	1732	200
468	Jacob Michaux	1732	150
468	Edward Scott	1732	200
468	John Sclater	1732	400
481	Charles Johnson	1732	400
481	Edward Scott	1732	100
483	Saml. Burk	1732	200
483	John Bolling	1732	400

484	Jacob Trebue	1732	117
516	Thos. Porter	1732	384
520	Wm. Creasy	1732	400
536	Chas. Allen	1732	1000
537	Jas. Nevil	1732	700

NEW KENT COUNTY

Book No. 3.

309	Arthur Nash	1654	950
310	Edward Simpson	1654	100
340	Ralph Green	1655	500
343	Robert Priddy	1655	400
345	Major Wm. Lewis	1655	2000
353	Wm. Blackey	1655	1300
354	Wm. Wyatt	1655	300
355	John Hodson and John Garratt	1655	300
355	Major Wm. Lewis	1655	100
358	Major Wm. Hoccaday	1655	3550
359	Same	1655	640
360	Anthony Langston	1655	1000
363	Richard, son of Arthur Price, decd	1655	600
380	Lazarus Thomas	1655	250
382	Richard Major	1656	1350
387	Francis Burnell	1655	300
388	Same	1655	1000

Book No. 4.

4	Dr. Giles Mode	1655	1000
18	Wm. Hall, surveyor	1655	350
19	Eliz. Gibbs, dau. of John Gibbs	1655	150
19	Capt. Geo. Floyd	1655	432
72	John Cosby	1656	760
72	Same	1656	1000
73	Same	1656	800
74	Wm. Pollam	1656	334
87	Howell Price	1656	1000

87	Henry Soanes	1656	2800
88	Ralph Green	1656	500
89	Thomas Merrideth	1656	380
94	Martin Baker	1656	1750
112	Richmond Terrell	1656	640
113	Major Wm. Hoccaday	1656	640
113	Wm. Blackey	1656	1000
114	Wm. Lacey	1656	
114	Rees Hughes	1656	410
142	Capt. Leonard Chamberline	1657	650
145	Capt. Leonard Chamberlin	1657	70
146	Lt. Col. Robert Abrall	1657	950
147	Henry Collier	1657	50
148	Thomas Merideth	1657	420
151	Charles Edmonds	1657	730
153	Col. Robt. Ellyson	1657	577
157	Anthony Arnell	1657	500
158	Thomas Bell	1657	250
162	George Smith	1657	850
163	George Chapman	1657	160
164	Francis Burnell	1657	500
165	Wm. Allen	1657	250
166	John Madison	1657	800
202	Thos. Pukles	1657	150
214	Capt. Geo. Lyddall	1657	2390
215	Wm. Pullam	1657	1000
220	Chas. Edmonds and Wm. Pullam	1658	830
221	Henry Goodgaine	1658	334
221	Chas. Edmonds and Wm. Pullam	1658	2520
222	Robert Priddy	1658	400
226	Major Joseph Croshaw	1659	500
243	John Basby	1657	50
249	John Handkin	1657	200
259	Lt. Col. Robert Abrall and John Pigg	1658	1280
259	Lt. Col. Robert Abrall	1658	550
263	George Morris	1658	208
269	Richard Wilikin	1658	600

270	Anthony Haynes	1658	640
271	John Pigge	1658	300
271	Geo. Chapman	1658	1500
271	John Axell and Anthony Haynes	1658	600
272	Nicholas Gibson, orphan of Thos. Gibson, decd.	1658	800
272	Ralph Leftwich	1658	300
273	John Madison	1658	300
274	Anthony Haynes	1658	500
274	Peter Ford and Edward Racle	1658	640
274	George Chapman	1658	1000
275	John Pigge	1658	700
276	Robert Jones, sd. Jones, assigned to Rowland Williams & Williams, assigned to Edwd. Gresham	1658	500
277	George Chapman	1658	1500
277	Wm. Woodland and Benj. Howard	1658	280
279	Rees Hughes	1657	860
308	Thomas Peck	1658	1000
308	Garrett Pigg	1658	350
309	Capt. Wm. Claiborne	1658	1000
310	Major Wm. Hoccaday	1658	1280
311	George Austin	1658	950
315	Martin Palmer	1658	1300
321	George Skipworth	1658	900
321	John Lewis and James Turner	1658	1000
322	Thos. Heckman	1658	1000
327	Wm. Goffe	1658	1000
327	John King	1658	1000
327	Thomas Ballard	1658	1300
335	Nathaniel Bacon	1658	300
342	Col. Mannering Hammond	1658	600
350	Edward Lockey	1658	1600
354	John Dorrant	1658	150
354	Thomas Bell	1658	500
355	Thomas Meredith	1658	450
355	John Fleminge	1658	250

356	Charles Edmonds	1658	132
356	Same	1658	2750
359	Nicholas Seabrell	1658	150
360	John Peteete	1659	500
367	Richard Major, Sr.	1659	350
369	George Brown	1659	200
369	John Adkeson	1658	74
373	Francis Burnell	1659	900
381	Elizabeth Kemp	1661	900
388	Edmund Machen	1662	1000
390	James Wilson	1661	700
394	Capt. Martin Palmer	1660	400
394	Richard Davis	1660	660
395	Thomas Holmes	1661	1100
395	Same	1661	1024
408	Wm. Pullam and Wm. Webb	1662	580
414	John Fleming	1661	493
424	Thomas Bell	1662	1100
432	Geo. Light and Thos. Spencer	1661	1127
437	Thos. Bell	1662	1100
444	Geo. Lyddall	1662	3306
445	Geo. Smith and Edmund Price	1662	800
445	George Smith	1662	1020
448	James Hurd	1660	1770
449	Francis Burnell	1660	2000
450	Geo. Morris and Jno. Pigge	1660	1000
467	Lt. Col. Robert Abrahall	1660	640
470	Major Genl. Hamond	1661	850
476	Lt. Col. Robert Abrahall	1660	500
477	Thos. Brereton, formerly granted to Geo. Chapman, 1658	1661	1500
478	Philip Freeman	1660	100
479	Francis Burnell	1661	2300
532	Eliz. Kemp, formerly granted to Sir Grey Skipwith, 1658	1661	900
558	Rees Hughes	1662	860
461	Edward Lockey	1662	1600

463	John Leggatt	1662	376
565	John Lewis and Thos. Mitchell	1662	1680
565	John Pigg	1662	300
566	Wm. Blackey	1662	1300
575	Ralph Green	1662	350
616	Edward Harris	1664	730

(Continued)

KING AND QUEEN COUNTY

Book No. 8.

188	Robert Bird	1691	134
189	Robert Bird	1691	100
189	Robert Bird	1691	321
190	Wm. Todd	1691	238
191	Wm. Cardwell and Wm. Fenney	1691	499
191	Joseph Wilsheare	1691	48
207	John Clerke	1691	104
208	John Bland	1691	108
209	Wm. Collins and Timothy Coniers	1691	620
248	John Williams	1693	410
264	Cornelius Vaughan	1693	288
266	Wm. Todd	1693	500
266	Capt. Joshua Story	1693	300
268	Capt. Joshua Story, James Taylor and Jonathan Fisher	1693	9150
269	Thos Vicaries	1693	360
277	Robert Bird	1693	225
317	Thomas Jones and Cornelius Vaughan	1694	420
317	James Taylor	1694	134
318	Zachary Lewis	1694	500
320	Geo. Dillard	1694	139
391	Robert Beverley	1694	6500
400	Wm. Gough	1694	70
414	James Taylor	1695	500
413	Major Peter Beverley	1695	4500

| 425 | Edward Guthrey, (formerly granted to Edward Simpson, by Patent Dec. 4, 1654)......1695 | 600 |
| 427 | Alex Campbell ....1695 | 195 |

Book No. 9.

1	Col. Edward Hill 1695	5060
3	Edward Guthrey 1695	753
8	Col. Richard Johnson 1695	3285
8	Bartholomew Fowler 1695	238
10	Margaret and Frances Todd, orphans of Wm. Todd, decd. 1695	500
11	Ralph Wormeley 1695	13,500
35	Robert Beverley 1696	2359
38	Sir Wm. Skipwith, Bart. 1696	710
39	Thos. Todd 1696	333
73	Edward Hill 1695	5060
75	Ralph Wormley 1695	13,500
76	Edward Jenings 1695	570
78	Col. Richd. Johnson 1695	3285
96	Wm. Gough 1697	1225
122	Timothy Ellis 1697	250
124	Edwin Thacker 1697	400
131	Roger Malory 1698	300
148	Barth. Fowler 1698	6500
186	John Carleton 1699	118
194	Geo. Clough 1699	620
196	Barth. Ramsey 1699	1300
196	Benj. Harrison of James City Co........1699	1500
197	Benj Harrison of James City Co........1699	1000
203	Henry Fox 1699	330
204	Edmund Jenings 1699	200
205	Edmund Jenings 1699	570
208	Col. Edward Hill 1699	1000
209	Wm. Jones 1699	700
211	Edward Hill 1699	5060
214	Wm. Leigh and Benj. Harrison.........1699	3474
216	Major Lewis Burwell 1699	5000

217	Sampson Darell	1699	5000
218	Richd. Whitehead of Gloster Co.	1699	5000
222	Honl. Ralph Wormeley	1699	5920
244	Chickeley Corbin Thacker	1700	1000
251	Henry Fox	1700	821
254	James Taylor	1700	333
260	Henry Fox	1700	584
261	Henry Fox	1700	580
262	Henry Goodloe	1700	321
269	Wm. Edwards	1700	238
293	James Boughan	1700	333
348	James Dabney	1701	204
348	Stephen Terry	1701	335
350	Nich. Meriwether	1701	459
350	Wm. Anderson and Dorothy, his wife	1701	179½
351	George Dabney	1701	293
352	Sarah Dabney	1701	179
352	Edward Hobdey	1701	263
354	Gideon Macon	1701	172
354	Gideon Macon	1701	425
355	Robert Davis	1701	208
356	William Maybank	1701	105
356	James Terry	1701	418
357	Thos. Cranshaw	1701	150
358	James Hayfield	1701	109
358	John Burrows	1701	430
359	John King	1701	211
360	Thomas Comer	1701	139
360	John Oliver	1701	446
363	John Thomson	1701	537
361	James Henderson	1701	155
362	Jane Gouch or Gouge	1701	80
362	Hance Hendrick	1701	594
364	Thomas Carr	1701	546
365	John Rapier	1701	185
365	Richard Littlepage	1701	2367
367	Mary Herbert, orphan of Thomas Herbert	1701	200

368	John Hayden 1701	196
368	Charles Fleming 1701	1184
369	James Adams 1701	437
370	James Edwards 1701	854
374	Peter White 1701	355
374	John Tremsir 1701	102
375	John Bresmer and Jane, his wife........1701	1000
375	Same 1701	100
384	Wm. Hurt, Sr. 1701	298
385	Geo. Slaughter 1701	200
386	Andrew Maccallester 1701	86
408	Robert Blackwell 1701	174
414	Susanna Page 1701	1419
416	Thos. Ellett 1701	157
417	Thos. Nichols 1701	183
418	Lewis Davis 1701	320
427	Chickley Corbin Thacker 1701-2	3080
428	Chickley Corbin Thacker 1702	980
428	John Ceesar 1702	405
436	Martin Slaughter and Lettice, his wife, one of the daus. of Ambrose Lipscombe, decd..1702	137
440	Wm. Hurt 1702	93
441	Wm. Morris 1702	366
444	John Buckner 1702	3080
445	Jas. Dabney 1702	1000
450	John Whitlock 1702	233
452	Morris Floyd 1702	100
464	Rowland Thomas 1702	100
466	Nathl. Burwell 1702	600
486	Wm. Seamor 1702	19
510	Mary Lane 1702	500
514	Thos. Pettis 1703	36
518	Jas. Taylor and Thos. Pettis 1703	576
531	John Rigg 1703	1000
536	Wm. Jones 1703	420
536	Harry Beverley and John Smith 1703	2300
538	Francis Major 1703	590

544	Chickley Corbin Thacker 1703		1130
552	Saml. Cradock, John Cave, John Eckholls, and		
	Wm. Glover 1703		1620
553	Edward Gadbury 1703		48
554	John Cave and John Eckholls 1703		600
554	Wm. Byrd 1703		1200
555	Henry Pigg 1703		61
556	Francis Major 1703		180
557	Wm. Jones 1703		350
558	Wm. Jones 1703		250
564	John Maddison 1703		80
579	Edwd. Ware 1703		116
590	Edwd. Lewis 1704		400
600	Robert Douglas 1704		150
610	Richd. Wyat 1704		760
630	James Taylor 1704		4500
641	John Baylor 1704		2717
645	Jas. Boughan, Jr., and John Boughan....1705		2000
654	John Wyatt 1705		700
654	Christopher Pearson, son of Thos. Pearson,		
	decd. 1705		106
655	Wm. Jones 1705		523
657	Mary Leigh, Val. Ware and Wm. Haines.1705		600
657	Mary Leigh, Val. Ware and Wm. Haines.1705		260
668	Timothy Conner 1705		1420
669	David Bray, Richd. Wharton, Hy. Lightfoot		
	and Robt. Ambrose 1705		6500
683	Thos. Austin 1705		35
624	Reynold Bocus 1705		146
685	Henry Pigg 1705		122
685	Hy. Baylor 1705		31
686	John Lankford 1705		228
686	Thos. Willbourne 1705		53
687	Robert Bell 1705		148
687	Philip Watkins 1705		1190
707	John Leigh 1705		484

721	Col. Jas. Taylor and John Baylor	1706	2763
736	John Major	1706	1245

Book No. 10.

5	Daniel King	1711	255
10	Capt. John Collier	1711	103
15	Timothy Conner	1711	60
39	Roger Gregory	1711	300
47	Guy Smith, Clerk of the county of—	1711	320
57	Larkin Chew of Co. of Essex	1712	2143
60	Larkin Chew of Co. of Essex	1712	220
61	Justephenica Bennett and Sawyer Bennett.	1712	230
91	Wm. Bird	1712	18
92	John Didlack	1713	800
94	Robt. Beverley	1713	2644
158	Jno. Richards	1714	758
194	John Guthery	1714	277
214	Wm. Lea	1714	100
220	Wm. Kilpin	1714	640
229	John Durham	1714	42
243	John Wills	1715	130
250	John Baylor	1715	1330
255	Michael Ginings and John Sutton	1716	200
256	Isaac Hill	1715	452
289	Robt. Beverley	1716	3420
299	Hy. Raines, Wm. Howard and John Sutton	1716	464
313	Mary Broche	1717	420
319	John Madison, John Rogers, Peter Rogers, Henry Pigg, Edward Pigg and John York	1717	1860
352	Bernard Paine	1717	350
417	Larkin Chew	1719	7100
426	Wm. Hall	1719	1080
453	Larkin Chew	1719	3000
455	Robert Beverley and Thos. Jones	1719	15,000

(Continued.)

RAPPAHANNOCK COUNTY WILLS

Brooks, Thomas. 29 Jan. 1675—21 Sept. 1681. William Barker, executor; witnesses, John English, Thomas Colby.

Howell, George. 4 March, 1680—2 Nov., 1681. Son George; my wife; witnesses Robert Clarke, Richard Peacocke, James Prichards.

Griffin, William. 25 Nov., 1681—1 March, 1681. Daughters Ann, Elizabeth and Joyce; son William; Mr. William Moss and Mr. William Sergeant overseers; witnesses William Lathoope, Thomas James, Thomas Williams.

Goose, Thomas. 27 Sept., 1680—3 May, 1682. George Eale, William Eale, Jr., Charity Eale, the children of Bridget Eale, she being my executrix; witnesses Richard Glover, Mary Glover, Henry Clark, Thomas Lewis.

Kirk, Elizabeth. 19 April, 1676—1 Jan., 1682. Son John; daughters Mary and Elizabeth; friend Henry Lucas; witnesses Thomas Taylor, Henry Lucas.

Bagwell, Roger. 26 March, 1679—6 July, 1679. Edward Jones executor; John Alloway; Samuel Samford; Giles, son of John Webb; Thomas Taylor; Edwin Conway; brother Andrew Bagwell of Apson, county of Devon, England; witnesses James Samford, Edwin Conway.

Cole, Robert. 7 Feb., 1681—6 Sept., 1682. Son Robert; wife Mary executrix; friend William Davis; witnesses Nicholas Yeates, Mary Yeates.

Ashton, John., Co. of Stafford. 10——1675. Prob. at Rappahannock, 26 Jan., 1682. Wife Elizabeth, providing she comes over here to live; to John Bimberry and his wife; to Capt. John Ashton; cousin John Ashton in Russell St., at the 'Adam & Eve' in London; executor brother James Ashton; witnesses Dominick Rice, Robert Massess.

Sargent, William. 13 Feb., 16——14 April, 1683. Son George; William Whitredge; William, son of John Warren; Henry, son of Abraham Field; William, son of Wil-

liam Griffin; Frances Sterne, daughter of David Sterne;
Rebecca Wells, daughter of Barnaby Wells; John, son
of John Deane; George Jones and Honoria, his wife;
John Weire; Mr. Daniel Gaines; Mr. Thomas Perkins;
Mrs. Jane Deane, wife of John Deane, one of my ex-
ecutors; Mrs. Martha Taylor; Capt. George Taylor;
John Deane, Jr., and Mrs. Elizabeth Jones executors;
witnesses Alexander Doniphan, Rees Evans, John Milles.

Clarke, Joane. 8 March, 1682—9 May, 1683. Daughters
Anne Gower and Elizabeth Jacobus; Stanley, son of
Francis and Ann Gower; Elizabeth Jacobus, daughter
of Angell and Elizabeth Jacobus; friend Col. Johnston of
Rappahannock; son John Clarke executor; witnesses
Isaac Wright, Edmund Northern, William Ward,
Thomas Hart.

Mills, John. 5 March, 1682-3—26 Jan., 1683. Sons John,
Robert, Henry and James; daughters Martha and Jane;
wife executrix; witnesses John King, John Roberts,
William Mackenny.

Crask, Edmund. 20 July, 1683—1 Aug., 1683. Elizabeth
and Frances Moss; daughter Ellen Crask; wife Elizabeth and son John to be executors; friends Lt. Col. William Loyd and Mr. Henry Awbrey; Thomas New; witnesses Henry Newton, Thomas Herbert, Thomas New.

Morrah, John. 14 Sept. 1682—26 Sept., 1683. Godson
Thomas Wardon of Barbadoes, land in the hands of
his father Joseph Wardon of Barbadoes; Thomas Chitty,
Jr.; John Jacob; Grace Bedford; Thomas Chitty, Sr.;
John Bayley.

Miller, Symon, Capt. 16 Feb., 1679—22 May, 1684. Son
Simon to be sent home next year to England; sons William and John; daughters Susannah, Isabella and Margaret; wife's son Anthony Prosser; to the sons of Mr.
Prosser; wife Margaret executrix; James Ashton overseer; witnesses Nathl. Tomlin, Francis Thornton, James
Taylor.

George, Thomas, 17 Aug., 1683—9 Oct., 1683. Wife Elizabeth; daughter Margaret; son Leroy; friends Edmund
Conway, Arthur Spicer and John Taverner overseers;
witnesses Dennis Carley, Philip Hennings, John Taverner.

Johnson, Peter. 4 Dec., 1683—23 Dec., 1683. Son-in-law
John Martin; son Peter; James Jackson executor; witnesses James Harrison, Susan Hammond.

Crask, Elizabeth. 18 Nov., 1683—23 Nov., 1683-4. Frances
Moss, daughter of my former husband Thomas Moss;
to Elizabeth Moss, daughter of the same; god-daughter
Elizabeth Moss, daughter of William Moss; sister Re-
becca Moss; Ellen, daughter of Richard Stoakes; Robert
son of Thomas Parker; Thomas Herbert of the Parish
of Sittingbourne and Elizabeth Moss to be executors;
Thomas New to account for all the concerns of my hus-
band Capt. Edmund Crask; Rebecca Stoakes wife of
Richard Stoakes; Elizabeth Newton, wife of Henry
Newton; godchild Ann daughter of Alexander Robins;
John Crask; Ellen Crask; Martha daughter of Abraham
Stepp; Dr. Green; Thomas Parker, Sr., brother William
Moss; witnesses Henry Tandey, Thomas Parker, Henry
Newton.

Motlin, John. 7 Feb., 1683-4—5 March, 1683-4. Sons Wil-
liam, Henry and John; Elizabeth Richardson; David
Stern and James Trent executors; son-in-law John
Spicer; Knight Richardson; Richard Mathews; Nathan-
iel Allen; Elizabeth Knight; witnesses Nathaniel Allen,
Martin Middleton, Knight Richardson.

Henley, Elizabeth, wife of Robert, formerly relict of John
English. 2 April, 1682—6 March, 1683-4. My husband
Robert Henley to be my heir; witness Alexander Dud-
ley, William Barber.

Watson, John. 6 Feb., 1683—2 April, 1684. Sons John and
Thomas; wife Priscilla and the child she now goes with;
daughters Susan and Elizabeth; friend Henry Gorman;
Capt. Daniel Gaines; Francis Slaughter; John Catlett

and William Underwood overseers; wife and son John
executors; witnesses David Hoomes, Samuel Henshaw,
William Heather.

Perkins, Thomas. 18 Dec., 1683—2 April, 1684. Thomas
Parker; Capt. Samuel Bloomfield executor; witnesses
Martin Johnson, Mary Johnson.

Peters, Randolph. 18 Feb. 1683—16 April, 1684. Margaret
Curtis to be executrix; witnesses George Colelough, Anthony Smith, Ann Smith.

Robins, Alexander. 16 Feb., 1683—16 April 1684. Eldest
daughter Rebecca; daughters Elizabeth, Judith and Ann;
son Alexander land bought of William Berry; my wife's
son John Cook; wife Judith and Thomas Parker executors; witnesses Thomas Parker, Susan Williams.

Harper, Thomas, Farnham Parish. 4 Dec., 1683—16 April,
1684. Wife Mary and eldest son John to be executors;
sons Solomon and Thomas; witnesses Henry Watkins,
John Bonner, John Stewart.

Gullock, Robert. 26 Feb. 1683—23 May, 1684. Daughter
Jane; Robert Payne; Elizabeth Rowzie; cousin Edward
Rowzie; Robert Brooke; wife and the child she now
goes with; John Foxhall and Robert Vaulx executors;
witnesses Edward Rowzie, Tobias Ingram, Robert
Brooke.

Morgan, Evan. 24 Aug., 1683—23 May, 1684. Wife Elizabeth; godson Maxfield Brown my wife's youngest son;
wife's son William Brown; wife's daughter Elizabeth
Brown; witnesses Josiah Mason, Thomas Jones, Thomas
Booth.

Barratt, Maggue. 23 Jan., 1683—28 May, 1684—Daughter
Sarah; daughter Patience Marks and her husband to be
executors; witnesses Henry Lawrence, James Blau.

Floyd, Samuel. 12 March, 1682-3—24 May, 1684. To Andrew
Boyer whole estate; witnesses Bridget Southwell; John
Beatson.

Smith, Henry. 15 April, 1684—4 June, 1684. Sons Toby
and Henry; wife and Edward Adcock executors; Col.

William Loyd and Samuel Peachey overseers; witnesses
George Colclough, Roger Waters, John Webb.

Skelderman, Harman. 12 March, 1683-4—3 Oct., 1684. My
children; my wife to be executrix; witnesses Alexander
Doniphan, John Garton; Susan Hamnon.

Gaines, Daniel, Capt., Sittingbourne Parish. 18 Aug., 1682—
16 Oct., 1684. To the orphans of Col. John Catlett,
decd.; son Bernard; daughters Margaret and Mary;
grandson-in-law John Smith; Ralph Rouzey; wife Margaret executrix; witnesses William Murrow, John Catlett, William Browne.

Stallard, Walter. 28 Dec., 1683—1 Oct., 1684. Son Samuel;
daughter Sarah; wife Winifred executrix; witnesses
John Evans, George Bachey, George Andrews.

Evans, John, Sittingbourne Parish. 29 Jan., 1683—20 Aug.,
1684. Sons John and William; father-in-law William
Veale; brother Martin Johnson; godchild Margaret
Ward daughter of Bryant Ward; wife Elizabeth executrix; witnesses Richard West, Thomas Johnson, William Heather.

Griffin, William. 1 Jan., 1683—5 Nov., 1864. Sons William and John; wife Janet executrix; witnesses Jane
Harrison, James Jackson.

White, Henry. 14 Feb., 1683—5 Nov., 1684. Daughter
Arabella; wife Dorcas executrix; witnesses Robert Moss,
John Googe.

Maffitt, John, Sittingbourne Parish. 26 March, 1682—25
Oct., 1684. Son and daughter; wife executrix; witnesses Mary Masson, John Masson, Thos. Webley.

Rice, Dominick. 28 Oct., 1683—11 March 1684-5. To William, John and Ann Time, children of James Time; son-
in-law Thomas Due; son-in-law Mark Time; son-in-law
Andrew Due; wife's niece Jane Duncombe; son Stephen
Rice to be sent to Ireland to my father when he is five
years old, there to be educated; to my eldest sister's eldest son in Ireland; wife Ann executrix; friends Col. William Loyd, Capt. Thomas Mathews and John Bayley

overseers; witnesses John Bayley, William Brockenborough, Andrew Dew.

Pritt, Robert. 25 Jan., 1684-5—11 March, 1684-5. Friends Richard Rice, Sr.; and his son Richard, Jr.; Ann Condon, widow; Elizabeth Rice; Richard Rice senior and junior to be executors; the sheriff of Rappahannock county, Col. William Taylor; witnesses, Thoroughgood Pate, Jeremiah Thornton.

Ffrack, William. 7 April, 1684—12 March, 1684-5. Wife Martha; my man Robert Vincent; godsons John Brown and William Pitman; witnesses Joseph Hemings, Robert Vincent.

NORTHAMPTON COUNTY WILLS

Moore, Gilbert, Northampton Co. 30 March, 1708—28 July, 1708. Sons Charles Ephraim and Isaac Moore; daughters Sarah and Elizabeth Moore; wife Katherine executrix; witnesses Thomas Eyre, John Maux.

Brewer, John, Northampton Co. 4 Nov., 1708—29 Nov., 1708. Grandson Edward Mills; Obedience Roberts, son of William Roberts to divide the estate. Witnesses Stephen Maxfield, Thomas Nutte.

Stott, David, Northampton Co. 2 Dec., 1708—28 Dec., 1708-9. Sons Nehemiah, Jonathan, David and Henry Stott; wife Tamazin executrix; witnesses Richard Turner, Thomas Bailie.

Davis, Isaac. 24 Dec., 1708—28 Jan., 1708-9. To Francis Roberts; Edward Kellam, Jonathan Ganison; Susanna Brown; Margaret, daughter of Francis Roberts; witnesses John Denton, Jonathan Stevens, Isaac Haggoman.

Johnson, Obedience, Northampton Co. 30 Nov., 1708—28 Jan. 1708-9. Sons Obedience and Richard; daughter Elizabeth and her husband John White; daughter Mary Parramore; granddaughter Temperance White; wife Temperance executrix; witnesses Mary Johnson, Luke Johnson, Geo. Marshall.

Robins, John, Snr. Major., Northampton Co. 5 Dec., 1707—28 May, 1709. Eldest son Obedience; sons John, Ed-

ward, Thomas and Littleton; daughter Esther, wife of
Arthur Denwood of Somerset Co., Province of Md.
my six grandchildren—Esther, Levin, John, Priscilla,
Arthur and Betty Denwood, children of above Arthur
and Esther; son-in-law Hillary Stringer and his wife
Grace, my daughter; daughter Elizabeth Robins; god-
daughter Margaret Waters, daughter of Col. William
Waters; four eldest children of my kinswoman Frances
Powell, wife of Samuel Powell; my five sons to be ex-
ecutors; witnesses Nathaniel Wilkins, Thomas Savage,
John Savage. Codicil 25 March, 1709.

Gelding, Charles, Northampton Co. 30 April, 1709—28 May,
1709. Son Charles; grandson Southey Rue; daughter
Comfort Rue; daughter Charity Stockly; daughters
Hope, Kezia and Agatha Gelding to be joint executors;
witnesses William Waters, Robert Warren, Elinor
Moore, Thomas Moore.

Wilkins, John, Northampton Co. 20 March, 1708-9—28
May, 1709. To Watkins Wilkins, son of my brother Ar-
goll Wilkins; my mother Esther Wilkins; friend George
Harmanson executor; witnesses John Shepard, John
Powell.

Smith, William. No date. 30 May, 1709. Brother John
Smith; Francis, Hillary and Thomas Hunt; Daniel, son
of William Foster; witnesses John Thompson, Thomas
Thompson.

Evans, Thomas. 20 Feb., 1708-9—8 May, 1709. Wife Elizabeth to be executrix; sons Thomas and Caesar; daughters Anne and Elizabeth; witnesses John Mapp, Thomas
Collier.

Sennor or Senior, John, Northampton Co. 7 March, 1708-9
—28 May, 1709. Wife Mary and son John; witnesses
Jos. Cowdry, John Tatum.

Harmanson, Thomas, Snr., Northampton Co. 31 March,
1709—28 May, 1709. Son Thomas; daughter Elishe
Stringer; brother Henry Harmanson; brother William;

brother John; wife Grace; son Thomas executor; witnesses William Dunn, James Hulton, Nathl. Capell.

Gascoigne, Robert, Northampton Co. 14 April, 1709—28 May, 1709. Wife Ann; children, Harman, Bridget, Tamar and Dent; sister Bridget Harmanson; John Micaell and his wife Sarah; wife to be executrix; Robert Scott, Benj. Nottingham and John Harmanson overseers; witnesses John Mathews, William Gascoigne, John Todd.

Luke, John, Northampton Co. 8 Dec., 1708—28 May, 1709. Sons Isaac, John and Daniel to be executors; daughter Susannah and her daughter Sarah; witnesses William White, John Frank.

Carpenter, Charles, Northampton Co. 18 Feb. 1708-9—28 May, 1709. Sons Stephen and Charles; wife Pamelia executrix; witnesses Jonathan Bell, Henry Scott, William Tankerd.

Tanner, Paul. ——— 28 May, 1709. Hillary Hunt; Susannah ———; John Smith; wife Ann executrix; witnesses Thomas Hunt, Sig. Short.

Twiford, William. 9 April, 1708—28 May, 1709. Sons Bartholomew, John and James; daughters Jane and Mary; wife Jane executrix; witnesses William Golding, John White.

Osman, Jane, Northampton Co. 16 Feb., 1708—28 May, 1709—Son Peter Clegg; son John Clegg; Ann Price; son Henry Clegg; son Ezekiel; daughter Elizabeth Clegg; daughter Rachael Clegg; son Peter executor; witnesses Michael Holford, Mary Holford, William Andrews.

Ellegood, John. 14 May, 1709—30 May, 1709. Sons John and William; Philip Jacob and John Jacob; wife Ann executrix; witnesses Benj. Gathere, Benj. Nottingham.

Belote, William, Northampton Co. 9 March, 1708-9—28 May, 1709. Sons Hillary and Hancock; daughter Elishe; wife Elizabeth executrix; brother John Belote and William Tankerd overseers; witnesses John Belote, Anne Belote.

Dunton, William, Northampton Co. 24 Jan., 1708-9—28 May, 1709. Sons William, Richard, Michael; wife Elizabeth; son Elias; daughters Joyce, Elizabeth and Sarah; Richard Jacob and Benj. Nottingham overseers; wife executrix; witnesses Michael Halbirt, Mary Halbirt.

Harmanson, Henry, Northampton Co. 15 April, 1709—28 May, 1709. Son Mathew; daughters Sarah, Elishe, Anne, Tabitha and Sophia Harmanson; wife Gertrude executrix; Capt. Thomas Savage and brother George Harmanson trustees; witnesses Thos. Savage, Argoll Wilkins, Geo. Harmanson.

Knight, John, Northampton Co. 2 April, 1709—28 May, 1709. Sons Charles, John and William Knight; my brother Dixon Knight; wife Ann to be executrix; witnesses Benj. Stratton, Richard Thorman.

Brooks, Francis, Northampton Co. 22 Feb. 1708-9—30 May, 1709. Wife Joan; cousin Jacob Brooks; witnesses Arthur Rascoe, Thomas Dent, Robert Lewis.

Brooks, Joan. No date. 30 May, 1709. My old friend Elizabeth Saman; Dorothea Roberts; cousin Jacob Brooks; Arthur Rascoe executor; witnesses Arthur Rascoe, Robert Lewis.

Branston, Francis, Northampton Co. 1 March, 1708-9—28 May, 1709. Son-in-law William Dolby; son David Dolby; son John Dolby; gd. son Branston Dolby; son-in--law Thomas Dolby; my wife executrix; witnesses William Kendall, John Kendall.

Grice, Peter, Northampton Co. 4 Dec., 1708—28 May, 1709. Sons Peter, Stott and William Grice; daughters Abigail, Mary, Sarah, Jane, Elizabeth and Tamar; wife Mary executrix; witnesses David Holt, David Edmunds, John Walker.

Walker, John (Nuncupative will). 7 Feb. 1708-9—28 May, 1709. Daughter Mary More; wife Mary Walker; witnesses Thos. Teague, John Cliffe.

Price, Walter, Northampton Co. 16 March, 1708-9—17 March, 1708-9. My grandmother; to Ann Berry; bro-

ther William Rabyshaw and sister Mary Kendall Rabyshaw; witnesses Michael Morgan, Thomas Sanderson,
Sarah Berry.

Price, Elinor, Northampton Co. 9 March, 1708-9—17
March, 1708-9. To William Berry; Mary Kendall
Rabyshaw; brother Walter Price; to my grandmother;
to Aunt Ann Berry; father-in-law William Rabyshaw;
witnesses Sarah Berry, Ann Berry.

Palmer, Samuel, Northampton Co. 17 Feb., 1708-9—28
July, 1709. Samuel Mapp, son of John Mapp; Sarah
Custis Mathews; Palmer Kendall, daughter of William
Kendall, Jr.; Robins Mapp; John Mapp, Jr.; son-in-law
Wm. Kendall, Jr.; William Waters; son-in-law John
Mathews; wife Sarah Palmer executrix; witnesses Rob-
ert Hudson, William Dyer, Wm. Munk, Wm. Munk, Jr.

Paine, Daniel, Northampton Co. 9 May, 1709—28 July,
1709. Sons John and Daniel; daughter Esther; wife
Hannah executrix; witnesses Hannah Capell, Nathl.
Capell.

1709. Son Parramore; daughters Elizabeth, Mary, Ann
and Tabitha; wife Rebecca executrix; witnesses Luke
Johnson, George Marshall, Jonah Jackson.

Roberts, Obedience, Northampton Co. 26 Oct., 1709—28
Nov., 1709. Brother Thomas Roberts; mentions John
Brewer, decd.; wife Elizabeth executrix; witnesses Wm.
Waterson, Henry Elligood, Wm. Waters.

Shepeard, Thomas, tanner, Northampton Co. 15 April, 1709
—28 Nov., 1709. Sons Michael, Thomas, John, George
and Smith Sheapeard; wife Ann executrix; witnesses
Smith Watt, Nathl. Capell.

Clark, Mary, Northampton Co. 29 Dec., 1703—28 Nov.,
1709. Daughters Mary, Ann and Elizabeth; sister Ann
Bentall; father Joseph Bentall, Sr.; brother Daniel
Bentall executor; witnesses William Bentall, Jane Mat-
man.

Bell, Robert, Northampton Co. 4 April 1709—28 Jan., 1709-
10. Brother Nathl. Bell; wife Tabitha executrix; wit-

nesses Edmund Scarburgh, Sr.; Edmund Scarburgh, Jr.; Morris Shepeard.

White, Henry, Northampton Cv. 3 Dec., 1708—28 July, Joshua; daughters Elizabeth and Susannah; daughter Fitchett, Joshua, Northampton Co. 5 May, 1709—5 Jan., 1709-10. Sons Witherinton, Thomas, John, Jacob and Comfort Sharp; wife Esther executrix; witnesses Sarah James, George ———.

Scott, John, Northampton Co. 17 Jan., 1708—28 May, 1709. Richard Smith; William Robins; John Tankard; Benjamin Scott; Wm. Belote; Arthur Robins; Benj. Dunton; Mary Scott; Brother Henry Scott; cousin John Scott; Thomas Scott; Edward, son of Wm. Robbins; George Scott. No witnesses.

Hanby, Daniel, Northampton Co. 3 Jan., 1709-10—28 Feb., 1709-10. Daughters Susanna and Elizabeth; brother Charles Hanby and Littleton Robins overseers; wife Mary executrix; witnesses Mordecai Holt, John Roberts.

Hunt, Ann, Northampton Co. 25 July, 1709-10—2 March, 1709-10. Sons Thomas and Gawton Hunt; grandchildren Elisha and Sarah, son and daughter to John and Mary Hunt; daughter Frances Benthall; witnesses John Thompson, Smart Hunt, Danl. Benthall.

Gittings, Thomas, Northampton Co. 5 Nov., 1709—28 March, 1710. Daughters Lucinia and Susan; grandson Lazarus Gittings; son Thomas; son William executor; witnesses Francis Wainhouse, Jr., Anthony Hardy.

Hanby, Richard, Northampton Co. 14 Nov., 1709—28 March, 1710. Daughter Sarah; brothers Daniel and Charles Hanby overseers; wife Sarah executrix. No witnesses.

Mozly Esther, Northampton Co., 28 Jan, 1710; 28 Sept., 1710. Daughter Esther Hawkins; grandson William Hawkins; son John Deer; grandson Dozman Lofland; daughter Mary Moore; daughter Elizabeth White; son William Hawkins executor; witnesses Mathew More.

Dolby, Ann, wife of Thomas Dolby. 18 Sept., 1708—28 Nov., 1710. Sister Amy Dolby, wife of Joseph Dolby; husband Thomas Dolby executor; witnesses Richard Smith, Joseph Dent.

RICHMOND COUNTY WILLS

Richmond county was formed in 1692, when "Old Rappahannock" was extinguished, the present counties of Richmond and Essex being formed from it. The earliest Will Book is marked No. 2. The first book is missing. The first Clerk was William Colston, who occupied this position from 1692 to 1701. The third Clerk was Sir Marmaduke Beckwith, Bart., from 1708 to 1748.

Book No. 2.

Carnaby, Anthony, Sittenburne Parish. ———1 Day Oct., 1699. My wife Sarah; son Anthony, and my daughter Sarah ———; witnesses Neb. Jones, John Jones.

Baylis, Thomas. 25 April, 1697—1 Oct., 1699. Five eldest children, Robert, Amandine, Frances, Katherine and Mary Baylis; my son Thomas; wife executrix; overseers Mr. John Webb, Samuel Sanford and Mr. Edward Jones; witnesses Phillip Hennings, George Bluford, Samuel Samford.

Baylis, Thomas, inventory of estate presented by Mrs. Sarah Baylis.

Parker, John. 13 December, 1699—30 January, 1699. To Elias Wilson, Sr.; to Terence Webb his freedom; to the children of John Upton, who died at my house; to John Burkett and his daughter Margarett Burkett; to John Jones, son of Nebuchednezzer Jones; to Richard Henry; Mr. William Colston to take care of Thomas Parker, the son of Thomas Parker; to Rawleigh Travers and Thomas Beale, who I appoint my executors.

Wilson, Elias, Parish of Sittenbourne. 2 March, 1697-8—6 March, 1699. To John H———; my son John; my sons Henry and James Wilson; to William Browne and

Frances his wife; son Elias Wilson; wife Susanna; daughter Elizabeth the wife of Edward Mosby; to my daughter,—— wife of E——; to Bridgett wife of Thomas ——; to daughter Martha; to grandchildren Edward Morris, Charles Snead, Jr., and Elias Snead, sons to my daughter Phebe, decd.; my wife Susanna, and son Elias to be executors. Codicil directs Capt. George Taylor, William Colston and Edwin Conway to be overseers; witnesses Thomas Longe, Thomas Bradley.

Ford, John. ————Probated 6 March, 1699. Wife Patience Ford; son John Ford; wife to be executrix; witnesses Henry Chappell, Edward Newton, Sr., Shelah Newton.

Mannering, Stephen, Sittingburne Parish. 6 Oct., 1699—6 March, 1699. Grandson John Jones; godson Stephen Trainum; wife Jane executrix. Codicil. Dr. Paul Micou, Rowland Thornton and Neb. Jones overseers; witnesses Rowland Thornton, Neb. Jones.

Spicer, Arthur, Sittingburne Parish. 18 Sept., 1699—3 April, 1700. To son John; to Lydia Spicer, eldest daughter of my brother John Spicer, late of London, decd.; youngest sister Elizabeth Spicer; o————Colston, Captain John Battaile, Mr. John Lloyd to be guardians to my dear child during his minority; Frances Robinson, daughter of Captain Samuel Bloomfield; my son to be sent to England for his better education, that of the Charter House I take to be best; Capt. Carter of Lancaster to accept the trouble of supervision; witnesses John Burkett, Mary Hardridge.

Smyth, William. 9 Feb., 1699—2 October, 1700. To Abraham Goard and his sons John and William, and daughter Catherine Goard; Hanna Goard, the daughter of Abraham and Katherine Goard; wife Eve Smyth to be executrix; witnesses John Phillips, Richard Sandfoe, Margaret Doson.

Mountjoy, Alvin. 28 Sept., 1700—1 Jan., 1700. Son Thomas; child my wife goes with; daughters Sibella and Mary

Mountjoy; wife Mary executrix; witnesses John Kelley, Amy Kelley.

Clarke, Henry. 29 August, 1700—1 January, 1700. Eldest son Henry; daughter Elizabeth; son William; son Alexander; wife to be executrix; my six youngest children; friend Charles Barber; witnesses Ralph Abington, Robert Hughes.

George, Leroy. 16 September, 1700—1 January, 1700. To kinsman Thomas White; friend Nicholas Smyth; my little brother Edward Read; to my mother; to John White and his wife Margaret, whom I name executors; witnesses Edward Read, Elizabeth Read.

Reynolds, William. 22 October, 1700—1 Jan., 1700. Sons Cornelius, John and William; daughter Elizabeth Reynolds; sons to be of age at 16 years; brother John Reynolds to be executor; witnesses Catherine Jackson, Cornelius Laffin, Ann Marshall.

Thomas, Rebecca. 28 December, 1700—5 March, 1700. My three godchildren; to Bridgett Mackcarthlin; Corbin Griffin; Thomas Griffin; William Griffin, Jr.; Winifred Griffin; Winifred Griffin, Jr., to be executrix; witnesses Thomas Griffin, Elizabeth Wright, Walter Wright.

Mealey, Humphrey. 14 December, 1700—5 March, 1700. To Alexander Huison; wife to be executrix; witnesses William Watson, John Dacocks.

Fisher, Martin, Sr. 11 January, 1699—7 May, 1701. Daughter-in-law Sarah; son Martin Fisher and daughter Elizabeth Kitchin executors; witnesses William Hudson, Richard Hayden, Thomas Pacey.

Hardy, John, St. Mary's Parish. 12 Dec., 1700—7 May, 1701. John Bowlin sole executor; to John Philpin; to Richard West; witnesses William Jackson, Richard West, Joseph Cotton.

Hammack, William. 11 July, 1700—2 July, 1701. Youngest son William; my daughter Elizabeth; son Richard to be executor; son William to be of age at 18 years;

daughter Elizabeth to be of age at 16 years; witnesses Rebecca Kertley, John Bohannah.

Ingoe, John, Sr., Parish of North Farnham. 3 June, 1701—2 July, 1701. Eldest son John; yougest son James; wife Mary executrix; daughter Elizabeth Ascough, wife of Thomas Ascough; to Mary Salisbury; witnesses Ann Ascough, Edward Read, Edward Jeffery.

Colston, William, clerk. 27 Oct., 1701—3 Dec., 1701. To be interred by the body of my wife Anne; daughter Susannah Colston; son William; son Charles; Thomas Read until he arrives at 18 years; to Mr. Rawleigh Travers, he and my son-in-law Mr. Thomas Beale to be executors; witnesses Daniel Hornby, Thomas Barlow, Ellen Foster.

Chappell, Henry. 10 January, 1701—3 December, 1701. To Elizabeth Hambleton, who shall be executrix of all my estate; to Anne, daughter of George and Anne Hopkins; witnesses George Hopkins, Anne Hopkins, Patrick Tiffe.

Ascough, Thomas, Parish of Farnham. 21 Aug., 1701—3 Dec., 1701. My mother Anne Ascough; wife Elizabeth; son Christopher; witnesses Luke Morgan, John Doyle.

Phillips, John, 17 July, 1701—3 Dec., 1701. Son John; to son Bryon, plantation in Lancaster county; son Thomas; son Tobias; daughters Mary and Anne Phillips; daughter Elizabeth Collin; Wife Mary; sons John and Bryan to be executors; witnesses John Stott, James Harley, James Hill.

French, Hugh, Parish of St. Maries. 20 Jan., 1699—3 Dec., 1701. Land in Maryland to be sold and produce paid to my son Hugh; daughter Mary; sons Daniel and Mason French; daughter Margaret French; wife Margaret executrix; witnesses John Battaile, William Marshall, Simon Miller, John Miller.

Evans, John. 3 August 1700—3 Dec., 1701. All my estate
to John Jones; witnesses John Johnson, Thomas Lewis,
Benjamin Lewis.

Radley, Thomas. 3 March, 1701—3 Dec., 1701. Son Thomas; daughters Patience and Isabella Radley; wife Isabella to be executrix; witnesses Dominick Dawson, Rice
Williams.

Williams, Rice. 4 August 1701—5 Feb. 1701. Wife Mary;
daughter Elizabeth Settle; grandson Francis Settle; son
Thomas Williams to be executor; witnesses Elizabeth
Jones, John Faver.

Triplett, Francis. 20 Nov., 1700—4 March, 1701. Wife Abigail; son Francis; son William; grandson Francis, son of
my eldest son Thomas, decd.; and in case he die to
grandson Thomas Triplett; Francis, son of John and
Elizabeth Jett; wife and son William executors; witnesses John Deane, Giles Matthews, Susan Cammack.

NORTHAMPTON COUNTY RECORDS.

Northampton was originally called Accawmacke—mod-
ern name—Accomac, and was one of the original eight shires
or counties into which Virginia was divided in 1634. In
1640, its name was changed to Northampton, and in 1663 its
limits were reduced by the formation of the present county
of Accomac.

Book No. 1. 1632-40.

A court held at Acchawmacke————1632, present; Captain Edmund Scarborough, Mr. Obedience Robins, Mr.
John Howe, Mr. Roger Sanders.

At this court was a suit brought by Mr. Edward Drew
against ——Bagwell.

At a court held 7 Jan., 1632. Present: Captain Thomas
Grayes, Captain Edmund Scarborough, Mr. Obedience
Robins, Mr. John Howe, Mr. Roger Sanders.

Suit brought by Jane Winlee against James Knott for mis-
usage of her son Pharoah, an apprentice to the said
James.

Alexander Bradburne acknowledges debt of two barrels of corn to Nicholas Gringer.

Suit of Elizabeth Hainie against Thomas Powell.

Acknowledgment of Edward Drew and Thomas Powell per Thomas Grayes.

Suit brought by Philip Chapman against Israel Hill for 470 lbs. of tobacco.

Court held Anno Domini, September 1632. President: Captain William Claiborne, Captain Thomas Grayes, Captain Edmund Scarborough, Obedience Robins, Gent., John Howe, Gent., Roger Sanders, Gent.

Ordered by the Court that John Major shall pay unto Prinstone Foster, administrator of William Harmanson, 466 lbs. of tobacco.

Petition to the Court against Edward Drew for calling William Whithart "a roage."

Petition by Robert Swinsonne for 14 days work which the Plantation oweth him. Ordered that Capt. Thomas Grayes and Capt. Edmund Scarborough shall act upon the request of this board.

Petition of John Wilkins for 14 days work on the Plantation. Ordered as above.

Suit of Philip Chapman against John Brown.

Suit of William Bibby against Rowland Williams.

Assignment of one cow from Capt. Edmund Scarborough to John Wilkins, last day of April, 1632. Test, Wm. Berryman.

Assignment as above between same parties, 10 Nov., 1632. Test. Wm. Berryman, Thomas Cole.

17 Sept., 1633. Acknowledgment of Daniel Cugley.
　　　　　Acknowledgment of John Neale.

17 Sept., 1633. Acknowledgment of Anthony Wills.

17 Sept., 1633. Acknowledgment of Thomas Powell.

20 Sept., 1633. Acknowledgment of George Travellor.

20 Sept., 1633. Acknowledgment of Nicholas Rainberte.

20 Sept., 1633. Acknowledgment of Walter Scott.

20 Sept., 1633. Acknowledgment of William Roper.

20 Sept., 1633. Acknowledgment of John Major.

24 Sept., 1633. Acknowledgment of Daniel Cugley.

24 Sept., 1633. Acknowledgment of the widow Hanna Savage.

27 Aug., 1633. Warrant issued to arrest the bodie of Francis Phillips.

10 Sept., 1633. Warrant issued to arrest the bodie of Anthony Wills.

Deposition of William Bibbie, aged 33 years or thereabouts. Examined the ——— day of Octo., 1633.

These presents witnesseth, that we, Francis Phillips, of Accomac, tailor and Edward Stockdell of same place, carpenter, do owe our Lord King Charles 50 pounds sterling.

Suit of Zachary Cripps against Francis Phillips.

Warrant issued to arrest the bodies of Premstone Foster, William Baseley and Charles Hartrey. Given at James City, 26 Aug., 1633.

Acknowledgment of Charles Hartry, John Vaughan and Pascho Crocker to answer to the suit of William Berryman.

At a Court held at Accomac, 30 Dec., 1633. President: Capt. William Claiborne, Esq., Capt. Edmund Scarborough, Mr. Obedience Robins, Mr. William Stone, Mr. William Burdett, Mr. William Andrews, Mr. John Wilkins.

The oath of the Commissioners of ye Plantation of Acchawmacke was first administered unto Wm. William Stone, Mr. William Andrewes, Mr. John Wilkins and Mr. William Burdett, according to an order by the Governor and Council dated 29 Aug., 1633.

At James City, 29 Aug., 1633.

Sir John Harvey, Knt., Gov. General.

Mr. John Brewer.	Mr. Henry ———
Capt. Francis West.	Capt. John Uty.
Capt. John West.	Capt. Hugh Bullocke.
Capt. Saml. Mathew.	Capt. Wm. Peirce.
Capt. Wm. Clayborne.	Capt. Wm. Perry.
Mr. Wm. ———	

Acknowledgment of Capt. Edmund Scarborough to William Bibby, 13 March, 1632.

Order of the Court against Liveinge Denwoode to pay William Ward 3 barrels of corn.

Order of the Court that Walter Scott pay Nicholas Grindger 430 lbs. of tobacco.

Order of the Court that Walter Scott pay to the widow Hellinge 100 lbs. of tobacco and 3 bushels of corn.

Ordered that Henry Lee perform the full term of his unexpired indenture to James Berry.

Order to William Berryman, Churchwarden.

Order for Roger Fyerbrasse to work for Mr. William Andrewes until satisfaction be made to the latter for 80 lbs. of tobacco.

Order that James Knott shall answer to suit preferred by Mr. William Stone in behalf of Capt. William Epes.

At this Court, Richard Worster, aged 26 years or thereabouts, deposeth that Jeffrey Sope came unto Mr. ———for 5 years as his servant in Saint Christopher.

At a Court held 13 Jan.,—— Present: Capt. Edmund Scarborough, Mr. Obedience Robins, Mr. Wm. Stone, Mr. John Wilkins.

At this Court it is proved that William Batts made his last will nuncupative 18 July, 1632, and that he gave to Robert Dye, Thomas Nuton and John Webster 300 lbs. of tobacco; to Garrett Andrews 3 barrels of corn and the rest of his estate to Nicholas Harwoode, whom he made his executor.

Deposition of Mr. William Cropp, aged 40 years, and Randoll Reavell, aged 26 years, that this is the true will of William Batts, decd.

Inventory of the estate of William Batts, decd., sworn to at this Court by Nicholas Harwoode, aged 30 years. Teste. Henry Bagwell.

Suit of Stephen Charlton against Richard North, who was Marshall of Acchawmacke.

Suit of Nicholas Harwood against Hugh Haies.

Deposition of William Basely, aged 25 years, that Solomon Greene paid unto Mr. Peddocke or his assigns 2 hogsheads of tobacco for the debt of Rowland Williams.

Suit of Stephen Charlton against Rowland Williams for a bill of tobacco which was due to Mr. Robert Tralany.

Acknowledgment of Walter Scott of debt to Stephen Charlton.

Court held 19 Feb., 1633. Present: Capt. William Clayborne, Esq., Mr. William Burdette, Capt. Edmund Scarborough, Mr. William Andrewes, Mr. William Stone, Mr. John Wilkins.

Complaint of Mr. William Cotton, minister, that the Churchwardens should gather his levy of tobacco and corn due from the parishoners.

Suit of John Wadlow and Arthur Eliott against Stephen Charlton for wages due.

Petition of Levyne Denwood for lease of 60 acres of land.

Petition of Henry Carsley for lease of 50 acres of land.

Deposition of Thomas Butler, aged 27 years, and William Payne, aged 27 years, that Mr. George Scovell did lay a wager with Mr Mountney of 10 shillings sterling to 5 shillings sterling that Mr. William Burdette should never match in wedlock with the widow Sanders while they lived in Virginia.

Petition of John Hollaway for ——acres of land.

Deposition of Thomas Morris, aged 24 years, that John the Frenchman came to William Douglas' house and did bargain with Philip Taylor to serve him one year, and the Frenchman did promise to give the said Taylor 220 lbs. of tobacco which William Humberstone owed him.

FAUQUIER COUNTY MILITIA

ORDER BOOK 1773-1780.

May 24, 1773.	Richard Covington, Lieut.
May 24, 1773.	Nicholas George, Captain.
Aug. 25, 1777.	Captain William Ball; Lieut. James Foley; Ensign —— Deering; Lieut. Joshua Tullos; Ensign Daniel Shumate; Captain Charles Williams.
May 25, 1778.	William Pope, Captain; Thomas Conway, Lieut.; William Kenton, Lieut.; John Combs, Ensign; Thomas Bronaugh, Capt.; James Withers, Lieut.; Berryman Jennings, Ensign; Turner Morehead, Capt.; Robert Layton, 1st. Lieut.; William Ransdell, Ensign; Armistead Churchill, Colonel of 2d Bat. of Fauquier Militia; Thomas Harris, 2d Lieut.; Richard Rixey, 1st Lieut.; Aylett Buckner, Major; Joseph Smith, Ensign; John Barker, Ensign.
June 22, 1778.	William Jennings, Capt.; Thomas Smith, Lieut.; William Donaldson, Ensign.
Aug. 24, 1778.	John French, 2d Lieut.
Sept. 28, 1778.	Francis Triplett, Capt.; Wharton Ransdell, Ensign; Martin Pickett and John Blackwell, Lt. Cols.; Samuel Blackwell, Major; Francis Atwell and Joseph James, Capts.; James Weathers and Augustine Jennings, 2d Lieuts.; Thomas Edwards and Rodham Tullos, Ensigns; Henry Peyton, 2d Lieut.
Nov. 23, 1778.	Daniel Shumate, 2d Lieut.; Tilman Weaver, Capt.
Feb. 22, 1779.	Francis Payne, Ensign.
April 26, 1779.	Francis Ash, 2d Lieut.
April 27, 1779.	Charles Chilton, Capt.
May 24, 1779.	Thomas James, 2d Lieut.

June 28, 1779. James Blackwell, 1st Lieut.; Benjamin Ball,
1st Lieut.; George Rogers, 2d Lieut.

July 26, 1779. Joseph Taylor, 1st Lieut.; Thomas Edwards and John Martin, 2d Lieuts.; John
Ball and Augustine Smith, Ensigns; William Blackwell, Capt.

Oct. 25, 1779. John Barbie, Sergt., 1st Va. Reg., Contl.
Army, served 3 years.

William Barber, soldier, 1st Va. Regt.,
Contl. Army, served 3 years.

John Jones, Sergt., in Corps of Guards,
served from beginning of campaign 1777
to Aug. 14, 1779. C. Gibbs, Commander
of the Guards.

Daniel Grant, soldier in Capt. Long's Co.,
of the Rifle Corps Contl. Army.

Nov. 22, 1779 William Keirnes, soldier 7th Va. Regt.

Feb. 28, 1780. John Ball, Capt. and John Barker, Lieut.

Richard Wilson, soldier in 1st Va. Regt. in
last war.

Thomas Malone, soldier in New Jersey
Regt. in last war under Col. Peter Schuy-
ler, has been an inhabitant of Va. upwards of seven years.

Mar. 27, 1780. William Smith, served in 5 or 6 campaigns
in 1st Va. Regt. in last war.

William Wright, William Provo, Vincent
Rollins and Robert Sherington, soldiers in
the last war in 2d Va. Regt. in Capt.
Eustace's Company.

Swanson Brown, Sergt., in Col. Byrd's Va.
Regt., in last war.

Joshua Jenkins, Sergt., in Capt. John Chilton's Co. 3d Va. Regt., killed at Brandywine. Thomas Jenkins, is his heir at law.
Certificate signed by Col. Thomas Marshall.

Robert Smith, soldier in 1st Va. Regt., in

last war.

Thomas Maccaboy, soldier in 47th British Regt. in Va. in last war.

John Nicholson, soldier in Col. Byrd's Regt. in last war.

John Hathaway, Capt.; Augustine Jennings, Lieut.; Minor Winn, Lieut.; William Heale, 2d Lieut.; Thos. Nelson, Ensign; Ambrose Barnett, Ensign; Peter Kamper, Ensign; all took the oath.

Joshua King produced a discharge from Genl. Washington and made oath that he served three years and then procured a substitute, to wit. Charles Neale, excepting and reserving his right lands; and that said substitute served until the Regt. was discharged.

John Hopper produced a certificate under the hand of Col. Edward Carrington, Colonel-Commandant of the 1st Regt. of Artillery, and that the said Hopper had duly served the time for which he listed.

Christopher McCannon, produced a certificate from Col. Allison of 1st Va. Regt., State, showing that he had served three years.

April 24, 1780.   Moses Rankin served as non-commissioned officer in last war. Certificate signed by Genl. Washington.

May 22, 1780.   Samuel Wise, soldier, 3 years being time for which he listed. Certificate signed by John Green, Colonel 6th Va. Regt.

Joseph Wheatley, Capt.; Joseph Smith, Lieut.; Baylor Jennings, Ensign; John Fletcher, Lieut.; and Joseph Nelson, Ensign; all took the oath.

William Hall served as a soldier in Col.

Byrd's Regt. in last war.

June 26, 1780. Mathew Caynor, soldier in 6th Va. Regt. for three years. Certificate signed by John Webb, Lieut. Col. of 5th Va. Regt.

July 24, 1780. Edward Shacklett, Sergt., 1st Va. Regt. of State Artillery. Served the time for which he listed. Certificate signed by Edward Carrington, Lieut. Col., commandant of said Regt.

Aug. 28, 1780. Samuel Bronaugh, Ensign. Took the oath.

Sept. 25, 1780. Thomas Conway, Capt. Took the oath.

VIRGINIA MILITIA LISTS.

FROM FORCE MSS. LIBRARY OF CONGRESS.

The following lists are contained in 'The Force Collection" in the Library of Congress. They are of great value, as a majority of the original records from which these are obtained were destroyed by the Federals. Peter Force was born near Little Falls, N. J., Nov. 26, 1790. His life work, entitled "American Archives" a valuable collection of 22,000 books and 40,000 pamphlets was bought by the U. S. Government in 1867, and placed in the Library of Congress. He died in Washington, D. C., Jan. 23, 1868.

GLOUCESTER COUNTY.

At a Committee meeting held at the Court House of Gloucester Co., 13th day of September 1775, the following gentlemen were nominated officers in the Militia of Gloucester County.

Warner Lewis, Esq., County-Lieut.; Sir John Peyton, Bart., Colonel; James Whiting, Gent., Lieut.-Col.; James Boswell, Gent., Major.

CAPTAINS.

Gibson Cuverius, John Camp, Richard Matthews, George Booth, Jasper Clayton, John Hubbard, John Whiting, John Billups, Sr., Benjamin Shackeford, John Willis, Robert Matthews, William Buckner, John Dixon, Richard Billups, William Smith.

LIEUTENANTS.

Samuel Cary Richard Hall, John Foster, James Baytop, Thomas Buckner, George Green, William Sears, James Bently, Edward Matthews, John Billups, Jr., Dudley Cary, Hugh Hayes, Churchill Armistead, Philip Tabb, John Foster, Jr., Robert Gayle.

ENSIGNS.

Henry Stevens, William Dawes, William Haywood, Thomas Baytop, John Fox, James Laughlin, William Bently, Christopher Garland, Peter Bernard, John Hayes, Samuel Eddis, Thomas Tabb, Richard Davis, Josiah Foster, George Plummer, John Gale.

CHESTERFIELD COUNTY.

At a meeting of the Committee for Chesterfield county at the Court House on the 25th day of October, 1775, the following gentlemen were chosen officers for the Militia of the county.

Edward Friend, County-Lieut.; John Bott, Colonel; Robert Haskins, Lieut.-Colonel; Joseph Bass, Major.

CAPTAINS.

Thomas Bolling, George Robertson, Robert Goode, Richard Baugh, James Elam, Benjamin Brance, Bernard Markham, Jesse Cogbill, Edward Moseley, James Harris, Creed Haskins, Joseph Royal.

LIEUTENANTS.

Richard Booker, Archibald Bass, David Patteson, John Osborne, Patrick Wright, Archibald Walthall, Stephen Pankey, King Graves, John Hill, Thomas Wooldridge, Samuel Goode, Benjamin Ward.

ENSIGNS.

John Archer, John Hill, John Fowler, Jr., Thomas Osborne, Branch Elam, Thomas Goode, Obadiah Smith, Jr., George Cogbill, Jr., Alex. Baugh, William Scott, Jr., Jesse Clark, Daniel Worsham.

HANOVER COUNTY

At a meeting of the Committee Monday, 29 Jan., 1776, the following gentlemen were chosen officers to the company of Regulars to be raised in this county.

Richard Clough Anderson, Capt.; John Anderson, 1st Lieut.; William Bentley, 2d Lieut.; Robert Tompkins, Ensign.

SPOTSYLVANIA COUNTY.

At a meeting of the select Committee September 12, 1775, for the District of this county, and the counties of Caroline, Stafford and King George, the following officers were elected.

REGULARS.

William Taliaferro, Capt.; John Willis, 1st Lieut.; Seymour Hooe, 2d Lieut.; Benjamin Holmes, Ensign.

MINUTE MEN.

Hugh Mercer, Colonel; Mordecai Buckner, Lieut. Col.; Robert Johnson, Major.

CAROLINE COUNTY.

CAPTAINS.

Thomas Lomax, Samuel Hawes, Thomas Robinson.

LIEUTENANTS.

William Lindsay, Richard Taylor, James Bankhead.

ENSIGNS.

James Upshaw, Thomas Buckner, William Wolfolk.

SPOTSYLVANIA COUNTY.

CAPTAINS.

Lewis Willis, George Stubblefield, Oliver Towles.

LIEUTENANTS.

Robert Carter Page, Larkin Chew, Francis Talliaferro.

ENSIGNS.

Henry Bartlett, Robert Dudley, Winslow Parker.

KING GEORGE COUNTY

CAPTAINS.

John Talliaferro, Jr., Andrew Buchanan.

LIEUTENANTS.

Francis Conway, Walter Vowell.

ENSIGNS.

Reuben Briscoe, James Hord.

STAFFORD COUNTY

CAPTAINS.

Townshend Dade, William Washington.

LIEUTENANTS.

William G. Stuart, Thomas Fitzhugh.

ENSIGNS.

William Fitzhugh, John Mountjoy.

Joseph Robinson, Commissary of Musters; Charles Washington, Commissary.

(To be continued.)

VIRGINIA REVOLUTIONARY SOLDIERS.

(Cont. from page 181.)

London, Wm., Private, State Line, 3 years' service.
Poe, Thos., Private, State Line, 3 years' service.
Collins, —— Private, State Line, 3 years' service.
Dandridge, Alex. Spotswood, Capt., Va. Cavalry, 3 years' service.
Daniel, Jno., Corporal, State Line, 3 years' service.
Minnes, Jno., Private, Contl. Line, 3 years' service.
Jones, Edwd., Private, State Line, 3 years' service.
Grig, Geo., Private, Contl. Line, 3 years' service.
Cypress, Andw., Private, Contl. Line., 7 years' service.
Jones, Jesse, Private, Contl. Line, 3 years' service.
Lipscomb, Hy., Fifer, Contl. Line, 3 years' service.
Simmons, Joshua, Fife Major, Contl. Line, 3 years' service.
Bridgman, Joseph, Drummer, Contl. Line, 3 years' service.
Thompson, Thos., Private, Contl. Line, 3 years' service.
Turk, Jas., Private, Contl. Line, 3 years' service.
Chambers, David, Private, Contl. Line, 3 years' service.
Shields, Jas., Private, Contl. Line, 3 years' service.
Wilson, Jas., Private, Contl. Line, 3 years' service.
Turk, Robert, Private, State Line, 3 years' service.
McMasters, Michael, Private, Contl. Line, 3 years' service.
Crawford, David, Private, Contl. Line, 3 years' service.
Perkinton, Wm., Sergeant, State Artillery, 3 years' service.
Dean, Jno., Sergeant, State Artillery, 3 years' service.
Simms, Isaac, Private, Contl. Line, 3 years' service.
Chisholm, Geo., Private, Contl. Line, 7 years' service.
Chilton, Jno., Capt., Va. Line. Killed at Battle of Brandywine 11 Sept., 1777; warrant to Jno. Chilton, heir at law, June 27, 1783.
Pugh, Lewis, Private, Contl. Line, 3 years' service.
Murray, Geo., Private, State Artillery, 3 years' service.
Clifton, Joshua, Private, Contl. Line, 7 years' service.
Simmons, Jas., Private, Contl. Line, 3 years' service.
Hines, Geo., Sergeant, Contl. Line, 3 years' service.

Buckley, Michael, Private, Contl. Line, 7 years' service.
Thomas, David, Private, State Line, for the war.
Fromaget, Roman, Private, Contl. Line, 3 years' service.
White, Rich., Private, State Line, for the war.
Burch, Saml., Private, Va. Cavalry, 3 years' service.
Roach, Wm., Corporal, Contl. Line, 7 years' service.
Wilson, Stacey, Sergeant, Contl. Line Oct., 1776—June 27, 1783.
Kavins, Jno., Corporal, Contl. Line, 3 years' service.
George, Francis, Private, Contl. Line, 3 years' service.
Canley, Asa, Private, Contl. Line, 3 years' service.
Sell, Geo., Private, Contl. Line, Dec., 1776—June 27, 1783.
Smithy, Benj., Private, Contl. Line, 3 years' service.
George, Jas. Mayo, Private, State Line, 3 years' service.
Walden, Jno., Corporal, State Line, 3 years' service.
Easten, Wm., Sergeant, State Line, 3 years' service.
Kidd, Benj., Private, Va. Artillery, 3 years' service.
Walden, Geo., Sergeant, State Line, 3 years' service.
Hackett, Jas., Private, Contl. Line, 3 years' service.
Burton, Hutchins, Lieutenant, State Line, 3 years' service.
Kein, Thos., Private, State Line, 7 years' service.
Hobbs, Fredk, Private, Contl. Line, 7 years' service.
Taylor, Isaac, Sergeant, Contl. Line, 7 years' service.
Hodges, Williamson, Private, Contl. Line, 7 years' service.
Kouts, Jacob, Private, Contl. Line, 7 years' service.
Murphy, Patk., Private, Contl. Line, 7 years' service.
Simmons, Williamson, Private, Contl. Line, 7 years' service.
Sample, Jas., Private, Contl. Line, 3 years' service.
Williams, Wm., Private, State Line, for the war.
McGuy, Bennett, Private, Contl. Line, 3 years service.
Thompson, Robt., Private, Contl. Line, 3 years' service.
Layne, John, Private, State Line, for the war.
Lewis, John, Private, Contl. Line, 3 years' service.
Klung, Henry, Private, Contl. Line, 3 years' service.
Groves, Thos., Drummer, Contl. Line, 3 years' service.
Morgan, David, Private, Contl. Line, 3 years' service.
Dollins, Wm., Private, State Line, for the war.

Roberts Ambrose, Private, State Line, 3 years' service.

English, Chas., Private, State Line, for the war.

Southworth, Thos., Private, State Line, 3 years' service.

Quarles, Abner, Private, Contl. Line, 3 years' service.

Macomber, Jno., Corporal Va. Cavalry, for the war.

Peyton, Valentine, Capt., decd., Contl. Line, 3 years' service; warrant to Timothy Peyton, heir at law, June 28, 1783.

Courtney, Saml., Private, Contl. Line, 7 years' service.

Keep, Jas., Private, Contl. Line, 3 years' service.

Darby, Nathl., Lieutenant, Contl. Line, 7 years' service.

Weedon, Aug., Sergeant, State Line, 3 years' service.

McCune, Patk., Private, State Line, 3 years' service.

Chapin, Jno., Private, State Line, 3 years' service.

Eastwood, Demsy, Private, Contl. Line, 3 years' service.

Best, Tucker, Sergeant, State Line, 3 years' service.

Field, Wm., Private, Contl. Line, 3 years' service.

Perry, Wm., Private, Contl. Line, 3 years' service.

Martin, Wm., Private, Contl. Line, 3 years' service.

Cooper, Wm., Private, State Line, 3 years' service.

Baker, Thos., Private, State Artillery, 3 years' service.

Driver, Edwd., Sergeant, Contl. Line, 3 years' service.

Muse, Geo., Sergeant, Va. Cavalry, 3 years' service.

Perkins, Joseph, Private, Contl. Line, 3 years' service.

Davis, Jno., Private, State Line, 3 years' service.

Griffin, Reuben, Private, Va. Cavalry, 3 years' service.

Scott, Wm., Drummer, Contl. Line, 7 years' service.

Hardin, John, Private, Contl. Line, 3 years' service.

Carter, Wm., Private, State Line, 3 years' service.

James, Elisha, Private, State Line, 3 years' service.

Skinner, Richd., Private, Contl. Line, 3 years' service.

Duneth, Jno., Private, State Line, for the war.

Thornburn, Jno., Private, State Line, for the war.

(To be continued)

CAROLINE COUNTY MARRIAGE BONDS.

(Contributed by Dr. Jos. Lyon Miller.)

Jan.	16, 1787.	Thomas Allen and Margaret Fields.
Jan.	16, 1787.	Thomas Ayres and Molly Noell.
Jan.	30, 1789.	James Andrews and Molly Broaddus.
July	7, 1789.	Thomas Allen and Jenny Hackney.
Feb.	21, 1795.	William Allen and Mary Collier.
Oct.	12, 1786.	Wm. Bridgford and Lucy Long.
Aug.	17, 1787.	John Baxter and Jane Tiller.
Aug.	17, 1787.	Wm. Bush and Nancy Kee.
Aug.	17, 1787.	Wm. Bell and Sally Doggett .
Aug.	17, 1787.	Samuel Butler and Patty Douglass.
Sept.	8, 1790.	George Burchell and Elizabeth Pemberton.
Aug.	17, 1787.	Carter Blanton and Susannah Snead.
Oct.	16, 1789.	David Bibb and Mary Chandler.
Jan.	— 1790.	James Berry and Nancy Buckner.
Mar.	6, 1791.	Lewis Ballard and Sukey Miller.
Jan.	29, 1792.	John G. Brown and Frances Eubank.
Mar.	31, 1792.	Thomas Barlow and Nancy West.
——	1789.	John Bond and Molly Sale.
Jan.	28, 1792.	Wm. Brown and Susannah Dyamett.
Sept.	1, 1797.	Anthony Baber and Rhoda Carlton.
Oct.	22, 1788.	John Bocock and Lucy Nonnent.
Dec.	25, 1793.	Thomas Burrow and Nelly Bibb.
Dec.	30, 1793.	Lewis Bell and Nutty Dillard.
Dec.	30, 1793.	Wm. Bullock and Lucy Timberlake.
Jan.	9, 1794.	Joseph Brame and Elizabeth Thomas.
Jan.	13, 1794.	John Broaddus and America Broaddus.
Nov.	10, 1794.	Andrew Broadus and Fanny Temple.
May	15, 1799.	Adam Beaseley and Fanny Vawter.
May	26, 1795.	Richard Bowlar and Elizabeth Skinner.
Dec.	22, 1795.	James Brown and Mary Farmer.
June	11, 1796.	Richard Boulware and Mary Narrett.
Feb.	1, 1796.	Frederick Bourne and Jenny Sampson.
Dec.	27, 1796.	Wm. E. Bowers and Fanny Jones.
Oct.	4, 1798.	David Bailor and Peggy Page.

June	4, 1797.	Walke Bowler and Elizabeth Self.
Nov.	26, 1798.	Edwin Broaddus and Frances Jerdon.
Dec.	24, 1798.	Thomas Belle and Sarah Grafton.
Mar.	13, 1794.	Thomas Blackburn and Sally Daniel.
Mar.	5, 1796.	John Barlow and Ursuly Southworth.
Dec.	13, 1799.	Hawes Barbee and Polly Jones.
May	25, 1799.	Thomas Blackburn and Nancy Green.
May	19, 1786.	John Carter and Nancy Carter.
Mar.	22, 1787.	Thomas Crenshaw and Elizabeth Saunders.
July	14, 1787.	Reuben Clift and Sally Stevens.
Dec.	17, 1786.	Wm. Cannon and Elizabeth Brown.
Mar.	5, 1788.	John Courts and Fanny Winn.
Mar.	5, 1788.	Lewis Collins and Martha Emmerson.
Mar.	5, 1788.	John Croucher and Martha Long.
Mar.	5, 1788.	John Cox and Patty Bush.
Dec.	16, 1788.	Wm. Crawford and Milly Chewning.
Aug.	17, 1789.	John Clark and Nancy Bird.
Sept.	8, 1790.	Isaac Croucher and Nancy Blanton.
Sept.	8, 1790.	John Chandler and Jenny McKee.
Jan.	22, 1792.	James Coleburn and Mary Crudle.
	1792.	James Collier and Nancy Pitts.
Dec.	22, 1792.	Ambrose Carlton and Nancy Slaughter.
May	20, 1793.	Thomas Terry Cook and Elizabeth Richeson.
July	10, 1793.	Samuel Chenault and Brune Pitts.
Jan.	3, 1795.	Reuben Crenshaw and Fanny Hundley.
Jan.	6, 1795.	Wm. Collins and Elizabeth Pitts.
July	18, 1795.	Edmund Carton and Sally Mourning.
July	18, 1795.	John Carpenter and Polly Duval.
Dec.	3, 1794.	Presley Carter and Elizabeth Pettus.
May	13, 1794.	John Cox and Polly Holloway.
Nov.	5, 1796.	Elijah Chenault and Molly Graves.
June	28, 1797.	James Chash and Susan Jeter.
June	28, 1797.	Elijah Camall and Jane Yarbrough.
June	28, 1797.	Thomas Camall and Elizabeth Harris.
Jan.	17, 1798.	James Camall and Anna Hetcher.
April	10, 1798.	Richmond Camall and Phoebe Jones.
Dec.	9, 1798.	Thomas B. Coleman and Elizabeth Coghill.

Dec. 26, 1799.	Edmund Clark and Sally Boulware.
No date.	Joel Dunn and Lucia Page.
No date.	Thomas Docotes and Elizabeth Sandland.
April 18, 1789.	Wm. Davenport and Milly Blackhall.
Sept. 19, 1789.	Garland Duke and Jane Roy Coleman.
Sept. 8, 1790.	Benj. Daniel and Peggy Brown.
Jan. 2, 1790.	Wm. Durrett and Sarah Conner.
	Joseph Duerson and Jennet Bowie.
	Thomas Donahoe and Patty Umbreckhouse.
	John Dodd and Lucy Poe.
Feb. 9, 1792.	Johnathon Dickerson and Crashe Seizer.
	Rueben Dear and Jenny Vawter.
	David Dillard and Susannah Stevens.
June 30, 1797.	Wm. Dunn and Sarah Coghill.
Mar. 12, 1798.	Wm. Douglass and Eliza Miller.
July 12, 1798.	Wm. Duval and Lucy Duvall.
Oct. 5, 1798.	Henry Dunn and Ann Dunn.
Nov. 1, 1799.	John Dye and Delphia Alsop.
No date.	Daniel Edmonds and Catharine Miller.
Dec. 14, 1788.	George Estes and Ann Sannell.
	———Edwards and Katy Boulware.
	George Este and Sarah Anderson.
May 12, 1793.	Wm. Elliot and Elizabeth Edwards.
May 20, 1794.	Daniel Edmonds and Ann Murry.

NORFOLK COUNTY MARRIAGE BONDS.

(Continued from Page 168.)

July 22, 1764.	Joseph Polett and Mary Sills.
July 28, 1764.	Jacob Lowry and Judith Hilman.
July 31, 1764.	Joel Moon and Elizabeth Nelson.
Aug. 7, 1764.	William Dale and Dinah Edwards.
Aug. 17, 1764.	Thomas Wakefield and Sarah Dunn.
Aug. 30, 1764.	Samuel White and Bithiah Bird.
Sept. 13, 1764.	Charles Wilkins and Mary Thompson.
Sept. 13, 1764.	John Smith and Priscilla Milner.
Sept. 20, 1764.	Willoughby Old and Martha Maning.

Nov.	5, 1764.	Joel Cooper and Courtney Roberts.
Nov.	15, 1764.	Captain Edward Davison and Martha, dau. of William Herbert.
Dec.	12, 1764.	George Braithwaite and Lucretia Williams.
Dec.	28, 1764.	Guivinies Marnes and Anna Maria Barnchhe of Reading, Berks County, Penna.
Feb.	17, 1765.	Henry Tucker and Mary Cole.
Feb.	20, 1765.	David Porter and Agnes, dau. of George Veale.
Feb.	28, 1765.	Richard Simms and Susannah Archer.
Mar.	23, 1765.	Thomas Redman and Mary Gibson.
Mar.	28, 1765.	Doctor Charles Mayle and Lydia, dau. of Thomas Nash, Sr.
April	2, 1765.	Jonathan Meredith and Elizabeth Hodgson.
April	11, 1765.	Joshua Davis and Sarah Mitchell.
April	20, 1765.	Robert Armstrong and Jemima Ballentine.
May	8, 1765.	John Pool and Mary Carter.
May	21, 1765.	William Smith and Sarah Stammars.
June	8, 1765.	Robert Forsyth and Anne Delson.
June	12, 1765.	John Montgomerie and Sarah Dyer Thelaball.
June	14, 1765.	Rueben Herbert and Betty Sparrow.
June	19, 1765.	Hardress Waller and Anne Godfrey.
July	25, 1765.	William Happer and Elizabeth, dau. of Simon Wilson.
July	29, 1765.	John Butt and Elizabeth Fairfield.
Aug.	17, 1765.	Hugh Watts and Margaret Williamson.
Aug.	24, 1765.	John Elleson and Mary Drury.
Sept.	7, 1765.	James Smith and Elizabeth Gregory.
Sept.	12, 1765.	Henry Wells and Elizabeth Case.
Sept.	14, 1765.	Jno. Gilchrist and Frances, dau. of Archibald Campbell.
Sept.	19, 1765.	Henry Lemon and Susannah Milburn.
Sept.	21, 1765.	Josiah Hodges and Mary Ewell.
Sept.	25, 1765.	Matthew Maund and Elizabeth, dau. of Jno. Williams.
Sept.	30, 1765.	Solomon Smith and Elizabeth Wilson.

Oct.   3, 1765.   Joseph Langley and Elizabeth Ashley.
Oct.   16, 1765.   Saml. Smith and Mary, dau. of Jeremiah
                      Forman.
Oct.   19, 1765.   Joseph Middleton and Elizabeth Ballentine.
Oct.   26, 1765.   Benjamin Bannerman and Mrs. Margaret
                      Streep.
May   28, 1766.   John Taylor and Sarah Tucker.
June   16, 1766.   William Wilkins and Tamer Burges.
July   8, 1766.   James Oswall and Rachel, dau. of John Mer-
Aug.   8, 1766.   James Miller and Elizabeth, dau. of Mary
                      cer, Sr., born Aug. 11, 1743.
                      Avery, born Dec. 5, 1744.
Aug.   26, 1766.   James Walker and Mary Duff, widow.
Sept.   30, 1766.   Arthur Butt and Martha, dau. of Jno. Rid-
                      dlehurst.
Oct.   2, 1766.   Matthew Crawford and Ann Turner.
Nov.   12, 1766.   Francis Hatton and Margaret, dau. of Ann
                      Manning, born Aug. 18, 1745.
Nov.   18, 1766.   John Edwards and Rebecca Whiddon.
Nov.   20, 1766.   Thomas Williamson and Margaret Wilson.
Nov.   24, 1766.   John Hutchings, Jr. and Ann Ramsay.
Nov.   29, 1766.   James Leitch and Susannah, dau. of Joanna
                      Terry, born Sep. 12, 1745.
Dec.   11, 1766.   Benjamin Dingley Gray and Sarah Bayne.
Jan.   3, 1767.   William Sley and Sarah Lancaster.
Jan.   21, 1767.   William Farrer and Mary, dau. of Adam
                      Lovett, decd., of P. Anne County
Jan.   22, 1767.   Duncan Campbell and Ann Wha———
Mar.   2, 1767.   Joseph Rives and Margaret Hatton.
Mar.   14, 1767.   Charles Bushnell and Catharine McGee.
Mar.   24, 1767.   John Murray and Abigail Cawson.
April   1, 1767.   William Verling and Elizabeth, dau. of Wm.
                      Conner.
April   6, 1767.   James Maxwell and Helen Calvert.
April   26, 1767.   George Gordon and Elizabeth Bruce, widow.
April   30, 1767.   John Brown and Sally, dau. of Ann Walker,
                      born Feb. 22, 1745.

May	12, 1767.	Thomas Herbert and Sophia Edwards.
May	22, 1767.	John Matthias and Mary Barrington.
June	6, 1767.	Nathan Denny and Bridget Guy.
June	9, 1767.	Captain Thomas Morris and Molly, dau. of Benjamin Bascome.
June	18, 1767.	Mathew Hubard and Anna Dungham.
Aug.	30, 1767.	Robert Shedded and Agatha Wells Goodrich.
Sept.	2, 1767.	Thomas Shepherd and Barthiah, dau. of Amos Etheredge.
Sept.	5, 1767.	Robert Banks and Sarah Symonds, widow.
Sept.	5, 1767.	John Randle and Elizabeth Wilkins.
Sept.	5, 1767.	Griffin Peart and Mrs. Elizabeth Fife.
Sept.	7, 1767.	Reuben Manning and Dinah McCay.
Oct.	6, 1767.	Thomas Newton, Jr., and Martha, dau. of Joanna Tucker.
Oct.	30, 1767.	Benjamin Newbould and Mrs. Elizabeth Davis.
Dec.	16, 1767.	John Collins and Frances Jones.
Dec.	24, 1767.	James Webb and Mrs. Aphia Langley.
Jan.	1, 1768.	John Baker and Sarah Jackson.
Jan.	6, 1768.	Thomas Holstead and Mrs. Sarah Northcott.
Jan.	8, 1768.	John Maclean and Suckie, dau. of Thomas Talbott.
Jan.	27, 1768.	Bassett Moseley and Rebecca Newton.
Jan.	31, 1768.	Peter Taylor and Margaret Wallace.
Feb.	8, 1768.	Charles Denby and Ann Owens.
Feb.	15, 1768.	John Hunter and Mrs. Mary Nicholson.
Feb.	25, 1768.	Gardner Fleming and Christian Smith.
April	19, 1768.	William Cosby and Mary, dau. of James Pasteur.
April	26, 1768.	Lemuel Langley and Sarah Butt.
June	1, 1768.	Alexander Moseley and Eleanora Kelsick.
June	16, 1768.	Josiah Hoffmire and Courtney, dau. of Alex. Foreman.
Aug.	24, 1768.	Nathaniel Hilton and Susannah Bailey.

Sept. 6, 1768. Caleb Herbert and Ann Nicholson.

Sept. 14, 1768. Robert Cawson and Lydia Herbert.

Oct. 15, 1768. Demcy Coffield and Westcoat Carney.

Oct. 24, 1768. John Cavender and Elizabeth, dau. of Robert Franks.

Oct. 29, 1768. Thomas Roberts and Frances Calvert.

Nov. 21, 1768. James Marsden and Polly Calvert.

Dec. 3, 1768. Thos. Williamson and Mary, dau. of William Talbot.

Dec. 6, 1768. Benjamin Bunting and Letta, dau. of Edward and Margaret Lewelling, born Oct. 24, 1747.

Jan. 16, 1769. Joshua Wright and Lucretia, dau. of Robert Fry.

Jan. 20, 1769. Solomon Shepherd and Elizabeth Osheal.

Jan. 21, 1769. William Brett and Rebecca Jacobs.

Jan. 31, 1769. George Farrer and Judith Dickson.

Jan. 31, 1769. John Bayne and Molly, dau. of William and Lydia Ashley.

Feb. 4, 1769. John Livingston and Ann Dunn.

Feb. 8, 1769. John Coles and Rebecca Tucker.

Mar. 16, 1769. Maxey Grims and Margaret Dale.

April 13, 1769. John McHerall and Frances Freeman.

April 28, 1769. William George and Ann Simpson.

May 13, 1769. William Brown and Mary, widow of William Smithson and dau. of Lemuel Coverly.

May 19, 1769. Richard Kelsick and Ann Porter.

May 20, 1769. David Chapman and Courtney Lowrey, widow.

June 19, 1769. Robert Steele and Sarah Cann, widow.

July 15, 1769. Samuel Bressie and Sarah Murden.

Aug. 10, 1769. Edward Allmon and Lucretia Braithwaite.

Sept. 2, 1769. John Oliffe and Mrs. Anne Knight.

Nov. 18, 1769. Thomas Larchin and Mrs. Elizabeth Holt, widow.

Nov. 25, 1769. Freer Armston and Elizabeth Gardner.

Dec.	21, 1769.	Benjamin Miller and Frances Odean.
Dec.	4, 1769.	John Lee and Jane Brazill.
Dec.	7, 1769.	George Webb and Peggy Cheshire.
Jan.	15, 1770.	Charles Cooper and Ann Dale, widow.
Jan.	29, 1770.	Roger Pearse and Teresa Boyd.
Feb.	1, 1770.	Aaron Barker and Elizabeth Maund.
Feb.	19, 1770.	John Edwards and Joice Carter.
Mar.	2, 1770.	Wright Brickell and Eliz., dau. of John Steel.
Mar.	5, 1770.	Absalom Keebel and Mildred Gwynn.
Mar.	28, 1770.	Thomas Burke and Mary, dau. of William Freeman.
April	13, 1770.	Dickerson Pryor and Mrs. Frances Frazier.
May	1, 1770.	William Callis and Hannah Dale.
May	21, 1770.	Slaughter Cofield and Mary Carney.
May	30, 1770.	Robert Jarvis and Sarah Manning.
June	1, 1770.	Francis Wright and Ann Godfrey Tatem.
July	2, 1770.	David Porter and Ann, dau. of Nicholas Wonycott.
July	4, 1770.	Lemuel Coverly and Mrs. Winea Dameron, widow.
Aug.	10, 1770.	James Wilson and Mary Wilson.
Aug.	10, 1770.	Robert Barron and Susannah Loyall.
Nov.	17, 1770.	Saml. Tomlinson and Ann, dau. of John Peirce.
Nov.	26, 1770.	Owen Morris and Elizabeth Walker.
Dec.	20, 1770.	James Champion and Rebecca Stackpole.
Dec.	20, 1770.	James Pasteur and Lelicy Langley.

FAMILY HISTORY

We shall publish from time to time under the above heading, data taken from the editor's note books, originally gathered from the Virginia records. In making special searches for Virginia pedigrees, it is advisable to note everything pertaining to the name, although eventually much of it may be cast aside as not being pertinent to the family in view. This unused material is of interest to some one of the name. In this issue of the magazine we print the first installment on Anderson, Taylor and Walton.

ANDERSON

Will of David Anderson, Trinity Parish, Louisa County. No date. Probated, 8 Oct. 1781. Wife Judith. Four sons John, Charles, Archilaus and David Anderson. Four daughters, Mary, Sarah, Susannah and Elizabeth. (under age). Witnesses. Elizabeth Johnson, Mary Lacy. Book 2, Page 392. Louisa Co.

Will of Pouncey Anderson, St. Martins Parish, Louisa County. Dated 24 Jan., 1781. Probated 13 August, 1781. Wife Elizabeth; sons Richard and Michael; the children of my daughter Judith Dabney; granddaughter Frances Anderson, daughter of Richard and Mary Anderson; granddaughters Mary Anderson and Judith Anderson, daughters of Richard and Mary Anderson; grandson Richard, son of Richard and Mary Anderson; granddaughter Christian Anderson daughter of Richard and Mary Anderson; granddaughter Jane, daughter of Richard and Mary Anderson; grandson Thomas Meriwether Anderson, son of Michael and Sarah Anderson; granddaughter Ann Anderson, daughter of Michael and Sarah Anderson; grandson Pouncey Anderson, son of Michael and Sarah Anderson; grandson Reuben Anderson, son of Michael and Sarah Anderson; grandson William Anderson, son of Michael and Sarah Anderson; grand-

son Edmond Anderson, son of Michael and Sarah
Anderson; grandson Richard Anderson, son of Michael
and Sarah Anderson; granddaughter Elizabeth Johnson,
daughter of James and Judith Dabney; granddaughters
Ciceley Dabney, Ann Anderson Dabney, Mary Dabney
and Charity Dabney daughters of James and Judith Dab-
ney; grandson William Dabney, son of James and Judith
Dabney; sons Richard and Michael Anderson; daughter
Judith Dabney; great-granddaughter Ann Anderson
Johnson, daughter of Christopher and Elizabeth Johnson;
grandson Richard Anderson, son of Michael and Sarah
Anderson. Executors, wife Elizabeth Anderson, sons
Richard and Michael, and my son-in-law James Dabney.
Witnesses: Nathan Sims, Mary Sims, Samuel Dabney.
Book 2, Page 379, Louisa Co.

David Anderson, Jr., administrator of the estate of Robert
Anderson, gentleman, decd., 9 April, 1782. Securities:
Turner Anderson and William Poindexter. Book 2,
Page 447, Louisa Co.

John Anderson administrator of David Anderson, decd., 14
Sept., 1785. Securities: Robert Anderson, Archibald
Moore, Waddy Thomson and Moses White. Book 3,
Page 111, Louisa Co.

Will of Elizabeth Anderson, St. Martins Parish, Louisa
County. Dated 7 July, 1791. Probated 8 December, 1794.
Grandson Richard, son of Michael Anderson; grand-
children Thomas M. Anderson, Connery Anderson, Reu-
ben Anderson, Edmund Anderson, David Anderson, Ann
Thomson, wife of Edmund Thomson and Elizabeth An-
derson, all children of Michael Anderson. Daughter Ju-
dith Dabney, wife of James Dabney. Sons Michael and
Richard Anderson, and the latter's son Richard Anderson.
Elizabeth, wife of Mathew Anderson; Frances Holland
wife to Christopher Holland; Mary Woodson wife to
John Woodson; Kitty Perkins wife to Robert Perkins.
Judith Anderson, Jane and Susannah Anderson, Richard
Anderson, Ann Anderson, Shandy Anderson and Joseph

Anderson children of Richard Anderson. Cicely Shelton
wife of Thomas Shelton; Ann Hardin wife of Thomas
Hardin; Polly Dabney, Charity Dabney and William Dab-
ney, children of Judith wife of James Dabney. Executors:
Son Michael Anderson, James Dabney and grandson
Thomas M. Anderson. Witnesses: John Thomson, Zach.
Pulliam. Book 3, Page 572, Louisa Co.

William Poindexter, administrator of Robert Anderson, gent.,
decd., 10 Oct., 1785. Security: John Poindexter, Louisa
County.

Milley Anderson, administratrix of Richard Anderson, decd.,
13 May, 1793. Securities: David Anderson and Matthew
Anderson, Louisa Co.

Will of Michael Anderson, Louisa County. Dated 14 Dec.,
1796. Probated 9 Oct., 1797. Wife Sally; sons Edmund,
Davy, Reuben, Richard, Pouncey and Thomas Clark Anderson; daughter Elizabeth; Edward Thompson. To son
Michael 500 acres in Kentucky; sons Pouncey, Reuben,
Richard and Edmund 400 acres each in Kentucky. Executors: Wife, and sons Thomas, Pouncey and Reuben. Witnesses: Andrew Kean, William Pulliam, Dudley Diggs.

Conveyance from Charles Anderson and Jennet his wife of
St. Pauls Parish, Hanover County, planter, to John Thomson of same place. 200 acres of land in Louisa County,
sold by Robert Anderson to said Charles Anderson as by
deed dated 5 July, 1738, being the remaining part of 400
acres granted by Patent dated 20 June, 1738 to said
Robert Anderson. Recorded 27 May, 1746. Louisa Co.

Conveyance from Matthew Anderson of St. Pauls Parish,
Hanover County, merchant, to Robert Anderson of same
parish and county, planter, 400 acres in Louisa (late Hanover County) granted by Patent to said Robert Anderson
and mortgaged by the latter to William Prentice, the said
Matthew Anderson having purchased the land from said
Prentice conveys same to said Robert Anderson. Recorded 27 January 1746. Louisa Co.

Conveyance from Robert Anderson of St. Pauls Parish, Hanover County, planter, to John Moore of St. Martins Parish, Hanover, 400 acres in Louisa County. Recorded 27 January, 1748. Louisa Co.

Conveyance from Robert Anderson of St. Martins Parish, Hanover County, to David Anderson of same county and Parish, 100 acres in Louisa County. Recorded 23 June, 1752. Louisa Co.

Conveyance from David Anderson and Elizabeth his wife of Hanover County, to Benjamin Bibb of Louisa County, 400 acres in Louisa, granted said David Anderson by Patent 16 August, 1750. Recorded 24 May, 1757. Louisa County.

Conveyance from Robert Estis, Jr., and Keziah his wife of Louisa County, to Robert Anderson of same place, 100 acres in Louisa County. Recorded 26 Oct., 1756. Louisa County.

Conveyance from Robert Anderson of Fredericksville Parish, Louisa County, gent., to Philip Buckner of same parish and county, gent., the said Anderson acting on P/ of atty. from Mary Arnold, widow of Jonathan Arnold of afsd. county, decd., dated 2 May, 1752, conveys 200 acres in Louisa. Recorded 27 September, 1757. Louisa Co.

Conveyance from William Anderson and Frances his wife of St. Martins Parish, Hanover County, to Hezekiah Sanders of same place, 400 acres in Fredericksville Parish. Recorded 22 May, 1759. Louisa Co.

Conveyance from Pouncey Anderson of St. Martins Parish, Hanover, to Samuel McClure of same place, 200 acres in Louisa County, being part of a tract granted to said Anderson by Patent 17 August, 1725. Recorded 28 July, 1761. Elizabeth wife of said Pouncey relinquishes her dower rights. Louisa Co.

Bond of Robert Anderson as Sheriff of Louisa County, 12 December, 1774. Sureties: Thomas Johnson, Jr., Richard Anderson, David Anderson, Richard Swift, John Robinson. Louisa Co.

Conveyance from David Anderson of Louisa County to his
brothers and sisters, Robert, John, Ann, Susannah, Kitty
and Sally Anderson, of all his right, title and interest, etc.
in a tract of land in Louisa County on Peters Creek,
whereon "our" father, the late Robert Anderson, was in
his lifetime possessed, the said David reserving to himself
1-7 part, and the residue to his six brothers and sisters.
Recorded 8 July, 1782. Louisa Co.

Conveyance from John Anderson of Trinity Parish, Louisa,
planter, to Richard Anderson, gent., of same place, 62
acres in afsd. parish. Recorded 10 August, 1767. Louisa
County.

Conveyance from Robert Anderson, gent., and Frances his
wife of Trinity Parish, Louisa, to John Nelson, gent, of
same place, 479 acres in afsd. county. Recorded 12
March, 1767. Louisa Co.

Conveyance from Robert Anderson of Louisa, to Robert Yancy
of same place. 1 negro girl. Recorded 11 Feb., 1771.
Louisa Co.

Conveyance from Robert Anderson of Louisa, to Richard
Poindexter of same place, 2 negroes in trust for the use
of Frances Anderson, wife of said Robert, and she to
have full power to deed them in her lifetime or by her
last will and testament. Recorded 8 Feb., 1773. Louisa
County.

(Continued.)

TAYLOR.

John Taylor, one of the legatees under the will of Richard
Lawson, dated ——ber, 1658. (Rappahannock Co.)

Captain George Taylor, one of the executors of the will of
William Sargent, probated 14 April, 1683. Mrs. Martha
Taylor is one of the legatees. (Rappahannock Co.)

James Taylor, a witness to the will of Capt. Symon Miller,
dated 16 Feb., 1679. (Rappahannock Co.)

Thomas Taylor, a witness to the will of William Lunn, dated

1 March, 1678. Age of witness is given as 27 years. (Rappahannock Co.)

Thomas Taylor, a witness to the will of William Hollister, dated 18 August, 1680. (Rappahannock Co.)

Thomas Taylor, a witness to the will of Elizabeth Kirk, dated 19 April, 1676. (Rappahannock Co.)

Thomas Taylor, a legatee under the will of Roger Bagwell, dated 25 March, 1679. (Rappahannock Co.)

Henry Taylor, a witness to the will of Nathaniel Gubb, dated 20 Nov., 1686. (Rappahannock Co.)

George Taylor, mentioned as the father-in-law of Elizabeth Jones in the will of Thomas Bliss, dated 7 Feb., 1676. (Rappahannock Co.)

Captain George Taylor, a Justice for Rappahannock 2 May, 1685.

Mr. James Taylor was this day sworn Under Sheriff for the County of Rappahannock, on the north side of the river, for the ensuing year, 1684. May Court 8th of the month.

Mr. James Taylor who intermarried with the relict and sole executrix of Evan Morgan, decd., petitions this court for his quietus from the estate of said Morgan, whereupon the said court granted quietus to the said Taylor. At a court held for Rappahannock, 7 May, 1785, there being present, Col. John Stone, Mr. Henry Awbrey, Capt. George Taylor, Capt. Samuel Blomefield, Mr. Samuel Peachy, Mr. James Harrison.

Will of Richard Taylor of Rappahannock County, dated 22 March, 1678-9. Probated 21 May, 1679. Son Richard Taylor; son Simon Taylor; daughter Constance; wife Sarah; friends John English, Peter Ellis and Edward Friar. Executor, Col. Leroy Griffin. Witnesses: John English, Elizabeth English, Elizabeth Wood.

Will of Thomas Taylor, Rappahannock County, dated 22 Jan., 1686. Probated 2 March, 1686. To godsons John Tavener, Jr., and Sanford Jones; Isaac son of John Webb; Rees Evans; Thomas White; Elizabeth Pond; my boy servant Thomas Hewett; friends Edward and Mrs. Jones;

Thomas Baylis; Catherine Baylis. Executors: James Sanford and William Orlston. Witnesses: Isaac Webb, John Blake, James Davis.

REGISTER OF FARNHAM PARISH, RICHMOND CO.

Sarah dau. of Simon and Elizabeth Taylor, born 28 Sept., 1692.
Peter son of William and Mary Taylor, born 26 Nov., 1689.
Catherine dau. of Charles and Anne Taylor, born 2 July, 1707.
Joseph Son of John and Catherine Taylor, born 18 May, 1717.
Anne dau. of Robert and Philadelphia Taylor, born 14 Jan., 1722.
John son of Robert and Philadelphia Taylor, born 6 July, 1725.
William son of Robert and Philadelphia Taylor, born 6 March, 1727.
Elizabeth dau. of John and Hannah Taylor, born 26 Sept., 1731.
Richard Taylor, died 23 Jan., 1716.
William Taylor, died 2 Nov. 1726.
Thomas Taylor, died 20 March, 1726.
Elizabeth Taylor, died 7 Oct. 1727.
Simon Taylor, died 10 Jan., 1728-9.
Thomas Taylor, died 9 Jan., 1730.
Simon son of John and Hannah Taylor, born 11 March, 1728.
Anne dau. of William and Elizabeth Taylor, born 9 Sept. 1734.
James son of James and Alice Taylor, born 13 Dec., 1734.
Harrison son of John and Hannah Taylor, born 14 Aug. 1735
Ann dau. of Septimus and Bridget Taylor, born 23 Sept., 1735.
Charles son of Septimus and Bridget Taylor, born 8 Jan., 1737.
William Taylor and Elizabeth Henderson, married 8 Oct., 1730.
Richard son of John and Hannah Taylor, born 8 Nov., 1738.
Katherine dau. of Septimus and Bridget Taylor, born 1 Oct., 1740.
John Taylor, died 28 Feb., 1740.
Tarpley son of George and Mary Taylor, born 24 Feb., 1742.
John son of Septimus and Bridget Taylor, born 25 Dec., 1742.

Simon son of George and Mary Taylor, born 9 March, 1744.

Septimus son of Septimus and Bridget Taylor, born 29 Sept., 1745.

George son of George and Mary Taylor, born 21 Oct., 1747.

Lucy dau. of George and Mary Taylor, born 19 Feb., 1749.

George Taylor, died 25 Oct., 1749.

William son of Charles and Caty Taylor, born 30 Sept., 1763.

(Continued.)

WALTON.

Will of John Walton of Accomac County. Dated 16 Sept., 1640. Leaves property to his son, John Walton, he being of the age of one year or thereabouts. Mentions his wife Grace Walton. Mentions his well beloved brother Mr. Stephen Charleton.

Att a Courte heald this 19 of Feb., 1634 at Acchawmacke. John Walton aged 24 years or thereabouts makes deposition that he heard Henry Charellton say "that if he had Mr. Colton without ye Church yard he would have kickt him over the Pallyzadoes, calling him a black cotted raskoll."

John Walton called as a witness, 8 Dec., 1634. (Accomac Co.)

Deposition of John Walton husband of Grace Walton, 25 Sept. 1637. (Accomac Co.)

Alice the wife of Henry Bagwell hath made to appeare unto our Court that there is dew unto her 200 acres of land for the transportation of herself and sonne Thomas Stratton upon her owne charges and likewise for two servants, John Walton and John Crowder. Atte a Court helde ye 1 Jan., 1636. (Accomac Co.)

Bond of John Walton, 6 June 1644. (Northampton Co.)

Deed of conveyance from Robert Walton of Rappahannock of 560 acres of land unto John Payne of same place. 8 Oct., 1666. (Rappahannock Co.)

Power of attorney given to Robert Walton by Nicholson Andrewes of London, dated 16 Oct., 1663. (Rappahannock
Co.)

Ordered that Mr. John Robins pay unto Edward Walton one
thousand pounds of tobacco. 27 Feb., 1671. (York Co.)

The difference between Edward Walton, plaintiff and James
Bullock, defendant, is at plaintiff's request referred to ye
next Court. 24 April 1673. (York Co.)

Conveyance from Thomas and Leonard Ballou of St. James
Parish, Goochland, to William Walton of same parish, 400
acres of land in same county and parish. 1 Jan., 1731.
(Goochland Co.)

Conveyance from William Cannon of St. James Parish, Goochland, to William Walton, 300 acres of land on North side
of James River on Rock Fish Creek. 19 March, 1738.
(Goochland Co.)

Conveyance from Joseph Ballenger and wife to Thomas Walton of St. James Parish, Goochland, 200 acres of land on
Fluvanna river. 15 Sept., 1741. (Goochland Co.)

Conveyance from Abel Croomof, St. James Parish, Goochland,
to Robert Walton, 100 acres on James River. 17 Oct.,
1741. (Goochland Co.)

Thomas Walton and Martha his wife of St. James Parish,
Goochland, to John Creasly and William Palmer, 200
acres and 100 acres in above county on south side of James
River on Little Deep Run, a branch of Muddy Creek,
which land is part of an order of Council for 700 acres of
land granted unto Thomas Walton by Patent. Recorded
16 Nov., 1742. (Goochland Co.)

Conveyance from John Alexander to Thomas Walton of
Goochland, 675 acres in above county. 16 March, 1741.
(Goochland Co.)

Conveyance from Joel and Joseph Chandler to Robert Walton
of Goochland, 33 acres in above county, adjoining land
of said Walton, William Mayo and others. 10 Feb., 1743.
(Goochland Co.)

Conveyance from Thomas Walton and Martha his wife to John Alexander, 475 acres of land in above county. 18 Oct., 1743. (Goochland Co.)

Conveyance from Thomas Walton and Martha his wife to Judith Ward, 200 acres in Goochland, formerly granted by Patent to Joseph Ballenger. 19 June, 1744. (Goochland Co.)

Conveyance from Sanborn Woodson of Southam Parish, Goochland, to Robert Walton of same parish, 130 acres of land. 18 Nov., 1746. (Goochland Co.)

William Walton of the county of Goochland, eldest son and heir at law of William Walton, late of the said county, decd., to James Hilton and Susanna his wife, one of the daughters of said William Walton, decd., 400 acres of land in Albemarle County formerly Goochland County, on both sides of the north branch of Walton's fork on State River. 16 Feb., 1758. (Goochland Co.)

Clayborn Rice and Susanna his wife, (late widow of William Walton, decd.,) and William Walton of the Parish and county of Amherst convey to Henry Mullins 400 acres of land in Goochland, lately held by William Walton, decd., the former husband of said Susanna Rice and father of said William Walton. 18 Oct., 1764. (Goochland Co.)

(Continued.)

Vol. VI   DECEMBER, 1909   Part 4

Virginia
County Records

PUBLISHED QUARTERLY

EDITED BY

William Armstrong Crozier, F. R. S., F. G. S. A.

Published by
The Genealogical Association
Hasbrouck Heights
New Jersey

Virginia County Records

Published Quarterly

CONTENTS

Virginia County Records

QUARTERLY MAGAZINE

VOL. VI.	DECEMBER 1909	No. 4

INDEX TO LAND GRANTS

LOUDOUN COUNTY

Book No. I

Page	Name	Date	No. acres
160	Dan'l Jones	1768	341
164	John Evans	1768	2211
165	John Dodd	1769	60¼
166	John Williams	1769	56
167	Gabriel Fox	1769	48
168	Francis Summers	1769	120
171	David Wilson	1769	106
186	Wm. Bartlet	1771	504
197	Thos. Kirkpatrick	1771	480
198	Joseph Gibson	1771	22
207	Isaac Brooke	1772	1046
214	Hampson Mason	1772	58
215	Capt. Wm. Ellzey	1772	358
218	Frances King and the heirs of Eliz. King, decd.	1772	1702
222	The Hon. Robert Carter	1772	14,847
232	John Hough	1773	104
238	Philip Ludwell Grymes	1773	1450
240	Leven Powell	1773	150
245	Wm. Douglass	1774	100
249	Wm. Morland	1774	36

255	Josias Clapham	1774	153
257	Same	1774	52
261	John Spencer	1775	88
263	Wm. Douglass	1775	8
277	John Sinclair	1776	346
286	Col. John Carlyle	1776	261
292	Thos. Kirkpatrick	1777	480
299	Isaac Humphreys	1777	227
309	John Spencer	1778	364
310	Jonathan Davis	1778	150
316	Elijah Major	1778	220
322	James Cross	1778	201
324	John Jones	1778	40
337	Joseph Marshon	1778	300
345	Wm. Hough	1779	24
381	Joshua Daniels	1780	703
386	John Hough	1780	180

Book K.

273	Jonathan Palmer	1761	180

Book O.

76	Thos. Bryan Martin	1767	119,927
80	Same	1767	26,535
92	Thos. Lewis	1767	359

Book P.

330	John Booth	1775	840

Book S.

212	Christopher Greenup	1787	38
345	Thos. Bryan Martin	1788	130
387	Christopher Greenup	1788	164

Book T.

129	John Hough	1788	360
132	John Oldacre	1788	120
146	Christopher Greenup	1788	235

Book U.

294	Wm. Elzey	1789	11
449	Edwd. Snicken	1789	411
501	Benj. C. Payne	1789	146
612	John Jackson	1790	101

Book V.

60	Joseph Combs	1790	206
122	Abraham Wykoff	1791	140
185	Thomazin Ellzey	1791	398
477	Wm. Ellzey	1792	18
557	Thomazin Ellzey	1792	29

Book W.

131	John Gibson	1792	102
133	Mary Stoker, Jr.	1792	97
137	Israel Jennings	1792	15
142	Jas. Claypole	1792	16½
241	Saml Love	1794	9¾
281	Wm. Rhodes	1794	40
446	Wm. Herbert	1794	118
535	Frances Hague	1794	14½
536	John Spencer	1794	238½

Book X.

101	Wm. Woolcut	1796	30
377	Jas. Coleman	1796	9
584	Reuben Settle	1797	320
612	John Tyler	1797	40

Book Y.

246	Benj. Grayson	1799	9
247	Rawleigh Colston	1799	21½
253	Joseph Lane	1799	1

NEW KENT COUNTY

Book No. 5.

Page	Name	Date	No. acres
5	John Prossier	1663	260
68	John Hogg	1663	140
85	Capt. Robert Priddy	1665	500
88	Susan Austin	1664	50
91	Thos. Meredith	1662	420
91	Thos. Meredith	1662	380
121	Wm. Jones	1663	150
122	Thos. Michaell	1662	1500
123	Thos. Gardner and John Crocker	1662	187
124	John Vaughan and John Rea	1662	130
131	John Maddison	1664	320
132	Jno. Pigg and Jno. Maddison	1664	1050
134	Mathew Hill	1663	470
135	Stephen Benbridge	1664	250
136	Benj. Strang and John Brockhurst	1663	200
146	Richd. Davis	1662	660
147	John Madison	1662	300
152	John Bunch	1662	450
153	Chas. Edmonds	1662	2750
158	John Stanup	1662	1350
161	Jno. Underhill and Wm. Bassett	1664	463
162	Jno. Underhill	1664	309
176	Philip Chesley	1662	1000
181	Capt. Martin Palmer	1665	608
185	Jno. Garrett and Nicholas Ware	1665	386
202	John Horsington	1663	1750
211	Wm. Stone	1663	750
264	Lt. Col. Robt. Abrahall	1662	1550
267	Thos. Hancks	1663	530
267	Same	1663	527
282	Peter Adams	1662	594½
285	John Adams	1662	220
288	Edward Simpson	1662	100

297	Martha Goffe	1663	650
312	Wm. Burford, Jnr.	1663	640
325	Thos. Brereton	1662	1500
334	Col. Robt. Abrahall	1664	500
343	Geo. Gill, Jnr.	1663	2000
349	Ralph Green	1663	650
349	Chas. Edmonds and Wm. ————	1662	2520
354	Peter Ford and Edward Racle	1663	640
358	Wm. Jones	1663	353
360	Stephen Tarlton	1664	453
368	Richard Major	1663	1350
373	Alex. Tyre and Jas. Read	1662	313
376	Richd. Littlepage and James Turner	1663-4	400
379	James Turner and Richard Littlepage	1663-4	
384	Lt. Col. Wm. Hockaday	1663	5470
406	Cornelius Debarry	1664	200
407	John Crocker	1664	100
408	Cornelius Reynolds	1664	640
408	John Madison	1664	200
413	Benj. Strang and John Brockhurst	1664	450
420	John Goffe	1664	400
438	Richard Harrison	1664	400
439	Major Wm. Wyatt	1664	1940
453	Major Wm. Wyatt	1664	300
485	Moysis Davis and Thos. Biggin	1665	1620
488	Ralph Mazey	1665	600
509	Wm. Woodward	1664	2100
522	Wm. Crump, Chas. Edmonds and Robt. Whitehaire	1665	2700
551	Thos. Clayborne	1665	500
552	Geo. Dillard	1665	250
552	Gabriel Hill	1665	727
553	Gabriel Hill	1665	134
553	Edward Dennis and Sam'l Mottersott	1665	500
554	Shirly Mandett	1665	100
555	Wm. Birch	1665	345
555	George Morris	1663	1350

557	Same	1663	933
585	Col. Nathl. Bacon	1665	2000
615	Henry Biggs	1665	100
615	Robert Harmon	1666	800
628	David Nowell	1665	324
644	Lt. Col. Wm. Hoccaday	1665	1000

Book No. 6.

3	Wm. Peasly	1666	390
13	Thos. Creeton and Hugh Roye	1666	2100
17	Mathew Jennings	1666	500
17	John James	1666	259
17	John Glen	1666	65
18	Chas. Loveing	1666	350
19	Moyses Davies	1666	220
19	Same	1666	1450
26	David Brand	1666	1178
45	Robt. Whitehaire, John Bowler and Edmonds	1667	3000
70	John Davis	1666	1000
86	Major Gen'l Manering Hamond	1667	4610
91	Thos. Bell	1667	160
95	Jonathan Newell and Ambrose Clare	1667	2500
95	John Duncomb	1667	600
96	John Cape	1667	650
96	John Pigg	1667	600
97	John Talbott and Elias Downes	1667	1600
99	Stephen Pettus	1667	350
107	John Page	1672	1900
108	Same	1672	1700
108	Richd. Tunstall	1667	1368
109	John Winsloe	——	600
114	John Sexton	1667	1000
114	Cornelius Dabney	1667	300
115	Wm. Woodward and John Barras	1667	179
143	John Lewis	1668	100
150	Wm. Fuzey	1668	1000
150	John Sexton	1668	700

150	Wm. Fuzey	1668	600
160	Domingo Mederis and James Johnson	1668	1000
160	Richard Davis	1667	700
161	Edward Bompas	1668	280
161	Richard Bullock	1668	100
162	Gabriel Michell	1668	182
162	Robert Pollard	1668	65

HALIFAX COUNTY
Book No. 33.

348	John Justice	1756	400
349	Same	1756	400
364	Benj. Dixon	1757	395
423	Matt. Manable	1758	175
429	George Walton	1758	2200
433	Wm. Clopton	1758	400
444	Michael McDaniel and Nath'l Hunt	1758	820
446	Thos. Smith	1758	400
455	Richd. Bland	1758	1394
476	Henry Stone	1758	73
502	Joseph Shelton	1758	98
505	Thos. Spraggin	1758	95
521	Jonathan Woodson	1758	402
554	Timothy Dalton	1759	150
582	Timothy Vaughan	1759	400
584	Timothy Dalton	1759	1180
586	John Cobb	1759	380
594	Abraham Maury	1759	1182
595	Mary Jennings	1759	272
596	Thos. Dilliard	1759	404
599	Isaac Martin	1759	400
623	Same	1759	400
652	Wm. Powell	1759	536
659	Adam Winder	1759	340
660	Nath'l Terry	1759	7050
673	Richd. Anderson, Pauling Anderson and John Watkins	1760	6200

675	John Atchison	1760	1000
676	Silvester Jones	1760	300
685	Thos. Chandler	1760	400
691	Benj. Childry	1760	790
698	John Estes	1760	1150
699	Jas. Foulis (clerk)	1760	2750
700	Same	1760	860
716	James Hunt	1760	700
717	Same	1760	750
718	John Hunter	1760	1025
727	John Justis	1760	404
729	Alex. Legrand	1760	2000
731	Joseph Minor	1760	428
732	Geo. Morris and John Collier	1760	1700
755	Richard Sullin	1760	400
756	John Sparrow	1760	403
756	Josiah Seal	1760	400
760	Wm. Thomas	1760	400
799	Robt. Pusey	1760	165
800	Francis Luck	1760	400
801	Same	1760	296
801	James Parish	1760	400
802	John Russell	1760	434
802	Richd. Murphey	1760	400
802	Jas. Parish	1760	330
823	James Seay	1760	400
811	Amos Richardson	1760	150
823	Wm. Wynn	1760	1810
824	Wm. McDaniel	1760	1000
882	Philip W. Claiborne	1760	320
882	Wm. Macby, Jnr.	1760	270
883	Alman Guin	1760	270
884	Peter Wilson	1760	400
885	Alman Guin	1760	280
935	John Dickinson	1760	120
941	Wm. Woodward	1760	400
941	Wm. Powell	1760	400

942	Richd. Griffin	1760	394
994	Thos. Watkins	1761	400
863	Thos. Billings	1760	404
996	Eliz. Eckhols	1761	409
1007	Wm. Roberts	1761	227
1011	Robert Wooding	1761	89
1017	Hugh Innis	1761	400
1018	Henry Green	1761	170
1023	Thos. Edwards	1761	48
1026	Revd. Robert Innis	1761	373
1027	Benj. Powell	1761	374

Book No. 34.

138	Robert Innes	1756	800
156	Thos. Mustain	1756	400
156	Wm. McDaniel	1756	370
171	Richd. Womack	1757	1270
177	David Greebhill	1757	400
179	John Justis	1757	400
183	Benj. Dickson	1757	2264
204	Wm. Vadien	1757	50
204	John Griere, Aquila Griere and Joseph Griere	1757	50
206	Ambrose Haley	1757	386
212	Francis Pollard	1758	404
212	Jas. Tinkler	1758	128
219	Wm. Glass	1759	400
229	Wm. Cooke	1759	225
270	Wm. Spragin	1759	400
289	Robt. Jones	1759	195
297	John Jones	1759	200
298	Robert Jones	1759	315
331	Christopher Bolling	1759	268
339	Thos. Bouldin	1759	765
345	Henry Chiles	1759	32
364	Sam'l Harris	1759	400
370	Benj. Childrey	1759	330
379	Richd. Dudgeon	1759	404

382	Charles Harris	1759	116
388	John Fargeson	1759	404
393	Wm. Rickle	1759	400
398	Zackariah Green	1759	330
411	Isaac Vanbibber	1759	170
442	James Southal	1759	400
451	John Parr	1759	400
459	Wm. Mobbarly	1759	150
473	Hugh Moore	1760	400
439	Thomas Williams	1759	400
487	Sam'l Harris	1760	325
494	Peter Hudson	1760	2100
496	Dan'l Terry	1760	2011
497	Sam'l Harris	1760	220
506	John Boyd	1760	366
512	James Careley	1760	400
512	Hannah Crunk	1760	166
514	Geo. Chadwell	1760	125
521	Edward Dean	1760	400
535	Luke Smith, Jr.	1760	112
541	Dan'l Terry	1760	400
544	Chas. Talbott	1760	400
549	John Wilcox	1760	400
550	Abraham Womack	1760	376
563	Wm. Carley	1760	170
570	Hy. Farmer	1760	400
577	Edwd. Hubbard	1760	290
580	Richd. Jones	1760	373
583	Benj. Lawlis	1760	400
584	Same	1760	200
592	Alex. Nelson	1760	400
606	Wm. Lax, Jr.	1760	400
612	Abraham Smith	1760	800
619	Joseph Williams	1760	604
624	Shadrach Treble	1760	400
640	Nicholas Hagle	1760	800
640	Sam'l Harris	1760	436

644	Joseph Shaw	1760	403
645	John Yeats	1760	154
646	John Sanders	1760	350
648	Robt. Warters	1760	400
655	Robt. Wooding	1760	330
656	John Vaughan	1760	392
682	Sam'l Bentley	1760	400
683	Thos. Smith	1760	400
683	Abraham Echols	1760	400
692	James Bates	1760	350
722	Archibald Gordon	1760	190
753	Wm. Cook	1760	400
759	Robert Jones, Jr.	1760	220
759	Robert Jones	1760	200
760	Same	1760	320
766	Hugh Moore	1760	400
771	Richard Parson	1760	386
774	Wm. Satterwhite	1760	240
798	John Irby	1761	2435
803	Wm. Chandler	1761	404
805	Wm. Mackbe	1761	580
808	Robt. Wording	1761	238
817	John Cargill	1761	315
818	Anthony Griffin	1761	244
821	Daniel Hankin	1761	380
832	Evan Stokes	1761	400
836	John Waters	1761	275
867	Jas. Cary	1761	190
869	John Justice	1761	400
870	Joseph Eckols, Jr.	1761	13
871	Thos. Tunstall	1761	430
873	Wm. McDaniel	1761	152
890	Hugh Corrin	1761	424
893	Richd. Dugen	1761	660
894	Richd. Eckhols	1761	400
895	Same	1761	550
901	John Logan	1761	383

902	John Light	1761	400
902	Henry Lansford	1761	400
910	John Pigg	1761	316
911	Same	1761	180
919	George Young	1761	400
937	James Gilliam	1761	94
939	Henry McDaniel	1761	285
950	Hannah Austin	1762	303
959	Thomas Callaway	1762	400
960	Thos. Carleton	1762	370
961	Thos. Finney	1762	800
961	Peter Overby, Jr.	1762	346
962	John Pigg	1762	390
965	Thos. Graven	1762	330
965	John Graven	1762	384
972	Patrick Vance	1762	260
973	George Walton	1762	977
974	Andrew Wade	1762	400
1026	Sherwood Walton	1762	2030
1035	Peter Wilson	1762	650
1039	Wm. Been	1762	179

ELIZABETH CITY COUNTY

Book No. 9.

Page	Name	Date	No. acres
52	Captn. Wm. Armistead	1696	130
63	Phillip Inoson	1696	400
102	John Heron	1697	124
113	Robert Holmes	1697	195
121	Henry Royall	1697	586
122	Mark Parrish	1697	35
158	Robert Beverly	1698	570
173	Robert Hollins	1698	195
192	Pasco Jennings	1698	143
213	Richard Crussell	1699	70
215	Henry Robinson	1699	188

229	Thomas Roberts, Jr.	1699	249
243	Robt. Beverly	1700	813
257	Wm. Armistead	1700	125
453	James Baker	1702	225
565	George Walker, Jr.	1703	25
610	Thomas Poole	1704	474
615	George Walker	1704	115
650	Matthew Watts	1705	50
650	Walter Bayley	1705	150
717	Robert Beverly	1705	120
723	Wm. Mallory	1706	274
727	Robert Taylor	1706	3 half acres

BOOK No. 10.

2	George Walker	—	126
3	Nicholas Curle	—	200
45	James Wallace	1711	583
54	Wm. Hachell	1711	74
69	Joshua Curle	1713	134
95	Wm. Armistead	1713	200
85	John Parsons, Jr.	1713	300
86	Charles Cellis	1713	124
139	Mark Johnson	1714	150
192	Thomas Allen	1714	328
197	John Hayward	1714	58
235	James Burtell	1714	½ acre
316	Thomas Wilcoks	1717	214
374	Joshua Curle	1718	45 A. & ½ poles.
375	George Walker	1718	1000 sq. ft.
416	John Ballie	1718	69 acres
450	Wm. Dandridge and Thomas Wythe	1719	32 poles
450	Henry Irwin	1719	19 pos.

BOOK No. 11.

24	Wm. Armistead	1720	9
84	John Dandridge	1722	32 pos.
142	Anthony Armistead	1722	93
143	Wm. Hatchill	1722	83

235 Wm. Allen 1723   150

BOOK No. 13.

359 Miles Cary 1729   200

BOOK No. 15.

249 John Casey 1734   62
286 Edward Andros 1734   50

BOOK No. 18.

444 Wm. King and Mary his wife and Judith
        Curle 1739   637
 12 Thomas Smith 1738   225

BOOK No. 28.

154 John Massenburgh 1747   75

BOOK No. 29.

361 Thos. Townsend Mingham 1750   90

BOOK No. 35.

111 Benjamin Lester 1763   214
327 George Wythe 1763   40

BOOK No. 38.

585 Wm. Morehead 1764   57
916 James Wallace Bayley...............1765   10½

BOOK No. 42.

745 Anne and John Smith 1774   94
        Commonwealth's grants or patents.

BOOK "O."

320 George Hope 1785   1A. 1R. 17P.
322 Robert Walker 1785   1A. 24P.

BOOK No. 17.

222 Worlick Westwood 1788   27

223	Miles King	1788	2 lotts
224	Same	1788	2 lotts
225	Same	1788	3 lotts
227	Same	1788	10 acres

ISLE OF WIGHT COUNTY

Book No. 7.

Page	Name	Date	No. acres
5	Thomas Wombwell	1679	650
6	Arthur Davies of Surrey Co.	1671	561
14	Wm. Collins	1679	1313
16	Roger Tarleton	1679	167
16	Wm. Powell	1679	257
16	Arthur Allen, Edward Thelwell and Robert Horneing	1679	337
18	Thomas Purnell	1679	150
18	Wm. Scott, Jr.	1679	24
19	Robt. King, ye Elder	1679	200
19	Francis Bridle	1679	422
20	Mathew Strickland	1680	1803
20	Giles Limscott	1680	1411
21	Josiah Harrison	1680	750
21	Thomas Parnell	1680	1100
25	Richard Booth	1680	560
28	Henry Wigges	1680	20
38	Colo. John Lear	1680	900
41	Robert Kae	1680	170
52	Gilbert Addams	1680	150
68	Richard Booth	1681	465
68	Wm. Powell	1681	400
68	John Moore	1681	300
69	Phill Wrayford	1681	350
69	Thomas Holder	1681	470
69	Robt. Johnson	1681	2150
70	George Pierce	1681	2500
70	John Watkins	1681	400

71	Richard Reynolds, Sr.	1681	380
71	Maj. Thos. Taberer	1681	400
71	George Pierce	1681	400
72	Jonathan Robinson, Richard Thomas and John Sanders	1681	1650
72	John Roberts	1681	1450
119	Capt. Henry Applewhaite	1682	1260
132	Wm. Mayo	1682	220
133	Hodges Councill	1682	320
134	Peter Vasser	1682	233
136	Thomas Powell	1682	480
137	Jacob Dardon	1682	435
139	Wm. Bush	1682	390
149	Thomas Ward	1682	350
155	Richard Hutchins	1682	226
156	Chas. Man	1682	22
156	Thomas Underwood	1682	400
158	John Thornton	1682	390
158	John Sellaway	1682	250
164	John Moor	1682	490
165	Thomas Mandue	1682	320
174	Richard Reynolds	1682	450
174	Daniel Long	1682	60
180	Thomas Mann	1682	300
182	John Drake	1682	100
236	Brigman Joyner	1683	300
239	John Sellaway	1683	650
240	Wm. Mayo	1683	366
252	James Bryan	1683	315
270	Peter Bainton	1683	200
293	Thomas Parker and James Bagnoll	1683	470
298	Hoptkins Howell	1683	110
302	Wm. Joyner	1683	520
311	Same (recorded in error)	1683	520
329	Capt. Henry Applewhaite	1683	902
329	George Wright and Thos. Wright, sons of Thos. Wright, deceased	1683	100
333	Colo. Arthur Smith	1683	1100

334	Captn. Henry Applewhaite	1683	1313
375	Christopher Wade	1684	92
375	James Garder	1684	200
378	John Nevell	1684	92
378	Christopher Hollyman	1684	1020
394	Wm. Boddie	1684	3350
395	James Tullagh	1684	270
396	Thomas Pitt	1684	150
407	Robert Thomas	1684	10
440	Anthony Matthews	1685	640
441	John and Thos. Harris	1680/5	365
446	Robert Flake	1685	170
448	Wm. Holleman	1685	132
465	John Procter	1685	250
489	Col. Arthur Smyth	1685	500
495	Humphry Clark	1685	300
510	Mathew Tomlin	1686	1227
514	Henry Hearne	1686	133
528	Same	1686	133
542	Walter Rutter	1686	150
544	Robert Williamson	1686	500
545	John Nevill	1686	246
566	Thomas Pitt	1687	550
568	Ambrose Bennet	1687	750
573	John Summerell	1687	420
574	James Adkinson	1687	216
576	Thomas Moore	1687	1150
614	Thomas Pitt	1687	550
636	James Allen	1688	230
665	Hopkins, Howell and Mary Howell, orphans	1688	200
672	Francis Davis	1688	100
672	Wm. Baldwin	1688	67
673	Mrs. Hester Bridger and James Tullah	1688	243
673	John Brown	1688	600
674	Peter Butler, James Butler, ye younger and John Butler	1688	678
695	John Sojourner	1689	162

Book No. 8.

8	James Bryan	1689	762
22	Col. Arthur Smith	1689	310
90	James Corlee	1690	187
91	Wm. Scott	1690	54
91	Robert King	1690	168
92	Hodges Councell	1690	200
128	Wm. Fowler	1691	100
174	Maj. Arthur Allen	1691	170
175	Wm. Chambers	1691	1150
176	Henry Pope	1691	187
176	Wm. Mayo	1691	170
220	John Browne	1692	220
220	Owen Daniel	1692	175
279	Wm. Cook	1693	250
374	Thomas Throp and Martha, his wife	1693	350
379	John Howell	1694	100
377	John Mackenny	1694	450
401	Robert King	1694	124
415	Hugh Campbell	1695	1311
422	Richard Pugh	1695	100
422	Robert Coleman	1695	80
428	Owen Daniel	1695	130
358	Hopkin Howell	1695	100

Book No. 9.

22	Thomas Underwood	1695	350
22	George Andrewson	1695	175
23	Wm. Carver	1695	45
23	John Parnell	1695	400
61	Captn. Hugh Campbell	1695	380
81	Jacob Darden	1697	330
84	Wm. Sykes of Nansemond Co.	1697	750
88	Thomas Mulford	1697	200
101	George Northworthy	1697	200
88	Humphrey Marshall	1697	100
104	John Mackmile	1697	200
123	Barth Fowler	1697	1260

135	John Giles	1698	300
138	Arth. Smith	1698	310
141	John Giles	1698	687
147	John Williams	1698	46
148	Henry Sanders	1698	118
150	James Doubtey	1698	198
165	John Giles	1698	100
177	Thomas Joyner	1698	1300
180	John Giles	1698	300
180	Stephen Smith	1698	500
181	Henry Applewaite	1698	600
188	Hugh Campbell	1699	1200
194	Henry Pope	1699	72
203	Hugh Campbell	1699	634
417	Robert Scott	1701	130
419	James Denson	1702	17
432	Thomas Howell	1702	100
446	Wm. West	1702	85
466	Anthony Lewis	1702	347
468	James Bryan	1702	100
468	Wm. Kintching	1702	170
469	Thomas Joyner	1702	440
469	Same	1702	300
470	Wm. Johnson	1702	428
471	Wm. Maye	1702	180
472	Barnaby Mackinnie	1702	308
471	Wm. Browne	1702	156
473	Arthur Purcell	1702	350
473	Thomas Mandrew	1702	390
474	Wm. Williams	1702	600
500	Henry Hart	1702	379
535	Arthur Smith	1703	500
74	John Powell	1703	313
658	Wm. Jolly	1705	634
700	Wm. West	1705	600
730	Nicholas Fulgham	1706	380
296	Thomas Cooper	1701	147

IMMIGRANTS TO VIRGINIA

(Continued from page 155)

15 May 1635

Theis underwritten names are to Virginia imbarqued in the "Plaine Joan," Richard Buckam, Master, the pties having brought attestation of their conformitie to the orders and discipline of the Church of England.

Names.	Years.	Names.	Years.
Robert Briers	21	Richard Fleming	24
John Johnson	20	Mathew Lem	20
Robert Coke	25	Henry Perpoynt	22
Jo. Alsopp	50	Thomas Hall	21
William Pigott	50	Edward Wilson	22
William Toplys	30	Jo. Palliday	23
Thomas Arnold	30	Richard Wolley	36
William Paulson	23	William Clark	27
Jo. Northin	22	William Baldwin	24
Thomas Turner	21	William Collins	20
Jo. Beddell	22	Thomas Pitcher	20
Jo. Barrowe	26	Joseph Nelson	26
Jo. Trent	27	Francis Gray	15
Jo. Coker	21	Samuel Young	14
Henry Donaldson	25	Robert Hutt	14
William Lavor	22	Jo. Raddish	23
Chri. Davies	22	Tho. Bulkley	32
Chri. Taylor	22	Robert Brooke	33
Daniel Clark	33	Rich. Downes	34
Richard Day	32	Arthur Peach	20
Robert Lewes	23	Wm. James	26
Luke Blund	20	Wm. Blackett	40
Ja. Warren	27	Roger Koorbe	25
James Ward	18	Ann Perks	27
Thomas Stamp	32	Tho. Britton	26
Tobias Frier	18	Wm. Colins	34
Wm. Steddall	26	Jo. Resburne	30
Chri. Thomas	26	Henry Jackson	24

Owen McCartie 18
Richd. Lawrence 20
Nico. Kent 16
Peter Subburroe 20
Wm. Hitchcock 27
Edward Wheeler 18
Jo. Shaw 21
Jo. Aris 19
Tho. Viper 26
Geo. Smith 34
Geo. Talbott 18
Jo. Bennet 18
James Wynd 23
Charles McCartie 27

Charles Flane 18
Tho. Godbitt 20
Thos. Newman 15
Thos. Lloyd 20
Francis Barber 18
Jas. Miller 18
Jo. Marshall 21
Robert Ward 22
Robt. Shinglewood 26
Jo. Hughes 30
Robert Gilbert 18
Jo. Rolles 22
John Marsh 26
Ralph Wray 64

WILL OF JOHN HOPKINS.

The following is a copy of a certified copy of the original will of John Hopkins of Hanover County, a son of Dr. Arthur Hopkins of Goochland. The copy was sent to Henry Laurens Hopkins, a grandson of John, in 1862. Nearly all of the records of Hanover County are lost, so that the publication of this will has added value to the descendants of John Hopkins.

Mary, daughter of John Hopkins married Captain John Otey, who served in the Revolutionary Army. Their son, Walter Hopkins, married Mary, a daughter of William Walton by his wife Mary Leftwich.

In the name of God, Amen: I, John Hopkins, of the parish of St. Martins, in the county of Hanover, being very sick and weak in body, but of perfect mind and memory, thanks be given to Almighty God; therefore calling to mind the mortality of my body, and knowing it is appointed unto all men once to die, do make and ordain this, my last Will and Testament.

That is to say principally and first of all, I give and recommend my soul to the hands of Almighty God that gave it, and my body I recommend to the earth, to be buried at the diversion (probably intended for direction) of my executors hereafter named, not doubting but that I shall receive the same by the mighty power of God; and as touching such worldly estate wherewith it pleased God to bless me in this life, I give, devise, and dispose of the same in the following manner and form.

Item: I will my just debts to be paid. I lend to my beloved wife, Susanna Hopkins during her widowhood my land and plantation I now live on, and also the following negroes: Moses, Robin, Tamar, Joseph, and Brewster Dick, together with my household furniture and stock of every kind. But if my wife should marry, then my will and desire is, that she shall have an equal share, during her life, of the said slaves and other estate before mentioned, with my eight children: David, Peter, Charles, William, Elizabeth, Mary, Sarah, and

Frances Hopkins. And after my wife's death, her part of the above mentioned estate to be equally divided between my said eight children, as also the aforesaid negroes in case she should not marry, which I give to them and their heirs forever.

Item: I lend to my said wife during her life my negro girl Jenny, and she and her increase to my daughter Elizabeth Hopkins after her mother's death, to her and the heirs of her body lawfully begotten forever.

Item: I give and bequeathe to my two sons Peter and Charles Hopkins four hundred acres of land that I purchased of John Tait lying in Louisa County to be equally divided between them and their heirs forever.

Item: I give and bequeathe to my son William Hopkins after my wife's death my land and plantation whereon I now live, also one feather bed and furniture, one dish, one basin, four plates and six spoons, to him and his heirs forever.

Item: I give to my daughter Mary Hopkins one negro girl named Dilly with future increase, to her and her heirs lawfully begotten forever, also one dish, one basin, four plates, and six spoons.

Item: I give and bequeathe to my daughter Sarah Hopkins one negro girl named Amey with her future increase to her and the heirs of her body lawfully begotten forever. Also one dish, one basin, four plates, and six spoons.

Item: I give and bequeathe to my daughter Frances Hopkins two negro boys, Ned and Patrick, to her and the heirs of her body lawfully begotten forever; also one dish, one basin, four plates, and six spoons.

Item: I give and bequeathe to each of my daughters: Elizabeth, Mary, Sarah, and Frances Hopkins, each of them a feather bed and furniture to them and their heirs forever.

Item: I will that if either of my children should die leaving no lawful issue that the estate so given shall be divided between the survivors.

Item: I will that if either of the negroes given to my daughters should die before they are possessed of them the negro so dying shall be valued as though he were living, and the valuation money be made up out of my estate and paid

to the owner of such negro so dying. And do appoint my
well beloved wife Susanna Hopkins Executrix, and my well beloved friends Robert Garland and David Shelton Executors
of this my last will and testament. And as I have given my
son, John Hopkins Thirty Pounds and one feather bed I will
that he should have no more except one Shilling sterling. In
witness whereof I have set my hand and seal, this 29 day of
August, one thousand seven hundred and sixty-five.

(signed) JOHN HOPKINS. (seal)

Signed sealed and published in the presence of Isaac Freeman, and Charles Mills.

At a court held for Hanover county on Thursday the third
day of July 1766, This last Will and Testament of John Hopkins deceased was offered for proof by Susanna Hopkins Executrix and Robert Garland Executor therein named, and was
proved by oath of Isaac Freeman and Charles Mills, the witnesses thereto, and also by the said executrix and executor, and
admitted to record.

(signed) William Pollard D. C. H. C.

A Copy,
   Teste.
(signed) R. O. Doswell,
Cl'k Pro Tempore.

NORFOLK CO. MARRIAGE BONDS

(Continued from page 253.)

Jan.	2, 1771.	Joseph Harding and Mary Herbert.
Jan.	4, 1771.	Bayley Warren and Elizabeth Dickenson.
Feb.	2, 1771.	William Donaldson and Eliza Arnott.
Feb.	9, 1771.	Robert Muter and Margaret Bell.
Feb.	16, 1771.	Peter Lewis and Margaret Eyre.
Feb.	19, 1771.	Robert Keeble and Miss Dorothy Reade.
Mar.	26, 1771.	Alex. Love and Miss Elizabeth Calvert.
May	7, 1771.	Geo. Watson and Anne Brucker.
May	11, 1771.	William Luke and Sarah Murray.
May	21, 1771.	James Blair and Catharine Eustace.
May	29, 1771.	Wm. Lewis and Sarah Taylor.
June	3, 1771.	John Shore and Ann Benn.
July	4, 1771.	Paul Proby and Miss Mary Pugh.
July	20, 1771.	John Harris and Mrs. Mary Scott.
July	21, 1771.	Bernard Babb and Jane Steel.
Aug.	7, 1771.	John Shaw and Mrs. Mary Arnott, widow.
Sep.	3, 1771.	Chas. Rothery and Eliz. Hanley.
Sep.	9, 1771.	Joshua Williamson and Susanah Biddle.
Sep.	21, 1771.	Richard Lishman and Agnes Thompson.
Sep.	21, 1771.	Robert Taylor and Miss Sarah Barrand.
Oct.	1, 1771.	James Langley and Eliz. Snale.
Nov.	16, 1771.	Capt. Bristol Brown and Sarah Cann.
Dec.	4, 1771.	Josiah Wilson and Margaret Cawson.
Dec.	11, 1771.	Wm. Wilson and Miss Ann Butt.
Dec.	21, 1771.	Ezekiel Cox and Miss Ann King.
Dec.	24, 1771.	Thomas Bayley and Rebecca Harmon.
May	29, 1772.	Sam'l Cotter and Miss Tamer Cherry.
Sep.	23, 1772.	John Garrick and Eliz. Gray.
Jan.	4, 1773.	John Bayne and Miss Mary Wishart.
Jan.	16, 1773.	Wm. Cornick and Mary Ashley.
Jan.	30, 1773.	John Boggess and Mary Ann Thelaball.
Jan.	—— 1773.	Jas. Sparrow and Mary Stanter.
Feb.	14, 1773.	Thos. Farrer and Eliz. Lovett, dau. of Adam Lovett, decd.

Feb.   17, 1773.   David Osheal and Catherine, dau. of George
                     Veale.
Feb.   23, 1773.   Alex. Gordon and Eliz. Hodges.
Mar.   11, 1773.   Thos. Langston and Clotilda Sawyer Jones.
Mar.   12, 1773.   John Braidfoot and Blandinah Moseley.
May   20, 1773.   John Owens and Sarah Wilkins.
May   28, 1771.   Baley Guy and Lockey, dau. of Wm. Talbot.
June   17, 1773.   John Hefferman and Eliz. Horton.
July   6, 1773.   Wm. Nicholson and Lovet, dau. of Nathl.
                     Tatem, decd.
July   9, 1773.   Thos. Mathews and Mary Miller.
July   28, 1773.   George Goll and Ann Skinner.
Aug.   11, 1773.   Mat. Shields and Sarah Corprew.
Sep.   4, 1773.   Richd. Bassett and Eliz. Moore.
Oct.   2, 1773.   Thos. Arnat and Sarah Steel, born Oct. 3,
                     1751.
Oct.   23, 1773.   Thos. Lowrey and Sarah Wildair.
Oct.   29, 1773.   Nathl. Tatem and Rebecca Portlock.
Nov.   3, 1773.   Wm. Ayles and Eliz. Hudson.
Nov.   14, 1773.   Labon Goffegon and Mary Veale.
Nov.   17, 1773.   Thos. Edwards, Jr. and Eliz. Southerland.
Nov.   19, 1773.   Hy. Wells, Jr. and Mary, dau. of Jass. Benn
                     of Nansemond.
Dec.   1, 1773.   Matthew McVie and Susannah Darby.
Dec.   23, 1773.   Henry Sparrow and Eliz. Tucker.
Dec.   23, 1773.   John Collins and Mrs. Dinah Dale.
Feb.   4, 1774.   Andrew Ronald and Mary Fry.
Feb.   7, 1774.   Robert McCully and Jane Sisson.
Mar.   2, 1774.   Jas. Herbert and Diana Tatem.
Mar.   12, 1774.   Wm. Alexander and Mary Tracey.
Mar.   30, 1774.   Jno. Tatem, Snr. and Alsey Smith.
April   21, 1774.   Thos. Nash and Ann Portlock.
April   23, 1774.   Wm. Jaques and Anne Watson.
April   27, 1774.   John Taylor and Mary Rhonald.
May   6, 1774.   Chas. Sayer Boush and Martha Sweney.
May   16, 1774.   James Thelaball and Ann Wishart.
May   30, 1774.   Alex. Montgomery and Margt Eaune.
June   13, 1774.   Wm. Eggleston and Ellen Whittle Davis.

June	29, 1774.	Sam'l Inglis and Ann, dau. of Wm. Aitchison.
July	23, 1774.	Nick Gauteir and Miss Frances Robinson.
Aug.	3, 1774.	Richd. Carney, Jr. and Sally Lewelling.
Aug.	6, 1774.	Michl. Freadly and Mrs. Direetor McLachlan.
Aug.	18, 1774.	Jas. Williamson and Eliz. Denby.
Sep.	1, 1774.	Jas. Leitch and Sarah Yewill.
Sep.	24, 1774.	Jas. Nicholson and Lydia Cowper.
Sep.	30, 1774.	George Leslie and Mary Williams, widow.
Oct.	15, 1774.	Thos. Ritson and Martha Willoughby.
Oct.	28, 1774.	George Robinson and Eliza. Baynes.
Oct.	31, 1774.	Jas. Lewis and Jane Wall.
Nov.	11, 1774.	Paul Owens and Janet Herbert.
Dec.	7, 1774.	Malachi Oldner, son of Geo. and Dinah Old-
Dec.	28, 1774.	ner and Ann, dau. of Nathl. Tatem, decd.
		Charles Hill and Eliz. Dale.
Jan.	3, 1775.	Robert Andrews and Eliza. Ballard.
Jan.	17, 1775.	Wm. Harvey and Frances Ker.
Jan.	23, 1775.	Benj. D. Gray and Mary Grimes, widow.
Feb.	9, 1775.	Danl. Stewart and Sarah Butler.
Feb.	21, 1775.	Alex. Guthery and Sophia Proby.
Mar.	20, 1775.	Wm. Marley and Anne Godfrey.
Mar.	25, 1775.	John Muirhead and Eliz. Warner.
Mar.	28, 1775.	Wm. Murden and Sarah Butt.
April	15, 1775.	Jonathan Eilbeck and Mary Talbot.
April	27, 1775.	Robert Jervis and Keziah Portlock.
May	30, 1775.	Francis Hodgson and Mrs. Mary Burton.
June	20, 1775.	John Lells and Eliz. Larchen.
Aug.	21, 1775.	John Hall and Eliz. Phillips.
Aug.	31, 1775.	John Hodgson and Ann Newton.
Sep.	5, 1775.	Francis Russell and Eliz. Dunn.
Sep.	12, 1775.	John Watson and Jane Rogers.
Oct.	7, 1775.	John Brickell, Jnr. and Eliz. Hudson.
Oct.	7, 1775.	Wm. Ingram and Ann Talbutt.

NORTHAMPTON COUNTY WILLS.

ORDER BOOK No. 16.

Benthall, Joseph, Northampton Co. — Jan., 1710-11; 1 Aug.. 1711. My children; wife Elizabeth entire estate and to be extx; witnesses John Frank, Thorn Wills.

Inch, Elizabeth, Northampton Co. 20 Oct., 1711; 18 Dec., 1711. Thomas Bullock; daus. Ann and Tamar; my loving mother; friend John Dowman; brother Richard; witnesses Anthony Hardy, Samuel Hardy.

Benthall, Joseph, Northampton Co. 6 Oct., 1712; 18 Nov., 1712. Sons Daniel and William; grandson Thomas, son of Joseph Benthall; dau. Elizabeth; wife Mary executrix; witnesses John Frank, Elisha Frank, Jos. Gilbourn.

Smith, John, Northampton Co. 22 Oct., 1711; 18 Nov., 1712. Sons Isaac, John and Jonathan; daus. Tabitha and Leah; friend John White, schoolmaster; wife Jean executrix; witnesses John Johnson, John White, Richard Johnson.

Stockley, John, Northampton Co. 13 Oct., 1711; 20 Jan., 1712-13. Sons John and Thomas; granddaughter Frances Wilkins; grandson Nathl. Wilkins; dau. Mary Wilkins; dau. Elizabeth Millin; wife Isabel executrix; witnesses William Willett, Ann Willett.

Tarbuck, Thomas, Northampton Co. 5 Jan. 1712-3; 20 Jan 1712-3. Arthur Rases; Andrew, son of John Snow; Marjory Senior; William Waterfield; Catherine, wife of John Robins; Sarah, mother of Andrew Snow; my brother John Tarbuck, his wife and their dau. Margaret; witnesses John Maux, John Gathony, Ann Gathony.

Core, John, Northampton Co. 1 Feb., 1709-10; 20 Jan., 1712-3. Sons John, Thomas, Edward, William and Edmund; wife Rebecca executrix. No witnesses.

Joyne, Edmund, Northampton Co. 18 July, 1712; 20 Jan., 1712-3. Sons Edward, Major, Thomas and Edmund; to my daughters one shilling to each of them; witnesses Gilbert Henderson, William Bell.

Littleton, Southy, Northampton Co. 31 Dec., 1712; 13 Feb., 1712-3. Mother-in-law Ann Eyre; sister Sarah Custis

Littleton; sister Esther Littleton; cousin Leah Littleton; my brother Joseph Maxfield; wife Mary executrix; witnesses Daniel Eyre, Benj. Gathors, Thos. Eyre, Luke Griffith, Elizabeth Ellegood, Esther Gathors.

James, Joan, widow; Northampton Co. 30 April, 1712; 17 Feb., 1712-3. Sons Francis, William, John and Robert; dau. Elizabeth James; dau. Mary Badger; dau. Sarah Parramore; grandson Philip James; son Thomas executor; witnesses Luke Layson, John Elson.

Corben, George, Northampton Co. 25 Sept., 1711; 16 June, 1713. Sons Ralph and Robert; son-in-law John Bloxom and Ann, his wife; grandson George Bloxom; wife Susanna; son Robert executor; witnesses Thomas Johnson, Francis Thompson, Nathl. Capell.

Laylor, Hannah, widow, Northampton Co. 21 April, 1713; 21 July, 1713. Son John Read; dau. Mary; granddaughter Sarah Edge; dau. Hannah; son-in-law Stephen Fletcher executor; witnesses John Marsh, Joseph Smith.

Evans, Elizabeth, Northampton Co. 24 Sept., 1713; 17 Nov., 1713. Sons Thomas and Ceasar Evans; granddaughter Abigail Belote; son John Belote; daus. Ann and Eliz. Evans; son John Belote executor; witnesses Hillary Stringer, Thomas Collier, Ann Belote.

Boyer, John, chirugeon. No date. 17 Nov., 1713. Wife Judith to divide estate at her death between my three children; wife executrix; witnesses Benj. Stratton, John Bowdon, Francis Allen.

Roberts, Thomas, Northampton Co. 8 Sept., 1713; 17 Nov., 1713. Sons Simon, Moses, Jacob and Mark; wife Fortune executrix; witnesses Henry Ellegood, Nathl. Capell, Sr.

Jacob, Philip, Northampton Co. 31 March, 1703; 17 Nov., 1713. Sons John, Richard, Philip and William; wife Martha executrix; witnesses John Clegg, Thomas Ward.

Brighouse, George, Northampton Co. 19 Sept., 1713; 17 Nov., 1713. Wife Mary; sons William, Major, Peter, Jedediah and John; dau. Hannah Brighouse; witnesses John Belotte, Anne Belotte.

Marshall, George, Northampton Co. 19 Nov., 1713; 15 Dec., 1713-4. Son William; my brother John Marshall; dau. Tamar Marshall; dau. Rachael Marshall; wife Mary executrix; witnesses William Baker, William Taylor, Obedience Johnson.

Newnam, Matthew, gentleman, Northampton Co. 4 Feb., 1713; 16 Feb., 1713. Friend Robert Howson to be executor; to Richard Nottingham, Jr., son of Richard Nottingham and my godson; brother Michaell Newnam, Esq.; Edward Newnam; witnesses Joseph Godwin, Daniel Godwin.

James, Robert, Northampton Co. 16 Nov., 1713; 16 Jan., 1713-4. Brother, John James; Philip, son of David James, decd.; brother Francis; brother Thomas; brother William James; Mary, wife of Rennold Badger; Nathl. Badger; brother Francis executor; witnesses Luke Johnson, John White, George Dewey.

Benthall, Mary, Northampton Co. 4 July, 1713; 16 Jan., 1713-4. Dau. Elizabeth Fisher; son Daniel; son William; granddaughter Sarah Jacob; granddaughter Ann Clegg; John Fisher; granddaughter Eliz. Jacob; son Daniel executor; witnesses Yardley Michaell, Francis Wainhouse.

Custis, John, Northampton Co. 3 Sept., 1708; 16 March, 1713. Wife Sarah; sons Hancock, John and Henry Custis; dau. Elizabeth Custis; dau. Sorrowful Margaret Kendall; John Adkisson; Yardley Michaell; Elias Taylor; Henry Toles; sons Hancock and Henry executors; William Harmanson; Henry Harmanson; Mr. Hillary Stringer; sister-in-law Elishe Frank; Robert Howson; witnesses Robert Howson, John Satchell, Sarah Palmer, Elishe Frank, Eliz. Atkinson.
Codicil same date; witnessed by John Atkinson, Eliz. Fox, Robt. Howson.

Betts, William, planter, Northampton Co. 28 July, 1714; Sept., 1714. Sons Isaac and William; wife Alice executrix; witnesses George Green, Jonathan Stevens.

Foster, John, Northampton Co. 2 Oct., 1714; 16 Nov., 1714. Brother William Roberts; brother Arthur Roberts; brother Robert Foster; William Kendall, Sr.; brother Mark Roberts; cousin William Roberts; cousin Diroetta Roberts; my mother Elizabeth Foster executrix; witnesses John Walker, Benj. Nottingham.

Dewey, George, Northampton Co. 7 Nov., 1714; 21 Dec., 1714. Son George; wife Elizabeth executrix; witnesses Abigail Boll, Mitchall Scarburgh, Mary White.

Foster, Elizabeth, Northampton Co. 6 Sept., 1712-3; 18 Jan., 1714-5. Son William Roberts and his wife Lucy; son . Mark Roberts; son John Foster; son Arthur Roberts; son Thomas Roberts; son John Roberts and his eldest son John; granddaughter Thamar Cassinett; son Robert Foster; Mary Roberts, dau. of my son Arthur Roberts; my daus. Bridget Jacob and Elizabeth Watts; son William Roberts executor; witnesses William Waterson, Elizabeth Waterson, William Waters.

Robinson, Benjamin, Northampton Co. 13 Dec., 1712; 20 March, 1715. Tully Robinson; wife Elizabeth executrix; witnesses Richard Waterson, John Clay.

Burr, Richard, Northampton Co. 9 Sept., 1715; 20 Sept. 1715. My little dau. Esther; son John; son-in-law Araton Capell; wife Esther executrix; witnesses Nathl. Capell, Hannah Capell.

Pitt, Andrew, carpenter, Northampton Co. 13 Feb., 1710-1; 20 Sept., 1715. Sons Thomas and Edward; daus. Mary, Ann, Margaret and Amy Pitt; wife Alice executrix; witnesses William Goulding, Richard Turner.

Sandor, James, Northampton Co. 8 May, 1715; 15 Nov., 1715. Son Richard; my brother John Sandor; wife Jane executrix; witnesses John Robins, Andrew Hooper.

Watts, John, Northampton Co. 20 Sept., 1715; 15 Nov., 1715. Luke Taylor; Daniel Luke; estate to be divided between John Lucas, Andrew Andrews and Arthur Rasco, the latter to be executrix; Mary Rasco.

Eyre, Thomas, Snr., Northampton Co. 23 Jan., 1713-4; 20 Dec., 1715. Son Severn; grandson ——Eyre, brother

John Eyre; son Thomas executor; witnesses John Harmanson, William Kendall, Snr., William Freshwater.

Smith, George, Northampton Co. 11 Jan., 1715; 20 March, 1715-6. Son George; daus. Sarah and Mary Smith; wife Mary executrix; witnesses Daniel Eyre, Mark Freshwater, Thomas Moore.

Dent, Thomas, tailor, Northampton Co. 10 April, 1713; 15 May, 1716. Cousin Joseph Dent; brother Marmaduke Dent; cousin Eliz. Moody and her sister Mary, daus. of James Dent, decd.; Joseph Ash; Bridget Bradford; cousin Joseph Dent executor; witnesses Arthur Roscoe, Jonathan Bell, John Dolby, Francis Wainhouse, Jnr.

FAMILY HISTORY

Strother of Fauquier County

Charles Burgess of Lancaster County, Va., and Alice his wife, to James Strother of Fauquier county, planter, for 40 pounds currency 218 acres in Fauquier county. 25 Sept., 1766. Book 2, P. 592.

20 Oct., 1774. Thomas, Lord Fairfax to William Strother and Milley his wife and Elizabeth his daughter, lease for and during their lives, etc., 110 acres in Fauquier part of the tract known by the name of the Manor of Leeds. Book 6, P. 64.

29 Sept., 1792. ——Fairfax etc., to Mary Strother, her daughter Dorothy and grandson George Gallagher. Lease ect. of Lot 120 Manor of Leeds in Fauquier. Book 11 P. 189.

22 Nov., 1793. Abram Gibson of Fauquier, being aged and infirm, and his wife Ann being also, and being unable to manage his estate, and all his children except Jane, wife of James Strother of Fauquier being removed very distant, said Gibson conveys to said Strother and Jane his wife, whole of the estate both real and personal. Book 14, P. 899.

28 Aug., 1815. George White and Judith Ann his wife and James Strother and Sally his wife to King George county for $370.00 convey to Charles Heirs of Fauquier county, 18½ acres of land "being their portion of the land devised by the last will and testament of Joseph Green, decd." Book 20, P. 8.

William Strother and Lucinda his wife to Fauquier sell land to Patrick Brady of same county.

17 May, 1823. George White, Jnr., and James and George Strother convey their reversionary interest in property of Joseph Green, decd., now in possession of his widow Mary Green, to Thomas Smith, trustee to secure a debt. Book 27, P. 181.

25 March, 1828. John and Lewis Strother, executors of James Strother, decd., to Mary Strother, widow of James Strother, who was Mary Green, widow of Joseph Green, decd., deeding to her one-third interest, etc. Book 30, P. 21.

25 April, 1837. Thomas B. Strother of Harrison county, Va., son of Reuben Strother late of Fauquier county, decd., power of attorney to his (Thomas B. Strothers) son James Strother of Harrison co. Book 37, P. 226.

14 Sept. 1837. Thomas B. Strother of Harrison county, Va. appoints his son Reuben Strother of Harrison county, his attorney. Book 37, P. 342.

6 Oct., 1838. Sarah Strother of Frederick county to Thomas O'Rear of Fauquier county for $30, any interest she may have in the land which was devised by the last will and testament of Abraham Cox, decd., to his son Zachariah Cox and his daughter Ann Cox, who both having departed this life without lawful heirs and the said land being devised in such event to William Cox and Thomas Cox and Mary Winn's heirs, of whom the said Sarah Strother is one, etc. Book 38, P. 264.

6 Dec., 1855. Phebe Urton of Fauquier county to Enoch Strother, Octavia Richards, Hedgeman Strother, Alexander Strother and Sarah Ann Strother, children of Jeremiah Strother, decd., and Susannah Strother wife of said

Jeremiah Strother, decd., and his administratrix for $250, all the undivided interest of said Phebe in and to the land of her father William Urton, decd., in Fauquier county. Book 28, P. 458.

Fitzhugh of Fauquier County

17 March, 1779.   Henry Fitzhugh and Sarah his wife of St. Pauls Parish, King George county. Deed of gift of 1185 acres in Fauquier county to their son George Fitzhugh. Book 7, P. 116.

18 June, 1779.   Henry Fitzhugh and Sarah his wife of St. Pauls Parish, King George county. Deed of gift of 1216 acres in Fauquier to their son William Fitzhugh. Book 7, P. 247.

29 March, 1780.   Henry Fitzhugh of King George county. Deed of gift of slaves to his son William Fitzhugh of Fauquier.

25 Dec., 1784.   William Fitzhugh, Snr. of King George county to nephew George Fitzhugh, Jnr. son of my brother Henry Fitzhugh. Deed of gift of slaves. Book 9, P. 30.

24 July, 1795.   Thomas Fitzhugh of Fauquier to John T. Fitzhugh and William Helm as trustees of his (Thomas) mother-in-law Lydia Moffett of Fauquier. Deed of cattle, etc., during her lifetime and afterwards to be divided between Susannah Moffett, Caroline Matilda Moffett, Helen Moffett and John Moffett. Book 12, P. 322.

Thomas Fitzhugh and Charlotte his wife of Prince William county. Deed of gift to Lydia Moffett, (William Helm and John Thornton Moffett, trustees.) Land in Fauquier county during her lifetime, and afterwards to John Helm Moffett, Susannah Moffett, Caroline Matilda Moffett, Helen Moffett, Louisa Moffett, Mildred Grigsby and Aaron Grigsby and their heirs. Book 12, P. 367.

2 April, 1818.   Cole Fitzhugh and Catherine Presley his wife of Jefferson county, Kentucky to Whiting Driggs of Fauquier, for $4600, 229½ acres in Fauquier. Book 22, P. 240.

31 July, 1824. Lynaugh H. Fitzhugh of Fauquier deeds to
Richard Foote of Prince William county, in trust for
his the said Fitzhughs children, viz.: Eliza Maria; Rowland Thornton; Harriet Lucinda; Caroline Matilda; Julia
Cornelia and Lynaugh Helm Fitzhugh, 280 acres of land
whereon said Lynaugh H. Fitzhugh now resides on Dor-
rels River, Fauquier county, Va. Book 28, P. 49.

18 Feb., 1848. Sarah B. Fitzhugh, George T. Fitzhugh, Henry
Fitzhugh, Thomas Fitzhugh, William L. B. Goodwin
who married Ann M. Fitzhugh, Rosalie Fitzhugh of Cul-
pepper county, to William A. Bowen of Fauquier county
for $4250 a tract of land near the Watery Mountains in
Fauquier and known as a part of the estate of George
Fitzhugh, decd., as may be seen by his will, etc. Book
47, P. 80.

VIRGINIA REVOLUTIONARY SOLDIERS.

(Cont. from page 245.)

Tapp, Vincent, Sgt. Major, Continental Line, 3 years' service.
Son, Anthony, Sergeant, Va. Cavalry, 3 years' service.
Bartlett, Jno., Sergeant, Va. Cavalry, 3 years' service.
Gill, Erasmus, Capt., Va. Cavalry, 7 years ending Sept., 1782.
Beno, Jno., Private, Va. Cavalry, 3 years' service.
James, Peter, Private, State Line, 3 years' service.
Harris, Edwd., Drum Major, Contl. Line, dschg. as unfit for
duty after 2 years' service.
Ewell, Thos., Capt. State Line, 3 years' service.
Tebbs, Thos., Capt., decd., Contl. Line, 3 years. Warrant to
John Tebbs, h. at law.
Waters, Rich., Capt.-Lt., Va. Artillery, 3 years' service.
Delaplane, Jas., Lieutenant, Contl. Line, 3 years' service.
Splann, Thos., Private, Contl. Line, 3 years' service.
McWilliams, Joshua, Midshipman, State Navy, 3 years' ser-
vice.
Dawson, Thos., Private, State Line, 3 years' service.
Wright, Rich., Private, State Line, 3 years' service.

Clayton, Joseph, Private, Va. Artillery, 3 years' service.
Marshall, Thos., Sgt-Major, Va. Cavalry, 3 years' service.
Edwards, Jno., Private, Contl. Line, 3 years' service.
Blalock, Zach., Private, State Artillery, 3 years' service.
Calfrey, Chas., Private, Va. Cavalry, 3 years' service.
Quirk, Thos., Major, State Line, 3 years' service.
Ridley, Jno., Sergeant, State Artillery, 3 years' service.
Palman, Wm., Sergeant, State Artillery, 3 years' service.
Allen, David, Lieutenant, Contl. Line, Mch. 1777—Nov. 30,
    1782.
Marshall, Thos., Colonel, State Line, 3 years' service.
McClain, Thos., Private, Contl. Line, 3 years' service.
Harrison, Joseph, Sergeant, State Line, 3 years' service.
Macklin, Jas., Private, Va. Cavalry, 3 years' service.
Peters, Thos., Private, State Line, 3 years' service.
Hagerty, Patk., Sergeant, Contl. Line, 3 years' service.
Boyle, Chas., Private, State Line, 3 years' service.
Cox, Wm., Sergeant, decd., Contl. Line.   Warrant to Francis
    Cox, his heir at law, July 12, 1783.
Ware, Wm., Private, Contl. Line, 3 years' service.
Fitzgerald, Jas., Private, State Line, 3 years' service.
Jones, Wm., Private, Contl. Line, 3 years' service.
Jones, John, Private, Contl. Line, for the war.
Allen, Moses, Private, Contl. Line, 3 years' service.
Grant, Dan'l, Private, Contl. Line, 3 years' service.
Snead, Holman, Private, Va. Artillery, 3 years' service.
Sullivan, John, Corporal, State Line, 3 years' service.
McIntosh, Wm., Private, State Line, 3 years' service.
Moore, Wm., Private, State Line, 3 years' service.
Usher, Wm., Private, State Line, 3 years' service.
Grymes, Wm., Corporal, State Line, 3 years' service.
Pickrel, Saml., Drummer, State Line, 3 years' service.
Murden, Peter, Private, State Line, for the war.
Proctor, Jno., Sergeant, Contl. Line, 3 years' service.
Davis, Jas., Private, Contl. Line, 3 years' service.
Chilton, Newman, Corporal, State Line, 3 years' service.
Poe, Wm., Private, State Line, 3 years' service.

White, Tarpley, Captain, Contl. Line, Feb., 1776 and resigned Jan., 1781.

White, Jno., Lieutenant, Contl. Line, 28 Dec., 1776, and is still in service, 1782.

Foster, Jno., Sergeant, State Line, 3 years' service.

Hudson, Jno., Captain, State Line, 3 years' service.

Blair, Dan'l, Private, Contl. Line, 3 years' service.

Dean, Joshua, Private, Contl. Line, 3 years' service.

Hutchings, Chas., Private, State Line, for the war.

Meriwether, Jas., Lieutenant, Contl. Line, for the war.

Kirk, Robt., Lieutenant, Contl. Line, 3 years' service.

Burfoot, Thos., Lieutenant, Contl. Line, 3 years' service.

Bristor, Saunders, Private, State Line, 3 years' service.

Eggleston, Joseph, Major, Va. Cavalry, 3 years' service.

Oneal, Ferdinand, Captain, Va. Cavalry, 3 years' service.

Grenstead, Jas., Private, State Artillery, 3 years' service.

Townsend, Wm., Private, Contl. Line, 3 years' service.

Bohannon, Hy., Private, Contl. Line, 3 years' service.

Pendleton, Nathl., Captain, Contl. Line, 7 years' service.

Cooper, Rich., Private, Contl. Line, 7 years' service.

Brayson, Robt., Private, Contl. Line, 3 years' service.

Terrell, Wm., Corporal, Contl. Line, 3 years' service.

Irby, Hardyman, Sergeant, State Line, 3 years' service.

Stokes, Jno., Captain, Contl. Line, 7 years' service.

Lynch, Jas., Private, Contl. Line, 3 years' service.

Allen, Reuben, Sergeant, Contl. Line, 7 years' service.

Downey, Jno., Sergeant, State Line, 3 years' service.

Langham, Elias, Lieutenant, Contl. Artillery, 3 years' service.

Stoneham, Hy., Corporal, Contl. Line, 3 years' service.

Murrah, Geo., Private, Contl. Line, 3 years' service.

Oust, Geo., Corporal, Contl. Line, 3 years' service.

Harris, Wm., Drum-Major, Contl. Line, 3 years' service.

Stephens, Thos., Corporal, Contl. Line, 7 years' service.

Evans, Philip, Private, Contl. Line, 3 years' service.

Elmore, Geo., Private, Contl. Line, 3 years' service.

Livingston, Justice, Surgeon, State Navy, 3 years' service.

McIntosh, Wm., Private, Contl. Line, 7 years' service.

Coverley, Thos., Lieutenant, Contl. Line, 7 years' service.

Powell, Peyton, Lieutenant, Contl. Line, 3 years' service.
Hayes, Thos., Lieutenant, State Line, 3 years' service.
Goodall, Jno., Sergeant, Contl. Line, 3 years' service.
Read, Wm., Corporal, Contl. Line, 3 years' service.
Bell, Irving, Private, Contl. Line, 3 years' service.
Smith, Elijah, Private, Contl. Line, 3 years' service.
Thompson, Landus, Corporal, Contl. Line, 3 years' service.
Angel, Jas., Drummer, Contl. Line, 3 years' service.
Knight, Jno., Private, State Line, 3 years' service.
Knight, Jno., Private, Contl. Line, 3 years' service.
Hutts, Leonard, Private, Contl. Line, 3 years' service.
Hutts, Jacob, Private, Contl. Line, 3 years' service.
Carpenter, Jno., Sergeant, State Line, 3 years' service.
Ballow, Chas., Sergeant, Contl. Line, 3 years' service.
Smith, Wm., Sergeant, Contl. Line, 3 years' service.
Rust, Benj., Lieutenant, State Navy, 3 years' service.
Mountague, Richd., Lieutenant, State Navy, 3 years' service.
Gilbert, Joseph, Private, State Line, 3 years' service.
Hutt, Read, Private, Contl. Line, 3 years' service.
Quin, Ptk., Private, Contl. Line, 3 years' service.
Gregory, Wm., Private, Contl. Line, 3 years' service.
Coleman, Jas., Private, Contl. Line, 3 years' service.
McKinley, John, Private, State Line, 7 years' service.
Foster, Peter, Sergeant, State Line, 3 years' service.
Murphy, Martin, Sergeant, Contl. Line, 3 years' service.
Fall, Henry, Private, Contl. Line, 3 years' service.
Turner, Wm., Private, Contl. Line, 3 years' service.
Goff, Philip, Musician, Contl. Line, 3 years' service.
Coran, Wm., Private, Contl. Line, 7 years' service.
Daves, Spilsby, Sergeant, Contl. Line, 3 years' service.
Carnal, Wm., Private, Contl. Line, 3 years' service.
Tillery, Jno., Private, Contl. Line, 3 years' service.
Wedgbar, Wm., Private, Contl. Line, 3 years' service.
Finley, Sam'l, Major, Contl. Line, 7 years' service.
Jones, Chas., Lieutenant, Contl. Line, 3 years' service.
Rhea, Matt., Lieutenant, Contl. Line, 3 years' service.
Smith, Jacob, Private, Contl. Line, 3 years' service.
Rains, John, Private, Contl. Line, 3 years' service.

Piper, Wm. Sergeant, State Line, 3 years' service.
Willis, Wm., Private, Contl. Line, 3 years' service.
Wilkins, Thos., Drummer, Contl. Line, 3 years' service.
Price, Geo., Corporal, Contl. Line, 3 years' service.
Steer, Thos., Sailor, State Navy, 3 years' service.
Maddox, Notely, Private, Contl. Line, 3 years' service.
Neucom, Solomon, Private, Contl. Line, 3 years' service.
Perry, Hy., Private, Contl. Line, 3 years' service.
Warren, Jno,, Private, Contl. Line, 3 years' service.
Allen, Thos., Private, Contl. Line, 3 years' service.
Lipscomb, Thos., Private, Contl. Line, 3 years' service.
Lipscomb, Mourning, Private, Contl. Line, 3 years' service.
Cyrus, Bartholomew, Private, Contl. Line, 3 years' service.
Moseley, Benj., Lieutenant, Artillery, Contl. Line, 2 May,
    1779—4 Mch., 1783.
Chaffin, Jno., Private, decd., Contl. Line, 3 years' service.
    Warrant to Stanley Chaffin, heir at law.
Hodge, Jas., Sergeant, Contl. Line, 3 years' service.
Aubany, Thos., Private, Contl. Line, 3 years' service.
Green, Wm., Private, Contl. Line, 3 years' service.
Duncan, Chas., Private, Contl. Line, 3 years' service.
Muir, Francis, Captain, Contl. Line, 3 years' service.
Eppes, Wm., Capt.-Lieut., Contl. Line, 3 years' service.
Edwards, Leroy, Captain, Contl. Line, 3 years' service.
Nickens, Rich., Seaman, State Navy, 3 years' service.
Church, Jno., Private, Contl. Line, 3 years' service.
Newby, Jno., Private, State Line, 3 years' service.
Major, Ironmonger, Private, State Line, 3 years' service.
Evans, Jno., Private, Contl. Line, 3 years' service.
Davis, Wm., Sergeant, Contl. Line, 3 years' service.
Rankins, Wm., Private, Contl. Line, 3 years' service.
Drummond, Jno., Drum-Major, Contl. Line, 7 years' service.
Rankins, Robt., Sergeant, Contl. Line, 3 years' service.
Dobson, Robt., Sailing Master, State Navy, 3 years' service.
Britain, Jno., Sailing Master, State Navy, 3 years' service.
Flippen, Robt., Private, Contl. Line, 3 years' service.
Smith, Jno., Private, Contl. Line, 3 years' service.
McGuire, Andrew, Private, Contl. Line, 7 years' service.

Grafton, Jno., Private, State Line, 3 years' service.
Carrol, Joseph, Private, Contl. Line, 3 years' service.
Crawley, Jas., Private, Contl. Line, 3 years' service.
Gamble, Robt., Captain, Contl. Line, 3 years' service.
Grattan, Jno., Lieutenant, decd., Contl. Line, 3 years' service.
 Warrant to Jno. Grattan, heir at law, Aug. 4, 1783.
Taylor, Ferguson, Fifer, Contl. Line, 3 years' service.
Robertson, Hugh, Sergeant, Contl. Line, 3 years' service.
Cooper, Ephraim, Sergeant, Contl. Line, 3 years' service.
Taylor, Jas., Sergeant, Contl. Line, 3 years' service.
Pride, Wm., Lieutenant, decd., Contl. Line, died in service.
 Jno. Pride, heir at law.
Rice, Wm., Sergeant, Contl. Line, 3 years' service.
Bulley, Jno., Seaman, State Navy, 3 years' service.
Ham, Wm., Seaman, State Navy, 3 years' service.
Banks, Jas., Sailing Master, State Navy, 3 years' service.
Banks, Wm., Sailor, State Navy, 3 years' service.
Carter, Thos. Dr., Surgeon, State Line, 3 years' service.
Rodden, Jno., Private, Contl. Line, 3 years' service.
Slate, Jas., Corporal, Contl. Line, 3 years' service.
Absolam, Edmund, Private, Contl. Line, 3 years' service.
Stewart, Patk., Private, Contl. Line, 3 years' service.
Rich, Wm., Private, State Line, 3 years' service.
Webb, Jas., Sailor, State Navy, 3 years' service.
Satterwhite, Jno., Sergeant, Contl. Line, 3 years' service.
Mush, Robt., Private, Contl. Line, 3 years' service.
Peterson, Israel, Private, Contl. Line, 3 years' service.
Shay, Dennis, Private, Contl. Line, 3 years' service.
Hudson, Jno., Private, Contl. Line, 3 years' service.
Cowherd, Jas., Sergeant, Contl. Line, 3 years' service.
Neil, Nicholas, Sergeant, Contl. Line, 7 years ending 5 Feb.,
 1783.
Bailey, Wm., Private, Contl. Line, 3 years' service.
Dillyard, Jno., Drummer, Contl. Line, 3 years' service.
Mahanes, Tapley, Private, State Line, 3 years' service.
Coppinger, Higgins, Private, Contl. Line, 3 years' service.
Rhoads, Wm., Corporal, Contl. Line, 7 years' service.
Loden, Wm., Private, State Line, 3 years' service.

Welch, Robt., Private, Contl. Line, 3 years' service.
Span, Rich'd., Private, Contl. Line, 3 years' service.
Span, Jas., Private, Contl. Line, 3 years' service.
Richard, Thos., Sergeant, Contl. Line, 3 years' service.

ERRATA

Page 7.   For Mr. Gyles Cate, read Cale.

Page 16.   For Joseph Clayton, read Jasper Clayton.

Page 16.   Will of Richard Simons, should read, brother and heir of Thomas Simons.

Page 71.   Hugh Fench, should read Hugh French.

Page 71.   For George Colelough, read Colclough.

Page 74.   For Vauly, read Vaulx.

Page 83.   For Waltham, read Walthall.

Page 84.   For Tidner, read Tignor.

Page 224.   After the will of Daniel Paine, the next line should read:—White, Henry, Northampton Co., 3 Dec., 1708; 28 July, 1709.

General Index

Index

INDEX

x